The Most Wanted Instant Pot Cookbook

SHOOT FOR CRAVEABLE MEALS

500 Recipes

BILL ROSE

CONTENTS

INTRODUCTION

POULTRY

BEEF & LAMB

PORK

FISH AND SEAFOOD

SNACKS AND APPETIZERS

EGGS AND SALADS

GRAINS AND PASTA

VEGETABLES AND VEGAN

SOUPS, BROTHS AND SAUCES

BREAKFAST AND BEVERAGES

DESSERTS

INTRODUCTION

Hello…and welcome to my book about the 500 Most Wanted Instant Pot Recipes. Let me share all my favorite and amazing recipes with you, so you can make delicious and scrumptious meals for your family and friends. I'll also let you know what the Instant Pot is all about, so you can see how easy it is to use.

Let me start by saying that I love my Instant Pot! This is the one kitchen tool I can't live without. I used to make meals for my family just because I needed to put something on the table. Now I make great and stunning meals because I'm love in again with cooking for my family.

I've perfected the art of using the Instant Pot…and now I'm sharing it all with you in my recipe book. The Instant Pot is a more than just a pressure cooker and air fryer combo. It elevates foods in ways you never imagined.

I've created recipes for every meal and occasion…all the way from breakfast to comforting weeknight dinners to elaborate Sunday dinners when you want to impress family and friends. I've got a recipe for you for all cuisines – fried chicken, stews, soups, and casseroles. And then there's those sweets and desserts that make the perfect finish to any meal. All here for you in one collection of my best recipes.

Just use the Instant Pot once, and you'll be hooked. You'll never go back to cooking food in the oven or on the stovetop ever again.

Before you get your pressure cooker ready to start cooking, let's find out what the Instant Pot is all about.

MY TOP 5 TIPS AND TRICKS FOR YOUR INSTANT POT!

1. Anyone can use the Instant Pot!

The technology of the Instant Pot makes this the perfect appliance for anyone to use...no matter how much you or your family think you can't cook! There are just three little things you need to do:

- Choose one of my amazing recipes.
- Gather the ingredients and get them all prepped.
- Put the ingredients into the Instant Pot– choose one of the multiple settings...and walk away until you hear the timer.

2. Forget to take the meat out of the freezer...no problem!

Did you forget to take dinner out of the freezer, so it can thaw in time for tonight's dinner? No problem at all. The Instant Pot takes frozen meats, such as chicken, and quickly pressure cooks it to defrost and cook at the same time.

3. Rice is nice

You may think that sticking to your old way of cooking rice on the stovetop is faster and easier than using the Instant Pot. You'll want to rethink that old cooking method! Not only is using the Instant Pot is faster and easier on the cleanup, you'll never mess up rice again when you don't get the proportions of rice to water just right. The pressure cooker cooks rice perfectly each time.

4. Read the digital screen

When you are pressure cooking using the Instant Pot, you have to guess at what the pressure level is inside the pot. With the Instant Pot, you can use the digital screen, so there's no more guessing! Make sure you take advantage of this handy little feature.

5. Use the steaming rack to make baked desserts

The Instant Pot is your perfect dessert-maker. Whip up the batter for a cheesecake or brownies...and layer the batter in the same pan you'd pop in the oven. But instead of using the oven, place that pan on the steaming rack or trivet that comes with the Instant Pot, which will hold the pan securely. Set the function to cake, and your favorite dessert will be done in no time.

WHAT IS THE INSTANT POT?

The buzz about the Instant Pot is true. It uses cutting-edge technology to let you cook foods fast as well as get all the benefits of a pressure cooker…all in one! You're probably wondering how that can be possible - to have several very different kitchen appliances in one. It's easy. The Instant Pot can be everything for everyone.

It won't take you long to learn how to use the Instant Pot. I'll let you know how to do that a bit later. But why would you want a pressure cooker? Because the Instant Pot is more than just a kitchen appliance. ! It can roast, broil, make soups and stews…and it can pressure cook as well.

Having this one amazing appliance means you can get rid of your dehydrator, roasting pan, slow cooker, even your oven. Just think of all the kitchen space you'll have when you just have one appliance, the Instant Pot, doing all the cooking for you.

Let's look a closer look at all the benefits of owning an Instant Pot.

BENEFITS OF USING THE INSTANT POT

Get rid of other cookbooks

Meal planning is so much easier with the Instant Pot. You don't have to look through three different cookbooks to find the recipe you want to use – Instant Pot, or maybe it's the slow cooker this time? Now you can use just one set of recipes…these 500 of the most cooked recipes that let you use the Instant Pot for every meal.

Prepare meals ahead of time

We all lead busy lives. The Instant Pot lets you prepare food ahead of time – when you have the time and not when you're under pressure to get dinner on the table. Prep in the morning or the night before. Just follow one of my recipes and get all the ingredients ready to go. If you're using the pressure cooker or slow cooker function, just put the ingredients into the Instant Pot, set to the right time, and dinner cooks on its own. Or have all the ingredients in the fridge, ready to go for when you arrive home at the end of the day.

Prepare budget-friendly and healthy meals

Eating meat every day can get expensive. When you have the Instant Pot, you can make delicious meals using lentil and beans. I use these ingredients in many of my recipes – and my meals are never dull or boring. The Instant Pot also lets you cook cheaper cuts of meat to perfection. When you pressure cook a beef shank, it comes out tender and juicy, cooked with sealed in moisture that you don't get when you cook it any other way.

Cooks faster than the slow cooker

With the slow cooker, beans take from 4 to 5 hours cook. With the Instant Pot, you can get that time down to under 30 with the pressure cooking functions. And that includes the time it takes for the Instant Pot to get the pressure up to the right level! What does this mean for you? Simple – you can come home and have a bean soup or stew on the table in no time at all.

USING THE INSTANT POT

When you first get your Instant Pot, it can look a little intimidating with all those functions and buttons to press. I certainly felt that way. But trust me…it won't take you long to get the hang of using the Instant Pot. Let's take a quick look at the basics of using the Instant Pot.

Easy to read display

The display on the Instant Pot is easy to read. All of the functions are there for you just to press and set. You'll also be able to select temperature, pressure levels, and time controls, as well as a start/stop button. As I said, don't let all these buttons make you think you'll never learn how to use the Instant Pot. The learning curve is fast – after making just one of my recipes you'll know what you're doing.

Pressure cooking

When you use the lid for the pressure cooker, you'll be able to cook all kinds of foods at low or high pressure. Just set the timer for one minute increments all the way up to one hour. After an hour, you'll be able to up the time in five minute increments and cook all the way to four hours for some foods, such as cheaper cuts of meat. Make sure to try one of my recipes for pressure cooked vegetables…. or cheesecake!

Slow cooker

You're never going to use your slow cooker again after you use this function on the Instant Pot. After putting all the ingredients in the pot, seal the pressure lid in the venting position. Then just use the Instant Pot the same as you would with the slow cooker, cooking foods for up to 10 hours. I like this function when I want to have the Instant Pot cook dinner for me overnight. It's perfect for chili or beef stew.

Steaming

Steaming fish and veggies is a breeze with the Instant Pot. And the great thing is that there will be no more over-steaming, causing foods to be limp and tasteless. The Instant Pot will cook the foods so that they're tender but still crisp and flavorful.

Sauté and Brown

I use the sauté or brown function for many of my favorite recipes. This setting lets you brown and sear foods before or after cooking them. After browning foods, you can add a bit of liquid, as per my recipes, and make some great tasting gravies. Sautéing foods in the Instant Pot is just like sautéing them on your stovetop.

Easy cleanup

Cleanup takes no time! Once the food is cooked, and the Instant Pot has cooled down, it's just a matter of cleaning the inner steel pot, in warm soapy water.

INSTANT POT RECIPES

The recipes in this book are my absolute favorite...and they're a great introduction to the Instant Pot, highlighting just what this amazing kitchen tool can do for you.

Before you start cooking, here's some valuable information for using my recipes in the Instant Pot.

Brown and sear some food before putting into the Instant Pot

Follow my recipes...in some of them I'll have you brown or sear some of the ingredients, particularly meats before you start the cooking process. This is so that the juices are sealed into the food, making it cook up that much more tender.

Check some foods to avoid over-cooking

Some foods are easy to over-cook, such as baked foods. In my recipes, I'll remind you if you need to check to avoid over-cooking.

Adding Ingredients at the end of cooking time

When layering food in the Instant Pot, lay them flat and close together so that you make the most of the space in the pot. I'll guide you in my recipes when there are any foods that shouldn't be stacked or overlapped.

Use hot water when pressure cooking

If you add a tablespoon or two of hot water when you're using the pressure cooker, the pressure will build up faster.

Adjusting cooking time

If you're using fewer ingredients, then my recipe calls for, remember to adjust the cooking time to a little less. The same goes if you're using more ingredients than my recipe calls for...adjust, so the Instant Pot cooks a little longer. Just be sure to check near the end of cooking time to see if needs to cook longer.

From Slow cooker to Instant Pot

Foods cooked in a slow cooker for 4 hours on high, can be quickly cooked in the Instant Pot for only 25 to 30 minutes! Follow my recipe...I might have you add a bit more liquid than if you were cooking in a slow cooker.

Always press Cancel when changing the functions

It may be omitted on some recipes, but right before releasing the pressure or changing the function from Sauté to any pressure cooking mode, always press Cancel, and then the function you'd like to use.

As you can see, the Instant Pot is just what you need in your life. You'll be cooking exceptional meals in no time! I hope you enjoy my favorite recipes...these are the ones I make over and over again for my family and friends. It's time to choose your first recipe...and get your Instant Pot cooking great food!

POULTRY

Thyme Chicken with Veggies

Serves: 4 | Ready in about: 40 min

INGREDIENTS

4 skin-on, bone-in chicken legs
2 tbsp olive oil
Salt and ground black pepper to taste
4 cloves garlic, minced
1 tsp fresh chopped thyme
½ cup dry white wine
1¼ cups chicken stock

1 cup carrots, chopped
1 cup parsnip, chopped
3 tomatoes, chopped
1 tbsp honey
4 slices lemon
Fresh thyme, chopped for garnish

DIRECTIONS

Season the chicken with pepper and salt. Warm oil on Sauté mode.

Arrange chicken legs into the hot oil; cook for 3 to 5 minutes each side until browned. Place in a bowl and set aside. Sauté thyme and garlic in the chicken fat for 1 minute until soft and lightly golden.

Add wine into the pot to deglaze, scrape the pot's bottom to get rid of any brown bits of food. Simmer the wine for 2 to 3 minutes until slightly reduced in volume.

Add stock, carrots, parsnips, tomatoes, pepper and salt into the pot. Lay steam rack onto veggies.

Into the pressure cooker's steamer basket, arrange chicken legs. Set the steamer basket onto the rack.

Drizzle the chicken with honey then Top with lemon slices. Seal the lid and cook on High Pressure for 12 minutes. Release pressure naturally for 10 minutes.

Place the chicken to a bowl. Drain the veggies and place them around the chicken. Garnish with fresh thyme leaves before serving.

Sticky Orange Chicken

Serves: 4 | Ready in about: 30 min

INGREDIENTS

2 chicken breasts, cubed
½ cup honey
½ cup orange juice
⅓ cup soy sauce
⅓ cup chicken stock
⅓ cup hoisin sauce

1 garlic clove, minced
2 tsp cornstarch
2 tbsp water
1 cup diced orange
3 cups hot cooked quinoa

DIRECTIONS

Arrange the chicken at the bottom of the pot. In a bowl, mix honey, soy sauce, garlic, hoisin sauce, chicken stock, and orange juice, until the honey is dissolved. Pour the mixture over the chicken.

Seal the lid and cook on High Pressure for 7 minutes. Release the pressure quickly. Take the chicken from the pot and set to a bowl. Press Sauté.

In a small bowl, mix water with cornstarch. Pour into the liquid within the pot and cook for 3 minutes until thick. Stir diced orange and chicken into the sauce until well coated. Serve with quinoa.

Za'atar Chicken with Lemony Couscous

Serves: 4 | Ready in about: 40 min

INGREDIENTS

4 chicken thighs
2 tbsp za'atar mix
1 tbsp ground sumac
Sea salt and ground black pepper to taste
2 tbsp butter
2 ½ cups chicken stock

1 onion, chopped
1 garlic clove, minced
1½ cups couscous
Juice from 1 lemon
Fresh parsley, chopped

DIRECTIONS

Season the chicken with salt, sumac, za'atar, and pepper.

Melt butter on Sauté and sear the chicken in batches for 5 minutes per batch until lightly browned. Set aside. Into the cooker, add ¼ cup chicken stock to deglaze the pan, scrape the bottom to get rid of any browned bits of food.

Add garlic and onion to the stock; cook for 3 minutes until soft. Add the remaining chicken stock into the pan; add lemon juice and couscous. Add in chicken.

Seal the lid and cook on High Pressure for 5 minutes. Naturally release the pressure for 5 minutes.

Transfer the couscous and chicken to a serving plate, and garnish with parsley.

Lettuce Carnitas Wraps

Serves: 6 | Ready in about: 50 min

INGREDIENTS

2 tbsp canola oil
2 pounds chicken thighs, boneless, skinless
1 cup pineapple juice
⅓ cup water
¼ cup soy sauce
2 tbsp maple syrup

1 tbsp rice vinegar
1 tsp chili-garlic sauce
3 tbsp cornstarch
Salt and freshly ground black pepper to taste
12 large lettuce leaves
2 cups canned pinto beans, rinsed and drained

DIRECTIONS

Warm oil on Sauté. In batches, sear chicken in the oil for 5 minutes until browned. Set aside in a bowl.

Into your pot, mix chili-garlic sauce, pineapple juice, soy sauce, vinegar, maple syrup, and water; Stir in chicken to coat.

Seal the lid and cook on High Pressure for 7 minutes. Release pressure naturally for 10 minutes. Shred the chicken with two forks. Take ¼ cup liquid from the pot to a bowl; Stir in cornstarch to dissolve.

Mix the cornstarch mixture with the mixture in the pot and return the chicken.

Select Sauté and cook for 5 minutes until the sauce thickens; add pepper and salt for seasoning.

Transfer beans into lettuce leaves, top with chicken carnitas and serve.

Juicy Orange Chicken

Serves: 6 | Ready in about: 50 min

INGREDIENTS

2 tbsp olive oil
6 chicken breasts, boneless, skinless, cubed
⅓ cup chicken stock
¼ cup soy sauce
2 tbsp brown sugar
1 tbsp lemon juice

1 tbsp garlic powder
1 tsp chili sauce
1 cup orange juice
salt and black pepper to taste
2 cups cooked gnocchi

DIRECTIONS

Warm oil on Sauté. In batches, sear chicken in the oil for 5 minutes until browned. Set aside in a bowl.

In your pot, mix orange juice, water, sugar, chili sauce, garlic powder, vinegar, and soy sauce; Stir in chicken to coat. Seal the lid and cook on High Pressure for 7 minutes. Release the pressure quickly.

Take ¼ cup liquid from the pot to a bowl; Stir in cornstarch to dissolve; mix into sauce in the pot until the color is consistent. Press Sauté. Cook sauce for 5 minutes until thickened. Season with pepper and salt.

Serve the chicken with gnocchi.

Chicken Fajitas with Avocado

Serves: 4 | Ready in about: 30 min

INGREDIENTS

4 chicken breasts, boneless and skinless
1 Taco Seasoning
1 tbsp olive oil
24 ounces canned diced tomatoes
3 bell peppers, julienned
1 shallot, chopped

4 garlic cloves, minced
juice of 1 lemon
Salt and pepper to taste
4 flour tortillas
2 tbsp cilantro, chopped
1 avocado, sliced

DIRECTIONS

In a bowl, mix taco seasoning and chicken until evenly coated. Warm oil on Sauté mode.

Sear chicken for 2 minutes per side until browned. To the chicken, add tomatoes, shallot, lemon juice, garlic, and bell peppers; Season with pepper and salt.

Seal the lid, press Poultry and cook for 4 minutes on High Pressure. Release the pressure quickly.

Move the bell peppers and chicken to tortillas. Add avocado slices and serve.

Winter Chicken Thighs with Cabbage

Serves: 4 | Ready in about: 35 min

INGREDIENTS

1 tbsp lard
4 slices pancetta, diced
4 chicken thighs, boneless skinless
salt and ground black pepper to taste

1 cup chicken broth
1tbsp Dijon mustard
1 pound green cabbage, shredded
Fresh parsley, chopped

DIRECTIONS

Warm lard on Sauté. Fry pancetta for 5 minutes until crisp. Set aside. Season chicken with pepper and salt. Sear in the pressure cooker for 2 minutes each side until browned. In a bowl, mix mustard and chicken broth.

In your pressure cooker, add pancetta and chicken broth mixture. Seal the lid and cook on High Pressure for 6 minutes. Release the pressure quickly.

Open the lid, mix in green cabbage, seal again, and cook on High Pressure for 2 minutes. Release the pressure quickly. Serve with sprinkled parsley.

Herby Chicken with Asparagus Sauce

Serves: 4 | Ready in about: 1hr

INGREDIENTS

1 (3 ½ pounds) Young Whole Chicken
4 garlic cloves, minced
1 tsp olive oil
4 fresh thyme, minced
3 fresh rosemary, minced
2 lemons, zested and quartered
Salt and freshly ground black pepper to taste
2 tbsp olive oil

8 ounces asparagus, trimmed and chopped
1 onion, chopped
1 cup chicken stock
1 tbsp soy sauce
1 fresh thyme sprig
cooking spray
1 tbsp flour
Chopped parsley to garnish

DIRECTIONS

Rub all sides of the chicken with garlic, rosemary, black pepper, lemon zest, thyme, and salt. Into the chicken cavity, insert lemon wedges. Warm oil on Sauté. Add in onion and asparagus, and sauté for 5 minutes until softened. Mix chicken stock, 1 thyme sprig, black pepper, soy sauce, and salt.

Into the inner pot, set trivet over asparagus mixture. On top of the trivet, place the chicken with breast-side up.

Seal the lid, select Poultry and cook for 20 minutes on High Pressure. Do a quick release. Remove the chicken to a serving platter.

In the inner pot, sprinkle flour over asparagus mixture and blend the sauce with an immersion blender until desired consistency. Top the chicken with asparagus sauce and garnish with parsley.

Greek-Style Chicken with Potatoes

Serves: 4 | Ready in about: 40 min

INGREDIENTS

4 potatoes, peeled and quartered
4 cups water
2 lemons, zested and juiced
1 tbsp olive oil
2 tsp fresh oregano
Salt to taste
¼ tsp freshly ground black pepper
2 Serrano peppers, stemmed, cored, and chopped
4 boneless skinless chicken drumsticks

3 tbsp finely chopped parsley
1 cup packed watercress
1 cucumber, chopped
½ cup cherry tomatoes, quartered
¼ cup Kalamata olives, pitted
¼ cup hummus
¼ cup feta cheese, crumbled
lemon wedges, for serving

DIRECTIONS

In the cooker, add water and potatoes. Set trivet over them. In a baking bowl, mix lemon juice, olive oil, black pepper, oregano, zest, salt, and red pepper flakes. Add chicken drumsticks in the marinade and stir to coat.

Set the bowl with chicken on the trivet in the inner pot. Seal the lid, select Poultry and cook on High for 15 minutes. Do a quick release. Take out the bowl with chicken and the trivet from the pot. Drain potatoes and add parsley and salt.

Split the potatoes among four serving plates and top with watercress, cucumber slices, hummus, cherry tomatoes, chicken, olives, and feta cheese. Each bowl should be garnished with a lemon wedge.

Creamy Chicken and Quinoa Soup

Serves: 6 | Ready in about: 30 min

INGREDIENTS

2 tbsp butter
1 cup red onion, chopped
1 cup carrots, chopped
1 cup celery, chopped
2 large boneless, skinless chicken breasts, cubed
4 cups chicken broth

6 ounces quinoa, rinsed
1 tbsp fresh parsley, chopped
Salt and freshly ground black pepper to taste
4 ounces mascarpone cheese, at room temperature
1 cup milk
1 cup heavy cream

DIRECTIONS

Melt butter on Sauté. Add carrot, onion, and celery and cook for 5 minutes until tender.

Add broth, mix in parsley, quinoa, and chicken. Season with pepper and salt.

Seal the lid and cook on High Pressure for 5 minutes. Release the pressure quickly. Press Sauté.

Add mascarpone cheese to the soup and stir well to melt completely; mix in heavy cream and milk. Simmer the soup for 3 to 4 minutes until thickened and creamy.

Creamy Chicken Pasta with Pesto Sauce

Serves: 8 | Ready in about: 30 min

INGREDIENTS

3½ cups water
4 chicken breast, boneless, skinless, cubed
8 oz macaroni pasta
1 tbsp butter
1 tablespoon salt, Divided
2 cups fresh collard greens, trimmed
1 cup cherry tomatoes, halved

½ cup basil pesto sauce
¼ cup cream cheese, at room temperature
1 garlic clove, minced
1 tsp freshly ground black pepper to taste
¼ cup Asiago cheese, grated
Freshly chopped basil for garnish

DIRECTIONS

Add water, chicken, 2 tsp salt, butter, and macaroni, and stir well to mix and be submerged in water.

Seal the lid and cook for 2 minutes on High Pressure. Release the pressure quickly.

Press Cancel, open the lid, get rid of ¼ cup water from the pot.

Set on Sauté mode. Into the pot, mix in collard greens, pesto sauce, garlic, remaining 1 teaspoon salt, cream cheese, tomatoes, and black pepper. Cook, for 1 to 2 minutes as you stir, until sauce is creamy.

Place the pasta into serving plates. Top with asiago cheese and basil before serving.

Chicken and Sweet Potato Corn Chowder

Serves: 8 | Ready in about: 40 min

INGREDIENTS

4 boneless, skinless chicken breast, diced
3 garlic cloves, minced
1 cup chicken stock
19 ounces corn kernels, frozen
1 sweet potato, peeled and cubed
4 ounces canned diced green chiles, drained

2 tsp chili powder
1 tsp ground cumin
2 cups cheddar cheese, shredded
2 cups creme fraiche
Salt and freshly ground black pepper to taste
Cilantro leaves, chopped

DIRECTIONS

Add chicken, corn, chili powder, cumin, chicken stock, sweet potato, green chiles, and garlic. Mix well.

Seal the lid and cook on High Pressure for 10 minutes. Release the pressure quickly.

Set the chicken to a cutting board and use two forks to shred it. Return to pot and stir well into the liquid.

Stir in cheese and creme fraiche; Season with pepper and salt. Cook for 2 to 3 minutes until cheese is melted. Place chowder into plates and top with cilantro.

Hawaiian-Style Chicken Sliders with Pineapple Salad

Serves: 12 | Ready in about: 1hr 55 min

INGREDIENTS

Pineapple Slaw:
¼ cup apple cider vinegar
¼ cup olive oil
1 pineapple, chopped
½ head red cabbage, shredded

4 cups arugula
¼ cup chopped fresh cilantro
4 green onions, choppe

Hawaiian-Style Chicken:
1 cup brown sugar
½ cup chicken broth
½ cup soy sauce
½ cup honey
¼ cup orange juice
2 garlic cloves, minced

2 tbsp grated fresh ginger
1 tsp freshly ground black pepper
6 skinless, boneless chicken breasts, halved
2 tbsp cornstarch
2 tbsp water
12 Hawaiian bread rolls

DIRECTIONS

In a bowl, mix oil and vinegar; add pineapple, green onions, cilantro, and arugula and toss well to coat. Refrigerate for 1 hour while the bowl is covered.

In the pot, mix in sugar, soy sauce, garlic, black pepper, ginger, honey, chicken broth, and orange juice.

Press Sauté. Allow the liquid to a simmer. Cook until the honey and sugar dissolves. Arrange chicken into the sauce and toss to coat. Seal the lid and cook on High Pressure for 16 minutes. Release the pressure quickly. Transfer chicken to a cutting board; use 2 forks to shred it.

Preheat your oven's broiler. In a small bowl, mix water and cornstarch; Stir into the sauce in the cooker.

Set cooker to Sauté mode and cook sauce for 2 to 3 minutes until it begins to thicken. Stir in the shredded chicken. Halve the loaf of Hawaiian rolls. Set the halves, cut-side up, onto a baking sheet.

Under the preheated broiler, toast the rolls for 3 minutes until golden brown.

Transfer the shredded chicken to the bottom half of the rolls and apply a topping of salad. Replace the top half of the rolls and cut into individual sliders before serving.

Honey-Garlic Chicken

Serves: 4 | Ready in about: 30 min

INGREDIENTS

4 boneless, skinless chicken breast, cut into chunks
1 onion, diced
4 garlic cloves, smashed
½ cup honey
3 tbsp soy sauce

2 tbsp Lime juice
2 tbsp sesame oil
1 tsp rice vinegar
salt and ground black pepper to taste
1 tbsp cornstarch

DIRECTIONS

Mix garlic, onion, and chicken in your instant pot. In a bowl, combine honey, sesame oil, lime juice, soy sauce, and rice vinegar; Pour over the chicken mixture.

Seal the lid and cook on High Pressure for 15 minutes. Release the pressure quickly. Mix 1 tbsp of water and cornstarch until well dissolved; Stir into the sauce. Press Sauté. Simmer the sauce and cook for 2 to 3 minutes as you stir until thickened.

Cajun Shredded Chicken and Wild Rice

Serves: 6 | Ready in about: 45 min

INGREDIENTS

6 chicken thighs, skinless
1 tsp salt
½ tsp ground red pepper
½ tsp onion powder
½ tsp ground white pepper
1 tsp Cajun Seasoning
1/8 tsp smoked paprika

2 tbsp olive oil
1 cup pumpkin, peeled and cubed
2 celery stalks, diced
2 onions, diced
2 garlic cloves, crushed
3 cups chicken broth
1 ½ cups wild rice

DIRECTIONS

Season the chicken with salt, onion powder, Cajun seasoning, white pepper, red pepper, and paprika. Warm oil on Sauté. Stir in celery and pumpkin and cook for 5 minutes until tender; set the vegetables on a plate. In batches, sear chicken in oil for 3 minutes each side until golden brown; set on a plate.

Into the cooker, add ¼ cup chicken stock to deglaze the pan, scrape away any browned bits from the bottom; add garlic and onion and cook for 2 minutes until fragrant.

Take back the celery and pumpkin the cooker; add the wild rice and remaining chicken stock. Place the chicken over the rice mixture.

Seal the lid and cook for 10 minutes on High Pressure. Release the pressure quickly. Place rice and chicken pieces in serving plates and serve.

Pulled Chicken and Peach Salsa

Serves: 4 | Ready in about: 40 min

INGREDIENTS

15 ounces canned peach chunks
4 boneless, skinless chicken thighs
14 ounces canned diced tomatoes
2 cloves garlic, minced

½ tsp cumin
½ tsp salt
Cheddar shredded cheese
Fresh chopped mint leaves

DIRECTIONS

Strain canned peach chunks, reserve the juice and set aside. In your instant pot, add chicken, tomatoes, cumin, garlic, peach juice (about 1 cup), and salt. Seal the lid, press Poultry and cook on High for 15 minutes. Do a quick pressure release.

Shred chicken with the use of two forks. Transfer to a serving plate. Add peach chunks to the cooking juices and mix until well combined. Pour the peach salsa over the chicken, top with chopped mint leaves and shredded cheese. Serve immediately.

Chicken with Beans and Bacon

Serves: 4 | Ready in about: 45 min

INGREDIENTS

1 tbsp olive oil
4 slices bacon, crumbled
4 boneless, skinless chicken thighs
1 onion, diced
4 garlic cloves, minced
1 tbsp tomato paste
1 tbsp oregano
1 tbsp ground cumin
1 tsp chili powder
½ tsp cayenne pepper

1 (14.5 ounces) can whole tomatoes
1 cup chicken broth
1 tsp salt
1 cup cooked corn
1 red bell pepper, chopped
15 ounces red kidney beans, drained and rinsed
1 cup shredded Monterey Jack cheese
1 cup cups red onion
¼ cup chopped cilantro

DIRECTIONS

Warm oil on Sauté. Sear the chicken for 3 minutes for each side until browned. Set the chicken on a plate. In the same oil, fry bacon until crispy, about 5 minutes and set aside.

Add in onions and cook for 2 to 3 minutes until fragrant. Stir in garlic, oregano, cayenne, cumin, tomato paste, bell pepper, and chili, and cook for 30 more seconds. Pour the chicken broth, salt, and tomatoes and bring to a boil. Press Cancel.

Take back the chicken and bacon to the pot and ensure it is submerged in the braising liquid.

Seal the lid and cook on High Pressure for 15 minutes. Release the pressure quickly.

Pour the kidney beans in the cooker, press Sauté and bring the liquid to a boil; cook for 10 minutes.

Serve topped with shredded cheese and chopped cilantro.

Chicken Cacciatore

Serves: 4 | Ready in about: 40 min

INGREDIENTS

2 tbsp olive oil
1 pound chicken drumsticks, boneless, skinless
2 tsp salt
1½ tsp freshly ground black pepper
1carrot, chopped
1 red bell pepper, chopped
1 yellow bell pepper, chopped
1 onion, chopped
4 garlic cloves, chopped

2 tsp dried oregano
1 tsp dried basil
1 tsp dried parsley
1 pinch red pepper flakes
1 (28 ounces) can diced tomatoes
½ cup dry red wine
¾ cup chicken stock
1 cup black olives, pitted
2 bay leaves

DIRECTIONS

Warm oil on Sauté mode. Season the drumsticks with pepper and salt. In batches, sear the chicken for 5-6 minutes until golden-brown. Set aside on a plate. Drain the pot and remain with 1 tablespoon of fat.

In the hot oil, Sauté onion, garlic, and bell peppers for 4 minutes until softened; add red pepper flakes, basil, parsley, and oregano, and cook for 30 more seconds. Season with salt and pepper.

Stir in tomatoes, olives, chicken stock, red wine and bay leaves. Return chicken to the pot. Seal the lid and cook on High Pressure for 15 minutes. Release the pressure quickly. Divide chicken into four serving bowls; Top with tomato mixture before serving.

Tandoori Chicken with Cilantro Sauce

Serves: 4 | Ready in about: 9hr

INGREDIENTS

Tandoori Chicken:
4 chicken thighs, skinless
½ cup Greek yogurt
1 tbsp olive oil
1 tbsp lemon juice
1 tbsp red chili powder
2 tsp salt

1 tsp garam masala
½ tsp ground turmeric
½ tbsp grated fresh ginger
½ tbsp minced garlic
1 cup water
cooking spray

Cilantro Sauce:
Handful fresh cilantro leaves
1 tsp cumin seeds
½ jalapeno pepper
2-3 garlic cloves

2 tsp honey
2 tsp lemon juice
¾ cup olive oil
Salt to taste

DIRECTIONS

In a bowl, mix yogurt, lemon juice, garam masala, garlic, turmeric, red chili powder, vegetable oil, salt, and ginger. Use a paper towel to pat-dry the thighs. Place them into a resealable plastic bag.

Add in yogurt mixture and seal. Massage bag to ensure the marinade coats the chicken completely and place in the refrigerator for 12 hours. Take out of the fridge and set aside for 30 minutes before cooking.

Add water into the cooker. Apply a cooking spray to your steamer and set it in over the water. Remove chicken from marinade and arrange on the trivet.

Seal the lid and cook for 15 minutes on High Pressure. Release the pressure quickly. In a blender, blend cilantro, water, garlic, honey, cumin, jalapeno pepper, salt, and lemon juice, until smooth. Over the chicken, drizzle sauce and serve.

Chicken Chickpea Chili

Serves: 4 | Ready in about: 25 min

INGREDIENTS

1 tbsp olive oil
3 large serrano peppers, diced
1 onion, diced
1 jalapeño pepper, diced
1 pound boneless, skinless chicken breast, cubed
1 tsp ground cumin
1 tsp minced fresh garlic

1 tsp salt
2 (14.5 ounces) cans chickpeas, drained and rinsed
2 ½ cups water,
2 tbsp chili powder
½ cup chopped fresh cilantro
½ cup shredded Monterey Jack cheese
1 Lime, cut into six wedges

DIRECTIONS

Warm oil on Sauté. Add in onion, serrano peppers, and jalapeno pepper and cook for 5 minutes until tender. Season with salt, cumin, and garlic. Stir chicken with vegetable mixture; cook for 3 to 6 minutes until no longer pink; add 2 cups water and chickpeas. Mix well.

Seal the lid and cook for 5 minutes on High Pressure. Release pressure naturally for 5 minutes. Stir chili powder with remaining ½ cup water. Press Sauté. Boil the chili as you stir and cook until slightly thickened. Divide chili into plates; garnish with cheese and cilantro. Over the chili, squeeze a lime wedge.

Indian Butter Chicken

Serves: 6 | Ready in about: 30 min

INGREDIENTS

2 tbsp butter
1 large onion, minced
1 tsp salt
1 tbsp grated fresh ginger
1 tbsp minced fresh garlic
½ tsp ground turmeric
1 tbsp kashmiri red chili powder
1 (14.5 ounces) can coconut milk, refrigerated overnight

2 pounds boneless, skinless chicken legs
3 tomatoes, pureed in a blender
½ cup chopped fresh cilantro, divided
2 tbsp. Indian curry paste
2 tbsp dried fenugreek
2 tsp sugar
1 tsp garam masala
Salt to taste

DIRECTIONS

Melt butter on Sauté mode. Add in 1 teaspoon salt and onion. Cook for 2 to 3 minutes until fragrant. Stir in ginger, turmeric, garlic, and red chili powder to coat; cook for 2 more minutes.

Place water and coconut cream into separate bowls. Stir the water from the coconut milk can, pureed tomatoes, and chicken with the onion mixture.

Seal the lid and cook on High Pressure for 8 minutes. Release the pressure quickly.

Stir sugar, coconut cream, fenugreek, curry paste, half the cilantro, and garam masala through the chicken mixture; apply salt for seasoning. Simmer the mixture and cook for 10 minutes until the sauce thickens, on Sauté mode. Garnish with the rest of the cilantro before serving.

Paprika Buttered Chicken

Serves: 6 | Ready in about: 45 min

INGREDIENTS

1 cup chicken stock
½ cup white wine
½ onion, chopped
2 cloves garlic, minced
3.5-pound whole chicken, patted dry with paper towel

1 tsp salt
½ tsp ground black pepper
½ tsp dried thyme
3 tbsp butter, melted
½ tsp paprika

DIRECTIONS

Into the pot, add onion, chicken stock, white wine, and garlic. Over the mixture, place a steamer rack.

Rub pepper, salt, and thyme onto chicken; lay onto rack breast-side up.

Seal the lid, press Poultry and cook on High Pressure for 26 minutes. Release the pressure quickly.

While pressure releases, preheat oven broiler. In a bowl, mix paprika and butter.

Remove the rack with chicken from your pot. Get rid of onion and stock.

Onto the chicken, brush butter mixture and take the rack back to the pot.

Cook under the broiler for 5 minutes until chicken skin is crispy and browned.

Set chicken to a cutting board to cool for about 5 minutes, then carve and transfer to a serving platter.

Buffalo Chicken and Navy Bean Chili

Serves: 6 | Ready in about: 45 min

INGREDIENTS

1 tbsp olive oil
1 shallot, diced
½ cup fennel, chopped
¼ cup minced garlic
1 tbsp smoked paprika
2 tsp chili powder
2 tsp ground cumin

½ tsp salt
½ tsp ground white pepper
1 (28 ounces) can crushed tomatoes
1 ½ pounds chicken sausage, chopped
1 (14 ounces) can diced tomatoes with green chilies
¾ cup Buffalo wing sauce
2 (14 ounces) cans navy beans, drained and rinsed

DIRECTIONS

Warm oil on Sauté. Add the sausages and brown for 5 minutes, turning frequently. Set aside on a plate.

In the same fat, sauté onion, roasted red peppers, fennel, and garlic for 4 minutes until soft. Season with paprika, cumin, pepper, salt, and chili powder.

Stir in crushed tomatoes, diced tomatoes with green chilies, buffalo sauce, and navy beans. Return the sausages to the pot. Seal the lid and cook on High Pressure for 30 minutes. Do a quick pressure release.

Spoon chili into bowls and serve warm.

Pesto Stuffed Chicken with Green Beans

Serves: 4 | Ready in about: 20 min

INGREDIENTS

4 chicken breasts
1 tbsp butter
1 tbsp olive oil
¼ cup dry white wine

For pesto:
1 cup fresh basil
1 garlic clove, smashed
2 tbsp. pine nuts

¾ cup chicken stock
1 tsp salt
1 cup green beans, trimmed and cut into pieces

¼ cup Parmesan Cheese
¼ cup extra virgin olive oil

DIRECTIONS

First, make the pesto - in a bowl, mix fresh basil, pine nuts, garlic, salt, pepper, and Parmesan and place in food processor. Add in oil and process until the desired consistency is attained.

Apply a thin layer of pesto to one side of each chicken breast; tightly roll into a cylinder and fasten closed with small skewers. Press Sauté. Add oil and butter. Cook chicken rolls for 1 to 2 minutes per side until browned.

Add in wine and cook until the wine has evaporated, about 3-4 minutes.

Add stock and salt, and top the chicken with green beans. Seal the lid, press Meat/Stew and cook at High Pressure for 5 minutes. Release the pressure quickly.

Serve chicken rolls with cooking liquid and green beans.

Chicken in Tikka Masala Sauce

Serves: 4 | Ready in about: 40 min

INGREDIENTS

2 pounds boneless, skinless chicken thighs,
1 tsp salt
¼ tsp freshly ground black pepper
1½ tbsp olive oil
½ onion, chopped
2 garlic cloves, minced
3 tbsp tomato puree
1 tsp fresh ginger, minced
1 tbsp garam masala
2 tsp curry powder

1 tsp ground coriander
½ tsp ground cumin
1 jalapeño pepper, seeded and chopped
29 ounces canned tomato sauce
3 tomatoes, chopped
½ cup natural yogurt
1 lemon, juiced
3 cups cooked basmati rice
¼ cup fresh chopped cilantro leaves
4 lemon wedges

DIRECTIONS

Rub black pepper and ½ teaspoon of salt onto chicken. Warm oil on Sauté. Add garlic and onion and cook for 3 minutes until soft. Stir in tomato puree, garam masala, cumin, curry powder, ginger, coriander, and jalapeño pepper; cook for 30 seconds until fragrant.

Stir in remaining ½ teaspoon salt, tomato sauce, and tomatoes. Simmer the mixture as you scrape the bottom to get rid of any browned bits; Stir in chicken to coat.

Seal the lid and cook on High Pressure for 10 minutes. Release the pressure quickly.

Press Sauté and simmer the sauce and cook for 3 to 5 minutes until thickened.

Stir lemon juice and yogurt through the sauce. Serve garnished with lemon wedges and cilantro.

Cajun Chicken with Rice and Peas

Serves: 4 | Ready in about: 30 min

INGREDIENTS

4 boneless, skinless chicken breasts, chopped
1 garlic clove, minced
½ tsp paprika
¼ tsp dried oregano
¼ tsp dried thyme
1 tsp cayenne pepper
1 tsp ground white pepper
Salt to taste

1 tbsp oil olive
1 onion, chopped
1 tbsp tomato puree
2 cups chicken broth
1 cup long grain rice
1 celery stalk, diced
1 cup frozen green peas

DIRECTIONS

Season chicken with garlic powder, oregano, white pepper, thyme, paprika, cayenne pepper, and salt.

Warm the oil on Sauté. Add in onion and cook for 4 minutes until fragrant. Mix in tomato puree to coat.

Add ¼ cup chicken stock into the cooker to deglaze the pan, scrape the pan's bottom to get rid of browned bits of food. Mix in celery, rice, and the seasoned chicken. Add in the remaining broth to the chicken mixture.

Seal the lid and cook on High Pressure for 8 minutes. Do a quick release.

Mix in green peas, cover with the lid and let sit for 5 minutes. Serve warm.

Spicy Chicken Wings with Lemon

Serves: 4 | Ready in about: 40 min

INGREDIENTS

2 tbsp olive oil
8 chicken wings
½ tsp chili powder
½ tsp garlic powder
½ tsp onion powder

½ dried oregano
½ tsp cayenne pepper
Sea salt and ground black pepper to taste
½ cup chicken broth
2 lemons, juiced

DIRECTIONS

Coat the chicken wings with olive oil. Season with chili powder, onion powder, salt, oregano, garlic powder, cayenne, and pepper.

In the pot, add the wings and chicken broth. Seal the lid and cook on High Pressure for 4 minutes. Do a quick pressure release. Preheat an oven to high.

Onto a greased baking sheet, place the wings in a single layer and drizzle over the lemon juice. Bake for 5 minutes until skin is crispy.

Chicken with BBQ Sauce

Serves: 6 | Ready in about: 20 min

INGREDIENTS

2 pounds boneless skinless chicken breasts
1 tsp salt
1½ cups barbecue sauce

1 small onion, minced
1 cup carrots, chopped
4 garlic cloves

DIRECTIONS

Rub salt onto chicken and place inside the instant pot. Add onion, carrots, garlic and barbeque sauce. Toss the chicken to coat. Seal the lid, press Poultry and cook on High for 15 minutes. Do a quick release.

Use two forks to shred chicken and stir into the sauce.

Spicy Salsa Chicken with Feta

Serves: 6 | Ready in about: 30 min

INGREDIENTS

2 pounds boneless skinless chicken drumsticks
¼ tsp salt
1 ½ cups hot tomato salsa

1 onion, chopped
1 cup feta cheese, crumbled

DIRECTIONS

Sprinkle salt over the chicken, and set in the instant pot. Stir in salsa to coat the chicken. Seal the lid and cook for 15 minutes on High Pressure. Do a quick pressure release.

Press Sauté and cook for 5 to 10 minutes as you stir until excess liquid has evaporated. Top with feta cheese and serve.

Chicken and Zucchini Pilaf

Serves: 4 | Ready in about: 40 min

INGREDIENTS

2 tbsp olive oil
1 zucchini, chopped
1 cup leeks, chopped
2 garlic cloves, minced
1 tbsp chopped fresh rosemary
1 cup rice, rinsed

2 tsp chopped fresh thyme leaves
salt and ground black pepper to taste
2 cups chicken stock
1 pound boneless and skinless chicken legs

DIRECTIONS

Warm oil on Sauté, add in zucchini and cook for 5 minutes until tender.

Stir in thyme, leeks, rosemary, pepper, salt and garlic. Cook the mixture for 3-4 minutes.

Add ½ cup chicken stock into the pot to deglaze, scrape the bottom to get rid of any browned bits of food.

When liquid stops simmering, add in the remaining stock, rice, and chicken with more pepper and salt.

Seal the lid and cook on High Pressure for 5 minutes. Do a quick release.

Chicken with Salsa Verde

Serves: 4 | Ready in about: 50 min

INGREDIENTS

Salsa Verde:
1 jalapeño pepper, deveined and chopped
½ cup capers
¼ cup parsley

1 Lime, juiced
1 tsp salt
¼ cup extra virgin olive oil

Chicken:
4 boneless skinless chicken breasts
2 cups water

1 cup quinoa, rinsed

DIRECTIONS

In a blender, mix olive oil, salt, lime juice, jalapeño pepper, capers, and parsley and blend until smooth.

Arrange chicken breasts at the bottom of the cooker. Over the chicken, add salsa verde mixture.

In a bowl that can fit in the cooker, mix quinoa and water. Set a steamer rack onto chicken and sauce. Set the bowl onto the rack. Seal the lid and cook on High Pressure for 20 minutes. Release the pressure quickly.

Remove the quinoa bowl and rack. Using two forks, shred chicken into the sauce; stir to coat.

Divide the quinoa, between plates. Top with chicken and salsa verde before serving.

Chicken Meatballs in Tomato Sauce

Serves: 5 | Ready in about: 35 min

INGREDIENTS

1 pound ground chicken
3 tbsp red hot sauce
1 egg
⅓ cup crumbled blue cheese
¼ cup breadcrumbs
¼ cup Pecorino cheese
1 tbsp ranch dressing

1 tsp dried basil
salt and ground black pepper to taste
15 ounces canned tomato sauce
1 cup chicken broth
2 tbsp olive oil
Handful parsley, chopped

DIRECTIONS

In a bowl, mix chicken, egg, pecorino, basil, pepper, salt, ranch dressing, blue cheese, 3 tbsp hot sauce, and breadcrumbs; shape the mixture into meatballs.

Warm oil on Sauté mode. Add in the meatballs and cook for 2 to 3 minutes until browned on all sides.

Add in tomato sauce and broth. Seal the lid and cook on High Pressure for 7 minutes. Release the pressure quickly. Remove meatballs carefully and place to a serving plate. Top with parsley and serve.

Shredded Chicken with Lentils and Rice

Serves: 4 | Ready in about: 45 min

INGREDIENTS

1 tsp olive oil
1 garlic clove, minced
1 small yellow onion, chopped
3 cups chicken broth,
4 boneless, skinless chicken thighs

1 cup white rice
½ cup dried lentils
salt and ground black pepper to taste
Chopped fresh parsley for garnish

DIRECTIONS

Warm oil on Sauté mode. Stir-fry onion and garlic for 3 minutes until soft. Add in broth, rice, lentils, chicken, pepper, and salt.

Seal the lid and cook on High Pressure for 15 minutes. Do a quick release. Remove and shred the chicken in a large bowl. Set the lentils and rice into serving plates, Top with shredded chicken and parsley.

Herby Chicken Breasts

Serves: 4 | Ready in about: 15 min

INGREDIENTS

4 boneless, skinless chicken breasts
½ tsp salt
1 cup water
¼ cup dry white wine

½ tsp rosemary
½ tsp mint
½ tsp marjoram
½ tsp sage

DIRECTIONS

Sprinkle salt over the chicken and set in the pot. Mix in mint, rosemary, marjoram, and sage. Pour wine and water around the chicken. Seal the lid, and cook for 6 minutes on High Pressure. Release the pressure naturally, for 10 minutes.

Sriracha Chicken with Black Beans

Serves: 4 | Ready in about: 25 min

INGREDIENTS

½ cup soy sauce
½ cup chicken broth
3 tbsp honey
2 tbsp tomato paste
1 tbsp sriracha
1 (1 inch) piece fresh ginger, grated
3 garlic cloves, grated

4 boneless, skinless chicken drumsticks
1 tbsp cornstarch
1 tbsp water
2 tbsp toasted sesame seeds
1 tbsp sesame oil
2 cups canned black beans
2 green onions, thinly chopped

DIRECTIONS

In the cooker, mix the soy sauce, honey, ginger, tomato paste, chicken broth, sriracha, and garlic. Stir well until smooth; toss in the chicken to coat.

Seal the lid and cook for 3 minutes on High Pressure. Release the Pressure immediately.

Open the lid and press Sauté. In a small bowl, mix water and cornstarch until no lumps remain, Stir into the sauce and cook for 5 minutes until thickened.

Stir sesame oil and 1½ tablespoons sesame seeds through the chicken mixture; garnish with extra sesame seeds and green onions. Serve with black beans.

Saucy Chicken Breasts

Serves: 4 | Ready in about: 45 min

INGREDIENTS

4 chicken breasts, boneless and skinless
salt and ground black pepper to taste
2 tbsp olive oil
2 tbsp soy sauce
2 tbsp tomato paste
2 tbsp honey

2 tbsp minced garlic
½ cup chicken broth
1 tbsp cornstarch
1 tbsp water
½ cup chives, chopped

DIRECTIONS

Season the chicken with pepper and salt. Warm oil on Sauté. Add in chicken and cook for 5 minutes until lightly browned.

In a small bowl, mix garlic, soy sauce, honey, and tomato paste. Pour the mixture over the chicken. Stir in ½ cup broth. Seal the lid and cook on High Pressure for 12 minutes. Release the pressure quickly.

Set the chicken to a bowl. Mix water and cornstarch to create a slurry. Briskly stir the mixture into the sauce left in the pan for 2 minutes until thickened. Serve the chicken with sauce and chives.

Chicken with Tomatoes and Capers

Serves: 4 | Ready in about: 45 min

INGREDIENTS

4 chicken legs
sea salt and black pepper to taste
2 tbsp olive oil
1 onion, diced
2 garlic cloves, minced

⅓ cup red wine
2 cups diced tomatoes
⅓ cup capers
¼ cup fresh basil
2 pickles, chopped

DIRECTIONS

Sprinkle pepper and salt over the chicken. Warm oil on Sauté. Add in onion and sauté for 3 minutes until fragrant. Add in garlic and cook for 30 seconds until softened.

Mix the chicken with vegetables and cook for 6 to 7 minutes until lightly browned.

Add red wine to the pan to deglaze, scrape the pan's bottom to get rid of any browned bits of food; Stir in tomatoes. Seal the lid and cook on High Pressure for 12 minutes. Release the pressure quickly.

To the chicken mixture, add basil, capers, and pickles. Serve the chicken in plates covered with the tomato sauce mixture.

Chicken in Pineapple Gravy

Serves: 4 | Ready in about: 25 min

INGREDIENTS

1 tbsp olive oil
4 boneless, skinless chicken thighs
¼ cup pineapple juice
2 tbsp ketchup
2 tbsp Worcestershire sauce

1 garlic clove, minced
1 tsp cornstarch
2 tbsp water
Handful fresh cilantro, chopped

DIRECTIONS

Warm oil on Sauté. In batches, sear chicken in oil for 3 minutes until golden brown; set aside on a plate.

Mix pineapple juice, Worcestershire sauce, garlic, and ketchup; add to the pot to deglaze, scrape the bottom to get rid of any browned bits of food. Place the chicken into the sauce and stir well to coat.

Seal the lid cook for 5 minutes on High Pressure. Release the pressure quickly.

In a small bowl, mix water and cornstarch until well dissolved. Press Cancel and set to Sauté mode. Stir the cornstarch slurry into the sauce; cook for 2 minutes until the sauce is well thickened.

Set in serving bowls and cilantro to serve.

Honey-Garlic Chicken and Okra

Serves: 4 | Ready in about: 25 min

INGREDIENTS

6 garlic cloves, grated
¼ cup tomato puree
½ cup soy sauce
⅓ cup honey
2 tbsp rice vinegar
1 tbsp olive oil
4 boneless, skinless chicken breasts, chopped
1 cup rice, rinsed

½ tsp salt
2 cups water
2 cups frozen okra
1 tbsp cornstarch
1 tbsp water
2 tsp toasted sesame seeds
4 spring onions, chopped

DIRECTIONS

In the pot, mix garlic, tomato puree, vinegar, soy sauce, ginger, honey, and oil; toss in chicken to coat in an ovenproof bowl that can fit in the instant pot, mix water, salt and rice.

Set the steamer rack on top of chicken. Lower the bowl onto the rack.

Seal the lid and cook on High Pressure for 10 minutes. Release the pressure quickly.

Use a fork to fluff the rice. Lay okra onto the rice. Allow the okra steam in the residual heat for 3 minutes.

Take the trivet and bowl from the pot. Set the chicken to a plate.

Press Sauté. In a small bowl, mix 1 tablespoon of water and cornstarch until smooth. Stir into the sauce and cook for 3 to 4 minutes until thickened.

Divide the rice, chicken, and okra between 4 bowls. Drizzle sauce over each portion; garnish with spring onions and sesame seeds.

Asian Turkey Lettuce Cups

Serves: 4 | Ready in about: 45 min

INGREDIENTS

¾ cup olive oil
4 cloves garlic, minced
3 tbsp maple syrup
2 tbsp pineapple juice
1 cup coconut milk
3 tbsp rice wine vinegar

3 tbsp soy sauce
1 tbsp Thai-style chili paste
1 lb boneless, skinless turkey breasts, cut into strips
1 romaine lettuce, leaves separated
⅓ cup chopped peanuts
¼ cup chopped fresh cilantro leaves

DIRECTIONS

In the pot, mix peanut butter, garlic, rice wine vinegar, soy sauce, pineapple juice, honey, coconut milk, and chili paste until smooth; add turkey strips and ensure they are submerged in the sauce.

Seal the lid and cook on High Pressure for 12 minutes. Release the pressure quickly.

Place the turkey at the center of each lettuce leaf; Top with cilantro and chopped peanuts.

Potato and Ground Turkey Chili

Serves: 6 | Ready in about: 55 min

INGREDIENTS

1 tbsp olive oil
1 small onion, diced
2 garlic cloves, minced
1 pound ground turkey
2 bell peppers, chopped
6 potatoes, peeled and chopped
1cup carrots, chopped

1 cups fresh or frozen corn kernels, roasted
1 cups tomato puree
1 cups diced tomatoes
1 cup chicken broth
1 tbsp ground cumin
1 tbsp chili powder
salt and fresh ground black pepper

DIRECTIONS

Warm oil on Sauté, and stir-fry onions and garlic until soft, for about 3 minutes. Stir in turkey and cook until thoroughly browned, about 5-6 minutes. Add the remaining ingredients, and stir to combine.

Seal the lid and cook for 25 minutes on High Pressure. Do a quick release. Set on Sauté and cook uncovered for 15 more minutes. Serve warm.

Greek Turkey Meatballs

Serves: 6 | Ready in about: 30 min

INGREDIENTS

1 onion, minced
½ cup plain breadcrumbs
⅓ cup feta cheese, crumbled
2 tsp salt
½ tsp dried oregano
¼ tsp ground black pepper
1 pound ground turkey

1 egg, lightly beaten
1 tbsp olive oil
1 carrot, minced
½ celery stalk, minced
3 cups tomato puree
2 cups water

DIRECTIONS

In a mixing bowl, combine half the onion, oregano, turkey, salt, crumbs, pepper, and egg, and stir until everything is well incorporated.

Heat oil on Sauté mode, and cook celery, remaining onion, and carrot for 5 minutes, until soft. Pour in water, and tomato puree. Adjust the seasonings.

Roll the mixture into meatballs, and drop into the sauce. Seal the lid.

Press Meat/Stew and cook on High Pressure for 5 minutes. Allow the cooker to cool and release the pressure naturally for 20 minutes. Serve topped with feta cheese.

Spicy Turkey Casserole

Serves: 5 | Ready in about: 45 min

INGREDIENTS

1 tbsp olive oil
½ sweet onion, diced
3 cloves garlic, minced
1 jalapeno pepper, minced
1 pound turkey breast, cubed
2 (14 ounces) cans fire-roasted tomatoes
1½ cups water

1 cup salsa
2 bell peppers, cut into thick strips
2 tsp chili powder
1 tsp ground cumin
sea salt to taste
5 tbsp fresh oregano, chopped

DIRECTIONS

Warm oil on Sauté. Add in garlic, onion, and jalapeño and cook for 5 minutes, until fragrant. Stir turkey into the pot; cook for 5-6 minutes until browned.

Add in salsa, tomatoes, bell peppers, and water. Season with salt, cumin, and chili powder. Seal the lid, press Soup, and cook for 10 minutes on High. Release the pressure quickly. Top with oregano and serve.

Turkey Meatballs with Rigatoni

Serves: 4 | Ready in about: 40 min

INGREDIENTS

2 tbsp canola oil
1 pound ground turkey
1 egg
¼ cup breadcrumbs
2 cloves garlic, minced

1 tsp dried oregano
salt and ground black pepper to taste
3 cups tomato sauce
ounces rigatoni
2 tbsp grated Grana Padano cheese

DIRECTIONS

In a bowl, combine turkey, crumbs, cumin, garlic, and egg. Season with oregano, salt, red pepper flakes, and pepper. Form the mixture into meatballs with well-oiled hands.

Warm the oil on Sauté. Cook the meatballs for 3 to 4 minutes, until browned on all sides. Remove to a plate.

Add rigatoni to the cooker and cover with tomato sauce. Pour enough water to cover the pasta. Stir well. Throw in the meatballs. Seal the lid and cook for 10 minutes on High Pressure. Release the pressure quickly. Serve topped with Grana Padano cheese.

Lemon Turkey Risotto

Serves: 4 | Ready in about: 40 min

INGREDIENTS

2 boneless turkey breasts, cut into strips
2 lemons, zested and juiced
1 tbsp dried oregano
2 garlic cloves, minced
½ tsp sea salt
1½ tbsp olive oil

1 onion, diced
2 cups chicken broth
1 cup arborio rice, rinsed
Salt and freshly ground black pepper to taste
¼ cup chopped fresh parsley, or to taste
8 lemon slices

DIRECTIONS

In a ziploc back, mix turkey, oregano, sea salt, garlic, juice, and zest of two lemons. Marinate for 10 minutes.

Warm oil on Sauté. Add onion and cook for 3 minutes until fragrant; add rice and chicken broth and Season with pepper and salt. Empty the ziplock having the chicken and marinade into the pot.

Seal the lid and cook on High Pressure for 12 minutes. Release the pressure quickly.

Divide the rice and turkey between 4 serving bowls; garnish with lemon slices and parsley.

Chicken Drumstick & Mushroom Salad

Serves: 4 | Ready in about: 60 min

INGREDIENTS

4 chicken drumsticks
3 cups chicken broth
6 oz button mushrooms, whole
1 tomato, roughly chopped
2 oz lettuce
1 cup kalamata olives
1 cucumber, chopped

3 tbsp olive oil
1 tbsp Dijon mustard
¼ cup white wine
1 tsp lemon juice
1 tbsp Italian Seasoning mix
1 tsp salt

DIRECTIONS

In a bowl, mix mustard, 2 tbsp olive oil, Italian mix, wine, and salt. Stir well and brush the meat. Wrap in aluminum foil and Refrigerate for 30 minutes.

Place the vegetables in a serving bowl. Add mushrooms and stir well. Set aside.

Remove the drumsticks from the fridge and transfer to the pot. Pour in the broth and seal the lid. Cook on Poultry mode for 15 minutes on High Pressure.

Do a quick release and remove the thighs. Preheat a non-stick grill pan over high heat. Brown the thighs for 6-7 minutes, turning once. Serve with the salad.

Spicy Chicken Thighs with Potatoes

Serves: 4 | Ready in about: 30 min

INGREDIENTS

4 chicken thighs, boneless
3 large potatoes, wedged
1 tbsp lemon juice
2 garlic cloves, crushed
1 tsp ginger, ground

1 tbsp cayenne pepper
1 tsp fresh mint, finely chopped
¼ cup olive oil
½ tsp salt

DIRECTIONS

In a bowl, combine oil, lemon juice, garlic, ginger, mint, cayenne, and salt. Brush each chicken piece with this mixture. Grease the inner pot with the remaining mixture. Place the potatoes and top with chicken.

Add 1½ cups of water and seal the lid. Cook on Manual/Pressure Cook mode for 15 minutes on High. When ready, press Cancel and release the pressure naturally, for 10 minutes.

Chicken with Steamed Artichoke

Serves: 3 | Ready in about: 35 min

INGREDIENTS

1 lb chicken breasts, boneless, skinless, chopped
2 artichokes, trimmed, halved
2 tbsp butter, melted
2 tbsp olive oil

1 lemon, juiced
1 tsp pink Himalayan salt
¼ tsp freshly ground black pepper

DIRECTIONS

Heat oil on Sauté and cook the chicken for a minute per side, until slightly golden. Pour in 1 cup of water, seal the lid, and cook on High pressure for 13 minutes. Do a quick release. Set aside the chicken.

Place the trivet and pour a cup of water. Rub the artichoke halves with half of the lemon juice, and arrange on top of the trivet. Seal the lid and cook on Steam for 3 minutes on High. Do a quick release.

Combine artichoke and chicken in a large bowl. Stir in salt, pepper, and lemon juice. Drizzle butter over.

Chicken Quinoa Pilaf

Serves: 4 | Ready in about: 60 min

INGREDIENTS

1 lb chicken breasts, boneless, skinless
1 cup quinoa
2 cups chicken broth

1 tsp salt
½ tsp freshly ground black pepper
Greek yogurt for topping

DIRECTIONS

Add chicken and broth to the pot and seal the lid. Cook on Poultry for 15 minutes on High. Do a quick release and remove the chicken. Add quinoa and seal the lid. Cook on Rice mode for 8 minutes on High.

Meanwhile, cut the chicken meat into bite-sized pieces and place in a large bowl. To the cooker, do a quick release. Stir in chicken, to warm, season with black pepper, and top with greek yogurt.

Chicken Risotto with Vegetables

Serves: 4 | Ready in about: 65 min

INGREDIENTS

10 oz chicken breasts, boneless, skinless, cubed
1 cup rice
6 oz button mushrooms, chopped, stems removed
1 red bell pepper, halved, seeds removed
1 green bell pepper, halved, seeds removed
1 yellow bell pepper, halved, seeds removed
6 oz broccoli, cut into florets
½ cup sweet corn

2 carrots, peeled and chopped
2 tbsp olive oil
1 tbsp butter
1 tsp salt
½ tsp freshly ground black pepper
1 tsp fresh basil, finely chopped
Parmesan cheese for topping

DIRECTIONS

Add rice and pour in 3 cups of water. Stir in butter, pepper and salt and seal the lid. Cook on Rice mode for 8 minutes on High. Do a quick release and remove the rice.

Heat oil on Sauté, and add carrots and broccoli. Sauté for 10 minutes. Add sweet corn and bell peppers and cook for 5 minutes, stirring constantly. Finally, stir in mushrooms, and cook for 3-4 minutes.

Remove the vegetables, mix with rice and set aside. Add the chicken to the pot and pour in 2 cups of water. Season with salt and pepper. Seal the lid and cook on High pressure for 7 minutes.

Do a quick release. Open the lid, stir in rice and vegetables and serve warm sprinkled with Parmesan.

Gingered Chicken Chili

Serves: 6 | Ready in about: 35 min

INGREDIENTS

2 pounds chicken thighs, with skin and bones
1 tbsp chili powder
1 tsp fresh basil
¼ tsp black pepper, freshly ground
1 tsp salt

6 cups chicken broth
1 tbsp ginger, freshly grated
1 tbsp coriander seeds
3 garlic cloves, crushed

INSTRUCTIONS:

Season the meat with salt, and place it in the instant pot. Add the remaining ingredients, and cook on Meat/Stew mode for 25 minutes on High. Do a natural release, for about 10 minutes. Serve immediately.

Instant Chicken with Swiss Chard

Serves: 4 | Ready in about: 30 min

INGREDIENTS

2 lb chicken breasts, boneless and skinless, cubed
2 lb Swiss chard, chopped
2 cups chicken broth

2 tbsp butter, unsalted
2 tbsp olive oil
1 tsp sea salt

DIRECTIONS

Add the meat, oil and broth to the pot. Season with salt, seal the lid and cook on Manual/Pressure Cook for 13 minutes on High. Do a quick release, open the lid and add swiss chard and butter. Seal the lid again and cook on High pressure for 2 minutes. Do a quick release and serve warm.

Italian Chicken with Mushrooms

Serves: 2 | Ready in about: 30 min

INGREDIENTS

2 chicken thighs, boneless and skinless
6 oz button mushrooms
3 tbsp olive oil
1 tsp fresh rosemary, finely chopped

2 garlic cloves, crushed
½ tsp salt
1 tbsp butter
1 tbsp Italian Seasoning mix

DIRECTIONS

Heat a tablespoon of olive oil on Sauté. Add chicken thighs and sear for 5 minutes. Set aside. Pour in the remaining oil, and add mushrooms, rosemary, and italian seasoning mix. Stir-fry for 5 minutes.

Add in butter, chicken, and 2 cups of water. Seal the lid and cook on Pressure Cook mode for 13 minutes on High. Do a quick release. Remove the chicken and mushrooms from the cooker and serve with onions.

Garlic and Thyme Chicken

Serves: 4 | Ready in about: 30 min

INGREDIENTS

1.5 lb chicken breast, boneless and skinless
4 cups chicken broth
A pinch white pepper
2 garlic cloves, crushed

Handful fresh thyme
2 tbsp olive oil
1 onion, peeled and finely chopped
Salt to taste

INSTRUCTIONS:

Warm oil on Sauté. Stir-fry the onions for 2 minutes. Stir in garlic and cook for 2 minutes, until fragrant. Add the other ingredients except for the thyme. Adjust the seasoning, seal the lid and cook on High pressure for 15 minutes. When ready, do a quick pressure release. Serve topped with fresh thyme.

Herbed Chicken Thighs

Serves: 4 | Ready in about: 1 hr 30 min

INGREDIENTS

4 chicken thighs
1 cup chicken broth
1 cup olive oil
¼ cup apple cider vinegar
3 garlic cloves, crushed
½ cup freshly squeezed lemon juice

1 tbsp fresh basil, chopped
2 tbsp fresh thyme, chopped
1 tbsp fresh rosemary, chopped
1 tsp cayenne pepper
1 tsp salt

DIRECTIONS

In a bowl, add oil, vinegar, garlic, juice, basil, thyme, rosemary, salt, and cayenne. Submerge thighs into this mixture and refrigerate for one hour. Remove from the fridge and pat dry with kitchen paper.

Pour the broth in the pot. Set the trivet and place the chicken on it. Seal the lid and cook on Steam mode for 15 minutes on High. Do a quick release and remove the chicken and broth; wipe clean.

Press Sauté, warm oil and brown the chicken thighs for 5 minutes, turning once, until nice and golden.

Chicken Thighs with Vegetables

Serves: 4 | Ready in about: 50 min

INGREDIENTS

4 chicken thighs, boneless and skinless
1 cup chicken stock
½ cauliflower head, roughly chopped
2 tomatoes, roughly chopped
½ pound Brussels sprouts

2 zucchinis, chopped
1 small onion, peeled and chopped
3 tbsp olive oil
1 tsp salt

INSTRUCTIONS:

Heat oil, and stir-fry onions for 2 minutes on Sauté. Add vegetables and stir-fry for 5 minutes. Add the remaining ingredients and seal the lid. Cook on Poultry for 15 minutes on High. Do a quick release.

Chicken Wings with Worcestershire Sauce

Serves: 8 | Ready in about: 40 min

INGREDIENTS

8 chicken wings, bones and skin on
3 cups chicken broth
1 tsp fresh ginger, grated
1 tbsp honey
2 tbsp oil

⅓ cup Worcestershire Sauce
2 spring onions, finely chopped
2 garlic cloves, crushed
1 tsp salt

DIRECTIONS

Add the meat to the pot and pour in broth. Seal the lid and cook on Poultry for 15 minutes on High. Do a quick release. Remove chicken and broth, and wipe the pot clean.

Heat oil on Sauté, and stir-fry onions and garlic for 2-3 minutes. Add Worcestershire sauce, honey, and ginger. Cook for a minute and return the wings. Stir well and cook for 2 minutes, until nice and crispy.

Coconut Chicken Stew

Serves: 4 | Ready in about: 55 min

INGREDIENTS

2 cups fire-roasted tomatoes, diced
1 lb chicken breast, boneless and skinless, cubed
1 tbsp fresh basil, chopped
2 cups coconut milk
1 cup chicken broth
1 tsp salt
¼ tsp black pepper, freshly ground

2 tbsp tomato paste
2 celery stalks, chopped
2 carrots, chopped
2 tbsp coconut oil
1 onion, finely chopped
3 garlic cloves, crushed
½ cup button mushrooms, chopped

INSTRUCTIONS:

Grease the inner pot with oil. Add celery, onions, and carrots and cook on Sauté for 7 minutes, stirring constantly. Add tomato paste, basil, garlic, and mushrooms. Continue to cook for 10 more minutes.

Add the rest, seal the lid and cook on Poultry for 15 minutes on High. Do a quick release.

Orange Chicken Stew

Serves: 4 | Ready in about: 50 min

INGREDIENTS

2 lb chicken breast, boneless and skinless
1 cup fire-roasted tomatoes, diced
1 tbsp chili powder
1 tsp salt

¼ tsp white pepper, freshly ground
1 cup orange juice
2 cups chicken broth

DIRECTIONS

Season the meat with salt and pepper, and place in your instant pot. Add the remaining ingredients, except for the orange juice and chicken broth, and cook on Sauté mode for 10 minutes, stirring occasionally.

Press Cancel, pour in the broth and orange juice. Seal the lid and cook on Poultry for 25 minutes on High. Release the pressure naturally, for 10 minutes. Serve immediately.

Chili-Lime Chicken Thighs

Serves: 4 | Ready in about: 50 min

INGREDIENTS

1 lb chicken thighs
2 tbsp oil
4 cups chicken broth
1 tsp salt

2 tsp Lime zest
1 tsp chili powder
½ cup tomato puree
1 tbsp sugar

DIRECTIONS

Season the meat evenly with salt and chili powder on both sides. Warm oil on Sauté, and add the thighs. Briefly brown on both sides and then set aside. Add the tomato puree, sugar, and lime zest.

Cook for 10 minutes to obtain a thick sauce. Add the chicken thighs and pour in the broth. Seal the lid and cook on Poultry mode for 20 minutes on High pressure. When done, do a quick release and serve.

Spring Chicken Stew

Serves: 4 | Ready in about: 55 min

INGREDIENTS

4 green onions, chopped
3 garlic cloves, peeled and crushed
3 new potatoes, peeled and chopped
8 baby carrots, chopped
4 oz can tomato sauce

1 tsp salt
8 oz chicken breast, cut into bite-sized pieces
2 cups chicken broth
2 tbsp olive oil

DIRECTIONS

Place the veggies in the instant pot and pour enough water to cover. Seal the lid and cook on Manual/Pressure Cook for 15 minutes on High. Do a quick release. Remove the vegetables along with the liquid.

Heat oil on Sauté and stir-fry the vegetables for 5 minutes. Add the remaining ingredients and seal the lid. Set on Poultry and cook for 15 minutes on High. Do a natural release, for 10 minutes and serve hot.

Chicken in Garlic Yogurt Sauce

Serves: 6 | Ready in about: 42 min

INGREDIENTS

12 chicken wings
3 tbsp olive oil
1 tsp salt
3 cups chicken broth

Yogurt sauce:
½ cup sour cream
1 cup yogurt
2 garlic cloves, peeled and crushed

DIRECTIONS

Heat oil on Sauté. Brown the wings for 6-8 minutes, turning once. Pour in the broth and seal the lid. Cook on Poultry mode for 15 minutes on High Pressure. Do a natural release, for about 10 minutes.

In a bowl, mix sour cream, yogurt and garlic. Chill the wings for a while and drizzle with yogurt sauce.

Italian-Style Chicken Stew

Serves: 4 | Ready in about: 20 min

INGREDIENTS

2 lb chicken wings
2 potatoes, peeled, cut into chunks
2 fire-roasted tomatoes, peeled, chopped
1 carrot, peeled, cut into chunks
2 garlic cloves, chopped
2 tbsp olive oil

1 tsp smoked paprika, ground
4 cups chicken broth
2 tbsp fresh parsley, chopped
1 tsp salt
¼ tsp black pepper, ground
1 cup spinach, chopped

DIRECTIONS

Rub the chicken with salt, pepper, and paprika, and place in the pot. Add in all remaining ingredients and seal the lid. Cook on High Pressure for 8 minutes. When ready, do a quick release. Serve hot.

Spicy Mushroom Chicken

Serves: 3 | Ready in about: 25 min

INGREDIENTS

1 lb chicken breasts, boneless, cut into pieces
1 cup button mushrooms, chopped
2 cups chicken broth
2 tbsp flour
1 tsp cayenne pepper, ground

1 tsp salt
1 tbsp olive oil
2 garlic cloves, chopped
¼ tsp freshly ground black pepper

DIRECTIONS

Grease the inner pot with oil. Add garlic and meat, season with salt, and stir-fry for 3 minutes. Add mushrooms and Pour the chicken broth. Seal the lid.

Cook on High Pressure for 8 minutes. Release the steam naturally, for 10 minutes and stir in flour, cayenne, and black pepper.

Stir-fry for 5 more minutes, on Sauté mode. Serve warm.

Mediterranean Chicken

Serves: 2 | Ready in about: 20 min

INGREDIENTS

1 lb chicken breast, cut into ½ -inch thick slices
1 cup olive oil
1 cup chicken broth
½ cup freshly squeezed lemon juice
½ cup parsley leaves, chopped

3 garlic cloves, crushed
1 tbsp cayenne pepper
1 tsp dried oregano
½ tsp kosher salt

DIRECTIONS

In a bowl, mix olive oil, lemon juice, parsley, garlic, cayenne, oregano, and salt. Submerge fillets in this mixture and cover. Chill for 30 minutes.

Remove from the fridge and place all inside the pot. Add in the broth.

Seal the lid and cook on High Pressure for 7 minutes. Release the pressure naturally, for about 10 minutes.

Chicken and Green Pepper Stew

Serves: 4 | Ready in about: 35 min

INGREDIENTS

1 lb chicken breasts, boneless, skinless, cubed
2 potatoes, peeled, chopped
5 green bell peppers, chopped, seeds removed
2 carrots, chopped
2 ½ cups chicken broth

1 tomato, roughly chopped
Handful freshly chopped parsley
3 tbsp extra virgin olive oil
1 tsp freshly ground chili pepper
1 tsp salt

DIRECTIONS

Warm the oil on Sauté, and stir-fry bell peppers and carrots, for 3 minutes. Add potatoes, tomatoes, and parsley. Sprinkle with cayenne, and salt, and stir well.

Top with the chicken, pour in broth and seal the lid. Cook on High Pressure for 13 minutes. When ready, do a quick pressure release, and serve hot.

Chicken & Veggie Stew with Beans

Serves: 4 | Ready in about: 50 min

INGREDIENTS

1 whole chicken, 3 lb
8 oz fresh broccoli
6 oz cauliflower florets
1 onion, peeled, chopped
1 potato, peeled and chopped
3 carrots, chopped

1 tomato, peeled and chopped
Handful yellow wax beans, whole
Handful fresh parsley, chopped
¼ cup extra virgin olive oil
2 tsp salt
½ tsp freshly ground black pepper

DIRECTIONS

Grease the bottom of the pot with 3 tbsp of olive oil. Stir-fry the onions, for 3-4 minutes, on Sauté mode. Add the carrot and sauté for 5 more minutes.

Add the remaining oil, vegetables, salt, black pepper, and top with chicken. Add 1 cup of water and seal the lid. Cook on High Pressure for 30 minutes. Release the pressure naturally, for about 10 minutes.

Tarragon Roasted Chicken with Orange Sauce

Serves: 8 | Ready in about: 45 min

INGREDIENTS

1 whole chicken (about 3.5 lb)
¼ cup oil
2 tbsp fresh tarragon, minced
2 tbsp lemon zest
1 tsp garlic powder
¼ tsp red pepper flakes

3 cups chicken broth
1 cup red wine
5 tbsp butter
1 cup orange juice
1 tsp sugar
½ cup flour

DIRECTIONS

Mix oil, tarragon, lemon zest, garlic, and red pepper. Rub the mixture onto chicken. Melt butter on Sauté. and brown the chicken for 3-4 minutes. Pour in broth and wine. Seal the lid and cook on Poultry mode for 30 minutes on High Pressure. Do a quick release and remove the chicken.

In a bowl, mix the orange juice, 1 cup of cooking liquid, flour, and sugar. Cook for 5 minutes on Sauté mode until sauce has thickened. Scatter the sauce over the chicken and serve.

Christmas Chicken with Bacon

Serves: 4 | Ready in about: 45 min

INGREDIENTS

1 whole chicken (3.5 lb)
3 tbsp butter
¼ cup Worcestershire sauce
2 cups chicken stock

6 oz bacon
1 tbsp flour
White pepper and salt to taste

DIRECTIONS

Rub the meat with salt and pepper. Place in the instant pot along with stock and Worcestershire sauce. Seal the lid and cook on High Pressure for 40 minutes. Do a quick release and remove to a bowl.

Melt butter on Sauté mode. Stir-fry the bacon for 2 minutes, until crispy.

Stir in flour and 1 cup of cooking juices and cook for 4 minutes, until the sauce thickens. Transfer the chicken to a platter and drizzle the gravy over.

Italian-Style Turkey with Vegetables

Serves: 4 | Ready in about: 45 min

INGREDIENTS

1 lb turkey breast, chopped into bite-sized pieces
1 tsp red pepper flakes
2 cups canned tomatoes, diced
3 cups chicken broth
1 tsp honey
2 cups zucchini, cubed

3 garlic cloves, chopped
1 cup onions, finely chopped
2 tbsp tomato paste
1 cup baby carrots, chopped
Salt and pepper to taste
2 tbsp olive oil

INSTRUCTIONS:

Mix all ingredients in your instant pot. Seal the lid and cook on Meat/Stew mode for 25 minutes on High Pressure. When ready, do a quick release and open the lid. Serve immediately.

Sage & Thyme Chicken with Peach Sauce

Serves: 4 | Ready in about: 45 min

INGREDIENTS

4 chicken breasts
¼ cup olive oil
1 cup onion, chopped
¼ cup celery stalks, chopped
2 peaches, cut into chunks

½ tsp dried thyme
½ tsp dried sage
1 cup cider
2 cups chicken stock

DIRECTIONS

Heat oil on Sauté, and stir-fry the onions for 2-3 minutes, until soft. Add celery stalks and peaches, and cook for 5 minutes, stirring occasionally. Meanwhile, rub the meat with thyme and sage. Add it in the pot along with cider and stock.

Seal the lid and cook on High Pressure for 35 minutes. Do a quick release.

Lemon & Mustard Chicken

Serves: 2 | Ready in about: 35 min

INGREDIENTS

1 lb chicken breasts, boneless and skinless
¼ cup apple cider vinegar
1 tsp garlic powder
2 tbsp Dijon mustard

¼ tsp black pepper, freshly ground
2 tbsp olive oil
2 cups chicken stock

DIRECTIONS

Season the meat with garlic and black pepper. Place in the instant pot and Pour in the stock. Seal the lid and cook on Poultry mode for 20 minutes on High.

Do a quick release and remove the meat along with the stock. In a bowl, mix olive oil, dijon, and apple cider. Pour into the pot and Press Sauté.

Place the meat in this mixture and cook for 10 minutes, turning once. When done, remove from the pot and drizzle with the sauce.

Juicy Turkey with Hazelnuts

Serves: 5 | Ready in about: 40 min

INGREDIENTS

1 lb turkey breast, boneless, skinless, cut into ½ -inch thick slices
3 tbsp butter, softened
2 cups fresh cranberries
1 cup toasted hazelnuts, chopped

1 cup red wine
1 tbsp fresh rosemary, chopped
2 tbsp oil
2 tbsp orange zest

DIRECTIONS

Rub the meat with oil and sprinkle with orange zest and rosemary. Melt butter in the pot, and brown turkey breast for 5-6 minutes, on Sauté mode.

Pour in wine, cranberries and 1 cup of water. Seal the lid. Cook on High Pressure for 25 minutes. Do a quick release. Serve with chopped hazelnuts.

Turkey Patties

Serves: 4 | Ready in about: 25 min

INGREDIENTS

1 lb ground turkey
2 eggs
1 cup flour
1 onion, finely chopped

2 tsp dried dill, chopped
½ tsp salt
½ tsp black pepper, ground
1 cup sour cream

DIRECTIONS

In a bowl, add all ingredients and mix well with hands. Form the patties with the previously prepared mixture. Line parchment paper over a baking dish and arrange the patties. Pour 1 cup of water in the pot.

Lay the trivet and place the baking dish on top. Seal the lid. Cook on Pressure Cook mode for 15 minutes on High. Release the pressure naturally, for 10 minutes. Serve with lettuce and tomatoes.

Turkey Casserole

Serves: 2 | Ready in about: 40 min

INGREDIENTS

1 lb turkey breast, boneless, cut into pieces
2 tomatoes, pureed
1 onion, finely chopped
2 potatoes, peeled and chopped

1 tsp dried oregano
1 tsp salt
2 cups chicken broth
½ tsp black pepper, freshly ground

DIRECTIONS

Place the tomato in a food processor. Add oregano, salt, and pepper. Pulse until pureed and set aside. Combine all ingredients in the pot and seal the lid. Cook on Manual/Pressure Cook mode for 30 minutes on High. When done, press Cancel and release the steam naturally, for 10 minutes.

Turkey Pepperoni Pizza

Serves: 4 | Ready in about: 25 min

INGREDIENTS

1 whole wheat Italian pizza crust
1 cup fire-roasted tomatoes, diced
1 tsp oregano
½ tsp dried basil

½ cup turkey pepperoni, chopped
7 oz Gouda cheese, grated
2 tbsp olive oil

DIRECTIONS

Grease a baking pan with oil. Line some parchment paper and place the pizza crust in it.

Spread the fire-roasted tomatoes over the pizza crust and sprinkle with oregano and basil. Make a layer with cheese and top with pepperoni.

Add a trivet inside the pot and pour in 1 cup of water. Seal the lid, and cook for 15 minutes on High Pressure. Do a quick release. Remove the pizza from the pot using a parchment paper.

Roast Turkey with Basil and Garlic

Serves: 6 | Ready in about: 50 min

INGREDIENTS

2 lb boneless turkey breast, halved
2 garlic cloves, crushed
1 tsp dried basil
1 tsp white pepper
3 whole cloves

½ cup soy sauce
½ cup lemon juice
1 tbsp cane sugar
¼ cup oil
3 cups chicken broth

DIRECTIONS

Place the meat in a Ziploc bag and add basil, cloves, soy sauce, oil, and lemon juice. Pour in 1 cup of broth and seal. Shake and Refrigerate for 30 minutes.

Heat oil on Sauté and stir-fry the garlic for 2 minutes. Add in the along with 2 tbsp of the marinade and the remaining broth. Seal the lid.

Cook on Poultry for 25 minutes on High. Release the pressure naturally, for 10 minutes.

White Wine Roast Goose

Serves: 10 | Ready in about: 40 min

INGREDIENTS

2 lb goose fillets, cut into 1-inch thick slices
1 cup onions, finely chopped
4 tbsp butter, softened
2 garlic cloves, crushed
1 cup white wine

2 tbsp fresh celery, chopped
1 tsp dried thyme
1 tsp sea salt
¼ tsp white pepper, ground

DIRECTIONS

Season the meat with salt and white pepper. Place in the pot and add wine and thyme. Pour in 2 cups of water, seal the lid and set on Meat/Stew.

Cook for 25 minutes on High Pressure. When ready, do a quick release and set aside. Melt butter on Sauté, and stir-fry onions and garlic, for 3-4 minutes.

Add the fillets, one at the time, and brown on both sides for 2 minutes.

Honey-Mustard Glazed Duck

Serves: 4 | Ready in about: 45 min

INGREDIENTS

1 lb duck breast
1 tbsp oil
1 tsp onion powder
1 cup honey

¼ cup soy sauce
¼ cup dry sherry
1 tbsp Dijon mustard
3 cups chicken broth

DIRECTIONS

Rub the meat with onion powder and place it in the instant pot. Pour the broth, seal the lid and cook on Meat/Stew mode for 35 minutes on High Pressure.

Do a quick release and remove from the pot. Heat oil on Sauté, add soy sauce, honey, sherry, and mustard. Stir well and cook for 3-4 minutes. Add the meat and coat well. Serve the meat topped with the sauce.

BEEF & LAMB

Beef and Garbanzo Bean Chili

Serves: 10 | Ready in about: 45 min

INGREDIENTS

1 lb garbanzo beans, soaked overnight
1 tbsp olive oil
2 onions, finely chopped
2 ½ pounds ground beef
1 small jalapeño with seeds, minced
6 garlic cloves, minced
¼ cup chili powder
2 tbsp ground cumin

2 tsp salt
1 tsp smoked paprika
1 tsp dried oregano
1 tsp garlic powder
¼ tsp cayenne pepper
2 ½ cups beef broth
6 ounces canned tomato puree

DIRECTIONS

Add the beans and pour in cold water to cover 1 inch.

Seal the lid and cook for 20 minutes on High Pressure. Release the pressure quickly.

Drain beans and rinse with cold water. Set aside. Wipe clean the pot and set to Sauté mode. Warm olive oil, add in onion, and sauté for 3 minutes until soft. Add jalapeño, beef, and minced garlic, and stir-fry for 5 minutes until everything is cooked through.

Stir in chili powder, salt, garlic powder, paprika, cumin, oregano, and cayenne, and cook until soft, about 30 seconds. Pour in broth, beans, and tomato puree.

Seal the lid and cook for 20 minutes on High Pressure. Release the pressure naturally, for about 10 minutes. Open the lid, press Sauté, and cook as you stir until desired consistency is attained. Spoon chili into bowls and serve.

Chipotle Beef Brisket

Serves: 4 | Ready in about: 1hr 10 min

INGREDIENTS

2 tsp smoked paprika
½ tsp dried oregano
½ tsp salt
½ tsp ground black pepper
1 tbsp Worcestershire sauce
½ tsp ground cumin
½ tsp garlic powder

1 tsp chipotle powder
¼ tsp cayenne pepper
2 pounds, beef brisket
2 tbsp olive oil
1 cup beef broth
¼ cup red wine
A handful of parsley, chopped

DIRECTIONS

In a bowl, combine oregano, cumin, cayenne, garlic powder, salt, paprika, pepper, Worcestershire sauce, and chipotle powder. Rub the seasoning mixture on the beef to coat. Warm olive oil on Sauté. Add in beef and cook for 3 to 4 minutes each side until browned completely.

Pour in broth and wine. Seal the lid and cook on High Pressure for 50 minutes. Release the pressure naturally, for 10 minutes. Place the beef on a cutting board and allow cooling for 10 minutes before slicing. Arrange the beef on a serving platter, pour the sauce over and scatter with parsley to serve.

Beef Bourguignon

Serves: 5 | Ready in about: 40 min

INGREDIENTS

1 pound boneless chuck steak, trimmed and cut chunks
¼ cup flour
1 tsp salt
1 tsp ground black pepper
1 cup pancetta, chopped
½ cup red burgundy wine

1¼ cup beef broth
1 carrot, diced
2 cups Portobello mushrooms, quartered
4 shallots, chopped
3 garlic cloves, crushed
A handful of parsley, chopped

DIRECTIONS

Toss beef with black pepper, salt, and flour in a large bowl to coat.

Set on Sauté mode. Cook pancetta for 5 minutes until brown and crispy.

Pour in approximately half the beef and cook for 5 minutes each side until browned all over. Transfer the pancetta and beef to a plate. Sear remaining beef and transfer to the plate.

Add beef broth and wine to the cooker to deglaze the pan, scrape the pan's bottom to get rid of any browned bits of food. Return beef and pancetta to cooker; stir in garlic, carrot, shallots, and mushrooms.

Seal the lid and cook on High Pressure for 32 minutes. Release the pressure quickly.

Garnish with fresh chopped parsley and serve.

Beef and Cherry Tagine

Serves: 4 | Ready in about: 1hr 20 min

INGREDIENTS

2 tbsp olive oil
1 onion, chopped
1 ½ pounds stewing beef, trimmed
1 tsp ground cinnamon
½ tsp paprika
½ tsp turmeric
½ tsp salt

¼ tsp ground ginger
¼ tsp ground allspice
1-star anise
1 cup water
1 tbsp honey
1 cup dried cherries, halved
¼ cup toasted almonds, slivered

DIRECTIONS

Set on Sauté mode and warm olive oil. Add in onions and cook for 3 minutes until fragrant.

Mix in beef and cook for 2 minutes each side until browned.

Stir in anise, cinnamon, turmeric, allspice, salt, paprika, and ginger; cook for 2 minutes until aromatic.

Add in honey and water. Seal the lid, press Meat/Stew and cook on High Pressure for 50 minutes.

Meanwhile, in a bowl, soak dried cherries in hot water until softened.

Once done with cooking, release pressure naturally for 15 minutes.

Drain cherries and stir into the tagine. Top with toasted almonds before serving.

Beef and Bacon Chili

Serves: 6 | Ready in about: 1hr

INGREDIENTS

2 pounds stewing beef, trimmed
4 tsp salt,
4 ounces smoked bacon, cut into strips
1 tsp freshly ground black pepper
2 tbsp olive oil
1 onion, diced
2 bell peppers, diced
3 garlic cloves, minced

1 tbsp ground cumin
1 tsp chili powder
½ tsp cayenne pepper
1 chipotle in adobo sauce, finely chopped
2 cups beef broth
29 ounces canned whole tomatoes
15 ounces canned kidney beans, drained

DIRECTIONS

Set on Sauté mode and fry the bacon until crispy, about 5 minutes. Set aside.

Rub the beef with ½ teaspoon black pepper and 1 teaspoon salt.

In the bacon fat, brown beef for 5-6 minutes; Transfer to a plate.

Warm the oil. Add in garlic, peppers, and onion and sauté for 3 to 4 minutes until soft. Stir in cumin, cayenne pepper, the extra pepper, salt, chipotle, chili powder and cook for 30 seconds until soft.

Return beef and bacon to the pot with vegetables and spices; add in tomatoes and broth.

Seal the lid and cook on High Pressure for 45 minutes. Release the pressure quickly.

Stir in beans. Let simmer on Keep Warm for 10 minutes until flavors combine.

Brisket Chili con Carne

Serves: 6 | Ready in about: 1hr 25 min

INGREDIENTS

1 tbsp ground black pepper
2 tsp salt
1 tsp sweet paprika
1 tsp cayenne pepper
1 tsp chili powder
½ tsp garlic salt
14 ounces canned black beans, drained and rinsed

½ tsp onion powder
4 pounds beef brisket
1 cup beef broth
2 bay leaves
2 tbsp Worcestershire sauce

DIRECTIONS

In a bowl, combine pepper, paprika, chili powder, cayenne pepper, salt, onion powder, and garlic salt; rub onto brisket pieces to coat.

Add the brisket to your instant pot. Cover with Worcestershire sauce and water.

Seal the lid and cook on High Pressure for 50 minutes. Release the pressure naturally for 10 minutes.

Transfer the brisket to a cutting board. Drain any liquid present in the pot using a fine-mesh strainer; get rid of any solids and fat.

Slice brisket, arrange the slices onto a platter, add the black beans on side and spoon the cooking liquid over the slices and beans to serve.

Caribbean Ropa Vieja

Serves: 6 | Ready in about: 1hr 10 min

INGREDIENTS

Salt and ground black pepper to taste
2 pounds beef skirt steak
3½ cups beef stock
2 bay leaves
¼ cup olive oil
1 red onion, halved and chopped
1 green bell pepper, chopped
1 red bell pepper, chopped

¼ cup minced garlic
1 tsp dried oregano
1 tsp ground cumin
1 cup tomato sauce
1 cup dry red wine
1 tbsp vinegar
¼ cup cheddar cheese, shredded

DIRECTIONS

Season the skirt steak with pepper and salt. Add water to the cooker; mix in bay leaves and flank steak. Seal the lid and cook on High Pressure for 35 minutes. Release the pressure quickly.

Remove skirt steak to a cutting board and allow to sit for about 5 minutes. When cooled, shred the beef using two forks. Drain the pressure cooker, and reserve the bay leaves and 1 cup liquid.

Warm oil on Sauté mode. Add onion, bell peppers, cumin, garlic, and oregano and continue cooking for 5 minutes until vegetables are softened.

Stir in reserved liquid, tomato sauce, bay leaves, and wine. Return shredded beef to the pot with vinegar; season with pepper and salt.

Seal the lid and cook on High Pressure for 15 minutes. Release pressure naturally for 10 minutes, then turn steam vent valve to Venting to release the remaining pressure quickly. Serve with shredded cheese.

Beef and Pumpkin Stew

Serves: 6 | Ready in about: 35 min

INGREDIENTS

2 tbsp canola oil
2 pounds stew beef, cut into 1-inch chunks
1 cup red wine
1 onion, chopped
1 tsp garlic powder
1 tsp salt

3 whole cloves
1 bay leaf
3 carrots, chopped
½ butternut pumpkin, chopped
2 tbsp cornstarch
3 tbsp water

DIRECTIONS

Warm oil on Sauté mode. Brown the beef for 5 minutes on each side.

Deglaze the pot with wine, scrape the bottom to get rid of any browned beef bits. Add in onion, salt, bay leaf, cloves, and garlic powder. Seal the lid, press Meat/Stew and cook on High for 15 minutes.

Release the pressure quickly. Add in pumpkin and carrots without stirring.

Seal the lid and cook on High Pressure for 5 minutes. Release the pressure quickly.

In a bowl, mix water and cornstarch until cornstarch dissolves completely; mix into the stew. Allow the stew to simmer while uncovered on Keep Warm for 5 minutes until you attain the desired thickness.

Beef Pho with Swiss Chard

Serves: 6 | Ready in about: 1hr 10 min

INGREDIENTS

2 tbsp coconut oil
1 yellow onion, quartered
¼ cup minced fresh ginger
2 tsp coriander seeds
2 tsp ground cinnamon
2 tsp ground cloves
9 cups water
2 pounds Beef Neck Bones
2 ½ tsp kosher salt

8 ounces rice noodles
3 tbsp sugar
2 tbsp fish sauce
10 ounces sirloin steak
A handful of fresh cilantro, chopped
2 scallions, chopped
2 jalapeño peppers
2 cups Swiss chard, chopped
Freshly ground black pepper to taste

DIRECTIONS

Melt oil on Sauté mode. Add ginger and onions, and cook for 4 minutes until the onions soften. Stir in cloves, cinnamon, and coriander, and cook for 1 minute until soft. Add in water, salt, beef meat, and bones. Seal the lid and cook on High Pressure for 30 minutes. Release the pressure naturally for 8 minutes.

Transfer the meat to a large bowl; cover with it enough water and soak for 10 minutes. Drain the water and slice the beef. In hot water, soak rice noodles for 8 minutes until softened and pliable; drain and rinse with cold water. Drain liquid from cooker into a separate pot through a fine-mesh strainer; get rid of any solids.

Add fish sauce and sugar to the broth. Transfer into the cooker and simmer on Sauté mode.

Place the noodles in four separate soup bowls. Top with steak slices, scallions, swiss chard, jalapeño pepper, cilantro, red onion, and pepper. Spoon the broth over each bowl to serve.

Beef and Turnip Chili

Serves: 6 | Ready in about: 30 min

INGREDIENTS

1 tbsp olive oil
1 yellow onion, chopped
Salt to taste
4 garlic cloves, minced
2 tbsp tomato puree
1 tbsp chili powder
2 tsp ground cumin
1 tsp dried oregano

½ tsp ground turmeric
1 pinch cayenne pepper
1 pound ground beef meat
1 (28 ounces) can whole tomatoes
2 cups beef stock
1 pound turnips, peeled and cubed
2 tomatoes, chopped
1 bell pepper, chopped

DIRECTIONS

Warm oil on Sauté mode. Add in onion with a pinch of salt and cook for 3 to 5 minutes until softened.

Stir in garlic, chili powder, turmeric, cumin, tomato paste, oregano, and cayenne pepper; cook for 2 to 3 minutes as you stir until very soft and sticks to the pot's bottom. Add beef and cook for 5 minutes until completely browned. Mix in tomatoes, turnips, bell pepper, and stock.

Seal the lid and cook on High Pressure for 15 minutes. Release the pressure quickly.

Beer-Braised Short Ribs with Mushrooms

Serves: 4 | Ready in about: 1hr

INGREDIENTS

2 pounds beef short ribs
1 tsp smoked paprika
½ tsp dried oregano
½ tsp cayenne pepper
Salt and ground black pepper to taste
1 tbsp olive oil
1 small onion, chopped

4 garlic cloves, smashed
1 cup beer
⅓ cup beef broth
1 cup crimini mushrooms, chopped
1 tbsp soy sauce
1 bell pepper, diced

DIRECTIONS

In a bowl, combine pepper, paprika, cayenne, salt, and oregano. Rub the seasoning mixture on all sides of the short ribs.

Warm oil on Sauté. Add mushrooms and cook until browned, about 6-8 minutes. Set aside.

Add short ribs to the instant pot, and cook for 3 minutes for each side until browned; set aside on a plate.

Throw in garlic and onion to the oil and stir-fry for 2 minutes until fragrant.

Add in beer to deglaze, scrape the pot's bottom to get rid of any browned bits of food; bring to a simmer and cook for 2 minutes until reduced slightly.

Stir in soy sauce, bell pepper, and beef broth. Dip short ribs into the liquid in a single layer.

Seal the lid, press Meat/Stew and cook on High for 40 minutes. Release pressure naturally, for about 10 minutes. Divide the ribs with the sauce into bowls and top with fried mushrooms.

Mississippi Pot Roast with Potatoes

Serves: 6 | Ready in about: 1hr 40 min

INGREDIENTS

1 tbsp canola oil
2 pounds chuck roast
2 tsp salt
½ tsp black pepper
¼ cup butter
1 onion, finely chopped
1 tsp onion powder
1 tsp garlic powder

½ tsp dried thyme
½ tsp dried parsley
6 cups beef broth
½ cup pepperoncini juice
10 pepperoncini
5 potatoes, peeled and chopped
2 bay leaves

DIRECTIONS

Warm oil on Sauté mode. Season chuck roast with pepper and salt, then sear in hot oil for 2 to 4 minutes per side until browned. Set aside.

Melt butter and cook onion for 3 minutes until fragrant. Sprinkle with dried parsley, onion powder, dried thyme, and garlic powder and stir for 30 seconds.

Stir in bay leaves, broth, pepperoncini juice, and pepperoncini. Nestle chuck roast down into the liquid. Seal the lid and cook on High for 60 minutes. Release pressure naturally, for about 10 minutes. Set the chuck roast to a cutting board and use two forks to shred. Serve immediately.

Italian-Style Pot Roast

Serves: 5 | Ready in about: 1hr 30 min

INGREDIENTS

2 ½ pounds beef brisket, trimmed
Salt and freshly ground black pepper
2 tbsp olive oil
1 onion, chopped
3 garlic cloves, minced
1 cup beef broth
¾ cup dry red wine

2 fresh thyme sprigs
2 fresh rosemary sprigs
4 ounces pancetta, chopped
6 carrots, chopped
1 bay leaf
A handful of parsley, chopped

DIRECTIONS

Warm oil on Sauté. Fry the pancetta for 4-5 minutes until crispy. Set aside. Season the beef with pepper and salt, and brown for 5 to 7 minutes per each. Remove and set aside on a plate.

In the same oil, fry garlic and onion for 3 minutes until softened. Pour in red wine and beef broth to deglaze the bottom, scrape the bottom of the pot to get rid of any browned bits of food.

Return the beef and pancetta to the pot and add rosemary sprigs and thyme.

Seal the lid and cook for 50 minutes on High Pressure. Release the pressure quickly.

Add carrots and bay leaf to the pot. Seal the lid and cook for an additional 4 minutes on High Pressure.

Release the pressure quickly. Get rid of the thyme, bay leaf, and rosemary sprigs. Place beef on a serving plate and sprinkle with parsley to serve.

Traditional Beef Stroganoff

Serves: 6 | Ready in about: 1hr 15 min

INGREDIENTS

¼ cup flour
Salt and ground black pepper to taste
2 pounds beef stew meat
2 tbsp olive oil
1 onion, chopped
2 garlic cloves, minced

1 cup beef broth
3 cups fresh mushrooms, chopped
8 ounces sour cream
1 tbsp chopped fresh parsley
1 cup long-grain rice, cooked

DIRECTIONS

In a large bowl, combine salt, pepper, and flour. Add beef and massage to coat beef in flour mixture.

Warm oil on Sauté mode. Brown the beef for 4 to 5 minutes. Add garlic and onion and cook for 3 minutes until fragrant. Add beef broth to the pot.

Seal the lid and cook on High Pressure for 35 minutes. Release the pressure quickly.

Open the lid and stir mushrooms and sour cream into the beef mixture.

Seal the lid and cook on High Pressure for 2 minutes. Release the pressure quickly.

Season the stroganoff with pepper and salt; scoop over cooked rice before serving.

Beef Stew with Veggies

Serves: 6 | Ready in about: 1hr 15 min

INGREDIENTS

¼ cup flour
2 tsp salt
1 tsp paprika
1 tsp ground black pepper
2-pound beef chuck, cubed
2 tbsp olive oil
2 tbsp butter
1 onion, diced
3 garlic cloves, minced
1 cup dry red wine

2 cups beef stock
1 tbsp dried Italian Seasoning
2 tsp Worcestershire sauce
4 cups potatoes, diced
2 celery stalks, chopped
3 cups carrots, chopped
3 tomatoes, chopped
2 bell pepper, chopped
Salt and ground black pepper to taste
A handful of fresh parsley, chopped

DIRECTIONS

In a bowl, mix black pepper, beef, flour, paprika, and 1 teaspoon salt. Toss the ingredients and ensure the beef is well-coated. Warm butter and oil on Sauté mode.

Add in beef and cook for 8- 10 minutes until browned. Set aside on a plate.

To the same fat, add garlic, onion, and celery, bell peppers, and cook for 4-5 minutes until tender.

Deglaze with wine, scrape the bottom to get rid of any browned beef bits. Pour in remaining salt, beef stock, Worcestershire sauce, and Italian seasoning.

Return beef to the pot; add carrots, tomatoes, and potatoes.

Seal the lid, press Meat/Stew and cook on High Pressure for 35 minutes. Release pressure naturally for 10 minutes. Taste and adjust the seasonings as necessary. Serve on plates and scatter over the parsley.

Greek Beef Gyros

Serves: 4 | Ready in about: 55 min

INGREDIENTS

1 pound beef sirloin, cut into thin strips
1 onion, chopped
⅓ cup beef broth
2 tbsp fresh lemon juice
2 tbsp olive oil
2 tsp dry oregano

1 clove garlic, minced
Salt and ground black pepper to taste
4 slices pita bread
1 cup Greek yogurt
2 tbsp fresh dill, chopped

DIRECTIONS

In the pot, mix beef, beef broth, oregano, garlic, lemon juice, pepper, onion, olive oil, and salt.

Seal the lid and cook on High Pressure for 30 minutes. Release pressure naturally for 15 minutes, then turn steam vent valve to Venting to release the remaining pressure quickly.

Divide the beef mixture between the pita bread slices, top with yogurt and dill, and roll up to serve.

Meatloaf and Cheesy Mashed Potatoes

Serves: 6 | Ready in about: 45 min

INGREDIENTS

Meatloaf:

1 ½ pounds ground beef
1 onion, diced
1 egg
1 potato, grated

¼ cup tomato puree
1 tsp garlic powder
1 tsp salt
1 tsp ground black pepper

Mashed Potatoes:

4 potatoes, chopped
2 cups water
½ cup milk
2 tbsp butter

1 tsp salt
½ tsp ground black pepper
1 cup ricotta cheese

DIRECTIONS

In a bowl, combine ground beef, eggs, 1 tsp pepper, garlic powder, potato, onion, tomato puree, and 1 tsp salt to obtain a consistent texture. Shape the mixture into a meatloaf and place onto an aluminum foil. Arrange potatoes in the pot and pour water over them.

Place a trivet onto potatoes and set the foil sheet with meatloaf onto the trivet.

Seal the lid and cook on High Pressure for 22 minutes. Release the pressure quickly.

Take the meatloaf from the pot and set on a cutting board to cool before slicing.

Drain the liquid out of the pot. Mash potatoes in the pot with ½ teaspoon pepper, milk, ricotta cheese, 1 teaspoon salt, and butter until smooth and all the liquid is absorbed.

Divide potatoes into serving plates and lean a meatloaf slice to one side of the potato pile before serving.

BBQ Sticky Baby Back Ribs

Serves: 6 | Ready in about: 40 min

INGREDIENTS

2 tbsp olive oil
1 rack baby back ribs, cut into bones
½ tsp salt
1 tbsp mustard powder
1 tbsp smoked paprika

1 tbsp dried oregano
½ tsp ground black pepper
⅓ cup ketchup
1 cup barbecue sauce
½ cup apple cider

DIRECTIONS

In a bowl, thoroughly combine salt, mustard, paprika, oregano, and black pepper. Rub the mixture over the ribs. Warm oil on Sauté mode.

Add in the ribs and sear for 1 to 2 minutes for each side until browned.

Pour apple cider and barbecue sauce into the pot. Turn the ribs to coat. Seal the lid, press Meat/Stew and cook on High Pressure for 30 minutes. Release the pressure quickly.

Afterward, preheat a broiler. Cook the ribs with the sauce under the broiler for about 7 until the ribs become sticky and have a dark brown color. Transfer the ribs to a serving plate. Baste with the sauce to serve.

Meatballs with Marinara Sauce

Serves: 6 | Ready in about: 35 min

INGREDIENTS

1½ pounds ground beef
⅓ cup warm water
¾ cup grated Parmigiano-Reggiano cheese
½ cup breadcrumbs
1 egg
2 tbsp fresh parsley

¼ tsp garlic powder
¼ tsp dried oregano
Salt and ground black pepper to taste
½ cup capers
1 tsp olive oil
3 cups marinara sauce

DIRECTIONS

In a bowl, mix ground beef, garlic powder, pepper, oregano, crumbs, egg, and salt; shape into meatballs. Warm oil on Sauté mode. Add meatballs to the oil and brown for 2-3 minutes and all sides.

Pour water and marinara sauce over the meatballs. Seal the lid and cook on High Pressure for 10 minutes. Release the pressure quickly. Serve in large bowls topped with capers and Parmigiano-Reggiano cheese.

Swedish Meatballs with Mashed Cauliflower

Serves: 6 | Ready in about: 1hr

INGREDIENTS

¾ pound ground beef
¾ pound ground pork
1 large egg, beaten
½ onion, minced
¼ cup breadcrumbs
1 tbsp water
Salt and freshly ground black pepper to taste
4 tbsp butter

2 cups beef stock
3 tbsp flour
½ tsp red wine vinegar
1 ¾ cup heavy cream
1 head cauliflower, cut into florets
¼ cup sour cream
¼ cup fresh chopped parsley

DIRECTIONS

In a bowl, mix beef, onion, salt, breadcrumbs, pork, egg, water, and pepper; shape meatballs. Warm 2 tbsp of butter on Sauté mode.

Add meatballs and cook until browned, about 5-6 minutes. Set aside to a plate.

Pour beef stock in the pot to deglaze, scrape the pan to get rid of browned bits of food.

Stir vinegar and flour with the liquid in the pot until smooth; bring to a boil. Stir ¾ cup heavy cream into the liquid. Arrange meatballs into the gravy. Place trivet onto meatballs. Arrange cauliflower florets onto the trivet. Seal the lid and cook on High Pressure for 8 minutes. Release the pressure quickly.

Set the cauliflower in a mixing bowl. Add in the remaining 1 cup heavy cream, pepper, sour cream, salt, and 2 tablespoons butter and use a potato masher to mash the mixture until smooth.

Spoon the mashed cauliflower onto serving bowls; place a topping of gravy and meatballs. Add parsley for garnishing.

Braised Short Ribs with Creamy Sauce

Serves: 6 | Ready in about: 1hr 55 min

INGREDIENTS

3 pounds beef short ribs
2 tsp salt
1½ tsp freshly ground black pepper
2 tbsp olive oil
1 onion, chopped
1 large carrot, chopped
1 celery stalk, chopped
3 garlic cloves, chopped

2 cups beef broth
1 (14.5 ounces) can diced tomatoes
½ cup dry red wine
¼ cup red wine vinegar
2 bay leaves
¼ tsp red pepper flakes
2 tbsp chopped parsley
½ cup cheese cream

DIRECTIONS

Season short ribs with 1 teaspoon black pepper and 1 teaspoon salt. Warm olive oil on Sauté.

Add in short ribs and sear for 3 minutes each side until browned. Set aside on a bowl.

Drain everything only to be left with 1 tablespoon of the remaining fat from the pot.

Set on Sauté, and stir-fry garlic, carrot, onion, and celery in the hot fat for 4 to 6 minutes until fragrant. Stir in broth, wine, flakes, vinegar, tomatoes, bay leaves, and remaining pepper and salt.

Set on Sauté and bring the mixture to a boil. With the bone-side up, lay short ribs into the braising liquid.

Seal the lid and cook on High Pressure for 40 minutes. Release the pressure quickly.

Set the short ribs on a plate. Get rid of bay leaves. Skim and get rid of the fat from the surface of braising liquid.

Using an immersion blender, blend the liquid for 1 minute; add cream cheese, pepper and salt, and blitz until smooth. Arrange the ribs onto a serving plate, pour the sauce over and top with parsley.

Italian Beef Sandwiches with Pesto

Serves: 4 | Ready in about: 1hr

INGREDIENTS

1 ½ pounds beef steak, cut into strips
Salt and ground black pepper
1 tbsp olive oil
¼ cup dry red wine
1 cup beef broth
1 tbsp oregano

1 tsp onion powder
1 tsp garlic powder
4 hoagie rolls, halved
8 slices mozzarella cheese
½ cup pepperoncini peppers
4 tbsp pesto

DIRECTIONS

Season the beef cubes with salt and pepper. Warm oil on Sauté and sear the beef for 2 to 3 minutes for each side until browned.

Add wine into the pot to deglaze, scrape the bottom to get rid of any browned beef bits.

Stir garlic powder, beef broth, onion powder, and oregano into the pot.

Seal the lid, press Meat/Stew and cook for 25 minutes on High. Release pressure naturally for 10 minutes. Spread each bread half with pesto, put beef on top, place pepperoncini slices over, add mozzarella cheese slices and cover with the second half of bread to serve.

Short Ribs with Mushrooms & Asparagus Sauce

Serves: 6 | Ready in about: 1hr 15 min

INGREDIENTS

3½ pounds boneless beef short ribs, cut into pieces
2 tsp salt
1 tsp ground black pepper
3 tbsp olive oil
1 onion, diced
1 cup dry red wine
1 tbsp tomato puree
2 carrots, peeled and chopped
2 garlic cloves, minced

5 sprigs parsley, chopped
2 sprigs rosemary, chopped
3 sprigs oregano, chopped
4 cups beef stock
10 ounces mushrooms, quartered
1 cup asparagus, trimmed chopped
1 tbsp cornstarch
¼ cup cold water

DIRECTIONS

Season the ribs with black pepper and salt. Warm oil on Sauté. In batches, add the short ribs to the oil and cook for 3 to 5 minutes each side until browned. Set aside. Add onions and sauté for 4 minutes until soft.

Add tomato puree and red wine into the pot to deglaze, scrape the bottom to get rid of any browned beef bits. Cook for 2 minutes until wine reduces slightly.

Return the ribs to pot and top with carrots, oregano, rosemary, and garlic. Add in broth and press Cancel.

Seal the lid, press Meat/Stew and cook on High for 35 minutes. Release pressure naturally for 10 minutes. Transfer ribs to a plate. Strain and get rid of herbs and vegetables, and return cooking broth to inner pot. Add mushrooms and asparagus to the broth. Press Sauté and cook for 2 to 4 minutes until soft.

In a bowl, mix water and cornstarch until cornstarch dissolves completely. Add the cornstarch mixture into the broth as you stir for 1 to 3 minutes until the broth thickens slightly. Season the sauce with black pepper and salt. Pour the sauce over ribs, add chopped parsley for garnish before serving.

East Asian Rice Porridge

Serves: 6 | Ready in about: 1hr

INGREDIENTS

1 cup jasmine rice
2 cloves garlic, minced
1 (1 inch) piece fresh ginger, minced
6 cups beef stock
1 cup kale, roughly chopped

1 cups water
2 pounds ground beef
Salt and ground black pepper to taste
Fresh cilantro, chopped

DIRECTIONS

Run cold water and rinse rice. Add garlic, rice, and ginger into the pot. Pour water and stock into the pot and Spread the beef on top of rice.

Seal the lid and cook on High Pressure for 30 minutes. Release pressure naturally, for 10 minutes.

Stir in kale to obtain the desired consistency. Season with pepper and salt. Divide into serving plates and top with cilantro.

Mustardy Beef Steak

Serves: 3 | Ready in about: 55 min

INGREDIENTS

3 rib-eye steaks, boneless
2 tbsp lemon juice
3 tbsp canola oil
3 tbsp Dijon mustard

1 tsp salt
½ tsp ground black pepper
3 cups beef broth

DIRECTIONS

In a bowl, mix lemon juice, oil, mustard, salt, and pepper. Brush the steaks with this mixture and set aside. Pour the beef broth in the instant pot.

Place the steamer tray and arrange the steaks on top. Seal the lid and cook on High Pressure for 35 minutes. Do a quick release and remove the broth.

Press Sauté and brown steaks on both sides for 3-4 minutes.

Peppery Beef with Parsley Butter

Serves: 6 | Ready in about: 50 min

INGREDIENTS

2 lb beef fillets, cut into bite-sized pieces
4 onions, peeled, chopped
3 tbsp tomato paste
2 tbsp oil

1 tbsp butter, melted
2 tbsp fresh parsley, chopped
½ tsp freshly ground black pepper
1 tsp salt

DIRECTIONS

Grease the instant pot with 2 tbsp of oil. Make the first layer of meat. Add onions, tomato paste, parsley, salt, and pepper. Stir and pour 2 cups of water.

Seal the lid and cook on Meat/Stew mode for 30 minutes on High. Release the steam naturally, for about 10 minutes. Stir in 1 tbsp of butter and serve warm.

Basil T-Bone Steak

Serves: 4 | Ready in about: 1 hr 35 min

INGREDIENTS

1 lb T-bone steak (2 pieces)
1 tsp pink Kosher salt
¼ tsp freshly ground black pepper

2 tbsp Dijon mustard
¼ cup oil
½ tsp dried basil, crushed

DIRECTIONS

Whisk together oil, mustard, salt, pepper, and basil. Brush each steak and refrigerate for 1 hour. Meanwhile, insert the steamer tray in the instant pot.

Pour 3 cups of water and arrange the steaks on the tray. Seal the lid and cook on Steam mode for 25 minutes on High. Do a quick release and open the pot.

Discard the liquid, remove the tray, and hit Sauté. Brown the steaks, one at the time, for 5 minutes, turning once.

Beef & Rice Stuffed Onions

Serves: 4 | Ready in about: 30 min

INGREDIENTS

10 sweet onions, peeled
1 lb lean ground beef
½ tbsp rice
3 tbsp olive oil
1 tbsp dry mint, ground
1 tsp cayenne pepper, ground

½ tsp cumin, ground
1 tsp salt
½ tbsp tomato paste
½ cup breadcrumbs
A handful of fresh parsley, finely chopped

DIRECTIONS

Cut a ¼-inch slice from top of each onion and trim a small amount from the bottom end, this will make the onions stand upright. Place onions in a microwave-safe dish, and pour one cup of water.

Cover with a tight lid and microwave for 10-12 minutes or until onions soften. Remove onions and cool slightly. Carefully remove inner layers of onions with a paring knife, leaving about a ¼-inch onion shell.

In a bowl, combine beef, rice, oil, mint, cayenne pepper, cumin, salt, and breadcrumbs. Use one tablespoon of the mixture to fill the onions. Grease the inner pot with oil. Add onions and pour 2.5 cups of water.

Seal the lid and cook on Manual/Pressure Cook for 10 minutes on High. Do a quick release. Top with parsley and serve with sour cream and pide bread.

Beef Stew with Eggplant & Parmesan

Serves: 6 | Ready in about: 50 min

INGREDIENTS

9 oz beef neck, cut into bite-sized pieces
1 eggplant, sliced
2 cups fire-roasted tomatoes
½ tbsp fresh green peas
1 tbsp beef broth

4 tbsp olive oil
2 tbsp tomato paste
1 tbsp ground chili pepper
½ tsp kosher salt
Parmesan Cheese, for garnish

DIRECTIONS

Rub the meat with salt, cayenne, and chili pepper. Grease the instant pot with oil and brown the meat for 5-7 minutes, or until golden, on Sauté mode.

Add all the remaining ingredients and seal the lid. Cook on Meat/Stew mode for 40 minutes on High. Do a natural release, for 10 minutes. Serve warm, sprinkled with freshly grated Parmesan Cheese.

Beef, Potato & Pea Stew

Serves: 4 | Ready in about: 50 min

INGREDIENTS

1 lb beef stew meat, chopped
2 onions, peeled, chopped
3 potatoes, peeled, chopped
1 cup green peas
1 tsp salt

1 tsp cayenne pepper
1 tbsp apple cider vinegar
3 tbsp olive oil
3 cups beef broth
A handful of freshly chopped parsley

DIRECTIONS

Heat oil on Sauté mode. Stir-fry the onions until translucent. Add the meat and potatoes, and brown for about 10 minutes. Add peas, and season with salt and cayenne pepper. Pour in broth and apple cider.

Seal the lid and set on Meat/Stew for 25 minutes on High. Do a quick release and top with parsley.

Beef & Cauliflower Stew

Serves: 6 | Ready in about: 20 min

INGREDIENTS

1 lb beef stew meat
1 tbsp cauliflower, chopped
1 medium onion, chopped
2 cups beef broth
2 cups heavy cream

1 cup water
1 tsp Italian Seasoning mix
1 tsp salt
½ tsp ground chili pepper

DIRECTIONS

Add all ingredients in your instant pot. Seal the lid and cook on High Pressure for 15 minutes. When ready, do a quick release and serve immediately.

Spicy Beef with Carrots & Potatoes

Serves: 4 | Ready in about: 35 min

INGREDIENTS

1 lb beef shoulder
1 lb potatoes, cut into chunks
2 carrots, chopped
1 onion, finely chopped
4 tbsp olive oil
2 tbsp tomato paste

1 tbsp flour
4 cups beef broth
1 tbsp fresh celery, chopped
1 tbsp fresh parsley, chopped
1 cayenne pepper, chopped
Salt and pepper

DIRECTIONS

Warm oil on Sauté. Stir-fry onions, carrots, and potatoes for 7-8 minutes. Stir in flour and press Cancel. Add the remaining ingredients. Seal the lid and cook on High pressure for 40 minutes. Do a quick release.

Beef & Vegetable Stew

Serves: 6 | Ready in about: 35 min

INGREDIENTS

2 lb beef meat for stew
¾ cup red wine
1 tbsp ghee
6 oz tomato paste
6 oz baby carrots, chopped
2 sweet potatoes, cut into chunks

1 onion, finely chopped
½ tsp salt
4 cups beef broth
½ cup green peas
1 tsp dried thyme
3 garlic cloves, crushed

INSTRUCTIONS:

Heat the ghee on Sauté. Add beef and brown for 5-6 minutes. Add onions and garlic, and keep stirring for 3 more minutes. Add the remaining ingredients and seal the lid. Cook on Meat/Stew for 20 minutes on High pressure. Do a quick release and serve immediately.

Winter Goulash Stew

Serves: 6 | Ready in about: 55 min

INGREDIENTS

2 lb beef stew meat
3 potatoes, cut into chunks
1 large onion, roughly chopped
1 large carrot, chopped
1 cabbage head, shredded
1 cup sun-dried tomatoes, diced

4 cups beef broth
3 tbsp tomato paste
1 tsp Tabasco
1 tsp salt
½ tsp freshly ground white pepper
3 tbsp butter

DIRECTIONS

Heat oil on Sauté and cook the onions, for 2 minutes. Add the tomato paste and stir. Add the remaining ingredients and seal the lid. Cook on High pressure for 35 minutes. Do a quick release.

Beef Pasta with Tomato Sauce

Serves: 5 | Ready in about: 45 min

INGREDIENTS

1 pack (16 oz.) macaroni
6 oz beef, braising steak cut into bite-sized chunks
1 onion, chopped
1 tomato, peeled, diced
1 tbsp tomato paste

3 tbsp butter, unsalted
¼ tsp freshly ground black pepper
1 tsp cayenne pepper
1 tbsp vegetable oil

DIRECTIONS

Heat oil on Sauté and stir-fry the onion, until translucent. Add tomato, paste, butter, a pinch of salt, black and cayenne pepper. Cook until tomato softens, stirring occasionally. Add beef chunks and 1 cup water.

Seal the lid and cook for 14 minutes on High Pressure. Do a quick release and set the meat aside. Add in macaroni and 2 cups of water. Seal the lid and cook on High Pressure for 4 minutes.

Do a quick release and transfer the macaroni to a large bowl, stir in the beef sauce and serve.

Beef Vegetable Steaks

Serves: 4 | Ready in about: 45 min

INGREDIENTS

2 large beef cutlets
3 potatoes, whole
1 onion, whole
3 carrots, whole
6 oz of cauliflower, into florets
3 tbsp olive oil

1 tbsp butter
1 tsp salt
¼ tsp black pepper
½ tbsp chili pepper, ground
3 cups beef broth

DIRECTIONS

Sprinkle the meat with salt and pepper, and place it in your instant pot: Peel onion, carrots, potatoes. Add the cauliflower. Pour broth, seal the lid and cook on High Pressure for 25 minutes.

Release the pressure naturally, for about 10 minutes. Remove the meat and vegetables. Melt butter on Sauté, and add chili pepper. Stir and add the meat. Brown on both sides and serve immediately.

Beef Steaks with Mushrooms

Serves: 4 | Ready in about: 35 min

INGREDIENTS

1 lb beef steaks
1 lb button mushrooms, chopped
2 tbsp vegetable oil
1 tsp salt

½ tsp freshly ground black pepper
1 bay leaf
1 tbsp dried thyme
6 oz cherry tomatoes

DIRECTIONS

Rub steaks with salt, pepper, and thyme. Place in the instant pot. Pour in 3 cups of water, add bay leaf, and seal the lid. Cook on High pressure for 13 minutes. Do a quick release and set the steaks aside. Heat oil on Sauté, and stir-fry mushrooms and tomatoes for 5 minutes. Add steaks and brown on both sides.

Crispy Beef with Rice

Serves: 4 | Ready in about: 55 min

INGREDIENTS

2 lb beef shoulder
1 cup rice
2 cups beef broth

3 tbsp butter
1 tsp salt
½ tsp pepper

DIRECTIONS

Rinse the meat and rub with salt. Place it in the pot and pour in broth. Seal the lid and cook on Meat/Stew for 25 minutes on High Pressure. Do a quick release, remove the meat but keep the broth.

Add rice and stir in 1 tbsp of butter. Seal the lid, and cook on Rice mode for 8 minutes on High. Do a quick release. Remove the rice and wipe the pot clean. Melt 2 tbsp of butter on Sauté.

Add meat and lightly brown for 10 minutes. Serve with rice and season with pepper and salt.

Beef & Eggplant Casserole

Serves: 2 | Ready in about: 35 min

INGREDIENTS

2 eggplants, peeled, cut lengthwise
1 cup lean ground beef
1 onion, chopped
1 tsp olive oil

¼ tsp. freshly ground black pepper
2 tomatoes
3 tbsp freshly chopped parsley

DIRECTIONS

Place eggplants in a bowl and season with salt. Let sit for 10 minutes. Rinse well and drain. Grease the inner pot with oil. Stir-fry onions for 2 minutes, until soft.

Add ground beef, tomato, and cook for 5 minutes. Transfer to a deep bowl. Make a layer with eggplant slices in the pot. Spread the ground beef mixture over and sprinkle with parsley. Make another layer with eggplants and repeat until you've used up all ingredients. Seal the lid and cook on High Pressure for 12 minutes. Do a quick release.

Beef and Wax Beans

Serves: 4 | Ready in about: 20 min

INGREDIENTS

1 lb ground beef
1 lb wax beans
1 small onion, chopped
1 tbsp tomato paste
2 cups beef broth
2 garlic cloves, crushed

2 tbsp olive oil
2 tbsp fresh parsley, finely chopped
1 tsp salt
½ tsp paprika
1 tbsp Parmesan Cheese, grated

DIRECTIONS

Grease the pot with olive oil. Stir-fry the onion and garlic, for a few minutes until translucent on Sauté. Add beef, tomato paste, parsley, salt, and paprika.

Cook for 5 minutes, stirring constantly. Add wax beans and beef broth. Press Cancel and seal the lid. Cook on High Pressure for 4 minutes. Do a naturally release, for 5 minutes. Top with Parmesan.

Beef Stew with Green Peas

Serves: 4 | Ready in about: 15 min

INGREDIENTS

2 lb beef, tender cuts, boneless, cut into bits
2 cups green peas
1 onion, diced
1 tomato, diced
3 cups beef broth
½ cup tomato paste

1 tsp cayenne pepper, ground
1 tbsp flour
1 tsp salt
½ tsp dried thyme, ground
½ tsp red pepper flakes

DIRECTIONS

Add all ingredients in the instant pot. Seal the lid, press Manual/Pressure Cook and cook for 10 minutes on High Pressure. When done, release the steam naturally, for 10 minutes and serve.

Chili Pepper & Beef Beans

Serves: 4 | Ready in about: 30 min

INGREDIENTS

14.5 oz canned beans
12 oz beef bones
1 onion, peeled, chopped
3 garlic cloves
1 carrot, chopped
1 tbsp fresh parsley, chopped

1 bay leaf
1 tsp salt
¼ tsp pepper
1 tsp cayenne pepper
3 tbsp vegetable oil

DIRECTIONS

Place all other ingredients in the instant pot. Pour water enough to cover. Seal the lid. Cook on High Pressure for 15 minutes. Release the steam naturally, for 10 minutes. Let it chill for a while before serving.

Easy Beef Casserole

Serves: 3 1 Ready in about: 20 minutes

INGREDIENTS

1 lb lean beef, with bones
2 carrots
1 potato, peeled, sliced

3 tbsp olive oil
½ tsp salt

DIRECTIONS

Mix all ingredients in the instant pot. Pour water enough to cover and seal the lid. Cook on High Pressure for 15 minutes. Do a quick release and serve hot.

Beef Stuffed Red Peppers

Serves: 4 | Ready in about: 35 min

INGREDIENTS

2 lb red bell peppers, stems and seed removed
1 onion, finely chopped
1 lb lean ground beef
¼ cup rice
½ cup tomatoes

1 tomato, chopped
½ tsp salt
1 tsp cayenne pepper
3 tbsp olive oil

DIRECTIONS

In a bowl, combine meat, onion, rice, tomatoes, salt, and cayenne. Stir well to combine. Use 2 tbsp of this mixture and fill each pepper.

Make sure to leave at least ½ inch of headspace. Grease the bottom of your instant pot with cooking spray. Make the first layer with tomato slices.

Arrange the peppers and add two cups of water. Seal the lid, and cook on High Pressure for 15 minutes. Do a natural pressure release, for 10 minutes.

Garlic Meatballs with Potatoes

Serves: 4 | Ready in about: 40 min

INGREDIENTS

1 lb lean ground beef
6 oz rice
2 onions, peeled, chopped
2 garlic cloves, crushed

1 egg, beaten
1 large potato, peeled, chopped
3 tbsp olive oil
1 tsp salt

DIRECTIONS

In a bowl, combine beef, rice, onions, garlic, egg, and salt. Shape the mixture into 15-16 meatballs. Grease the inner pot with 1 tbsp of olive oil. Press Sauté and cook the meatballs for 3-4 minutes.

Remove the meatballs. Add the remaining oil and make a layer of potatoes. Top with meatballs, cover with water and seal the lid. Adjust the release steam handle. Cook on Meat/Stew mode for 15 minutes on High. Do a quick release.

Sour Potato Beef Lasagne

Serves: 4 | Ready in about: 30 min

INGREDIENTS

2 lb potatoes, peeled, chopped
1 lb lean ground beef
1 onion, peeled, chopped
Salt and black pepper to taste

½ cup milk
2 eggs, beaten
Vegetable oil
Sour cream for serving

DIRECTIONS

Grease the bottom of the pot with oil. Make one layer of potatoes and brush with milk. Spread the ground beef on top and make another layer of potatoes. Brush well with the remaining milk, 2 cups.

Seal the lid, and cook for 15 minutes on High Pressure. When ready, do a quick release.Open the lid, and make the final layer with the beaten eggs. Seal the lid and let it stand for about 10 minutes. Top with sour cream to serve.

Eggplant Stew with Almonds

Serves: 4 | Ready in about: 30 min

INGREDIENTS

3 eggplants, halved
2 tomatoes, chopped
2 red bell peppers, chopped, seeds removed
¼ tbsp tomato paste

3 oz toasted almonds, chopped
2 tbsp salted capers, rinsed, drained
¼ cup extra virgin olive oil
Sea salt and pepper to taste

DIRECTIONS

Grease the instant pot with 2 tbsp of olive oil. Make the first layer with halved eggplants tucking the ends Gently to fit in. Make the second layer with tomatoes and red bell peppers. Spread the tomato paste evenly over the vegetables, sprinkle with almonds and salted capers.

Add the remaining olive oil, salt, and pepper. Pour 1 ½ cups of water and seal the lid. Cook on High Pressure for 13 minutes. Do a quick release.

Russian Beef & Mushroom Stew

Serves: 6 | Ready in about: 45 min

INGREDIENTS

1 lb beef steak, cut into bite-sized pieces
1 cup button mushrooms, chopped
1 cup sour cream
2 cups beef broth
3 tbsp Worcestershire sauce

3 tbsp olive oil
1 tbsp flour
1 onion, chopped
2 garlic cloves, minced
¼ tsp freshly ground black pepper

DIRECTIONS

In a bowl, mix flour, a pinch of salt and pepper. Coat steaks with this mixture. Place the meat and broth in the inner pot. Seal the lid and cook for 10 minutes on High Pressure. Do a quick release. Add mushrooms, onions, and garlic, and Worcestershire sauce. Seal the lid and cook on High Pressure for 15 minutes. Do a quick release. Stir in sour cream. Let simmer for 10 minutes, and serve.

Red Wine Beef Sirloin

Serves: 4 | Ready in about: 25 min

INGREDIENTS

2 lb beef sirloin
1 cup red wine
2 cups beef consomme
2 bay leaves
2 tbsp olive oil
Salt and black pepper to taste

1 large onion, chopped
1 stalk celery, diced
1 tbsp tomato puree
2 cloves garlic, minced
2 sprigs fresh parsley

DIRECTIONS

Rub the meat with salt and pepper on all sides. Heat oil on Sauté and sear the beef for 4-5 minutes. Set aside. In the same oil, add onion, celery, garlic, and tomato puree. Cook for 4-5 minutes, until soft. Pour in wine to deglaze the bottom of the pot, scrape to remove browned bits.

Bring the meat back to the pot, and add parsley and bay leaf. Seal the lid, and cook on High Pressure for 50 minutes. Do a natural pressure release, for 10 minutes and serve immediately.

Peppery Beef

Serves: 6 | Ready in about: 45 min

INGREDIENTS

2 lb lean beef, cut into bite-sized pieces
5 onions, peeled, chopped
5 garlic cloves, peeled, crushed
1 tsp salt
1 jalapeno pepper, deveined and chopped

1 bell pepper, deveined and chopped
Freshly ground black pepper, to taste
1 tsp cayenne pepper
2 tbsp tomato sauce
2 tbsp vegetable oil

DIRECTIONS

Heat oil on Sauté. Stir-fry onions, garlic, for 2-3 minutes. Add the meat, salt, pepper, cayenne pepper, and tomato sauce. Mix well and pour enough water to cover. Seal the lid and cook for 20 minutes on High Pressure. Do a quick pressure release.

Rosemary Meatloaf

Serves: 6 | Ready in about: 60 min

INGREDIENTS

2 lb ground beef
2 large eggs
½ tsp minced garlic
1 cup all-purpose flour

1 tsp dried thyme, ground
3 tbsp olive oil
1 tsp dried rosemary, ground
½ tsp salt

DIRECTIONS

In a bowl, combine the meat, flour, and eggs. Sprinkle with thyme, rosemary, and salt. Mix until well incorporated, and set aside. Grease a baking dish with olive oil. Form the meatloaf at the bottom. Add 1 ½ cups of water and place a trivet in your cooker. Lay the baking dish on the trivet.

Seal the lid, press Meat/Stew and cook for 40 minutes on High. Do a quick release. Carefully transfer the meatloaf to a serving dish. Garnish with vegetable salad or mashed potatoes, to serve.

Buttered Roast Beef with Bearnaise Sauce

Serves: 6 | Ready in about: 30 min

INGREDIENTS

2 lb beef scotch fillet
3 tbsp oil
6 tbsp butter
1 cup white wine
1 onion, chopped

1 tsp fresh basil, chopped
4 egg yolks
2 tbsp lemon juice
4 peppercorns

DIRECTIONS

Melt butter on Sauté, and stir-fry the onions until translucent, for about 3 minutes. Add wine, basil, peppercorns, and lemon juice. Stir well and seal the lid.

Cook on High Pressure for 3 minutes. Do a quick pressure release and stir in egg yolks. Add beef fillets, pour 2 cups of broth and seal the lid. Cook on Meat/Stew mode for 25 minutes on High Pressure. Do a quick release.

Italian-Style Calf's Liver

Serves: 2 | Ready in about: 10 min

INGREDIENTS

1 lb calf's liver, rinsed
3 tbsp olive oil
2 garlic cloves, crushed
1 tbsp fresh mint, finely chopped

½ tsp cayenne pepper
1 tsp salt
½ tsp Italian Seasoning

DIRECTIONS

In a bowl, mix oil, garlic, mint, cayenne, salt, and Italian seasoning. Brush the liver and chill for 30 minutes. Remove from the fridge and pat dry with paper.

Place the liver into the inner pot. Seal the lid and cook on High Pressure for 5 minutes. When ready, release the steam naturally, for about 10 minutes.

Veal and Chicken Stew

Serves: 4 | Ready in about: 53 min

INGREDIENTS

1 lb lean veal cuts, cut into bite-sized pieces
1 lb chicken breast, boneless, cut into pieces
12 oz button mushrooms, chopped
3 carrots, chopped
2 tbsp butter, softened
1 tbsp olive oil

1 tbsp cayenne pepper
1 tsp salt
½ tsp freshly ground black pepper
A bunch of fresh celery leaves, chopped
3 oz celery root, finely chopped

DIRECTIONS

Grease the bottom of the pot with 1 tbsp of oil. Add chops, carrot, salt, pepper, cayenne pepper, and celery root. Stir well, and add 2 cups of water. Seal the lid, and cook on High pressure for 13 minutes.

Do a quick release and add chicken breast, butter, and 1 cup of water. Continue to simmer for 15 minutes, or until the meat tenders, on Sauté. Add mushrooms and celery, and cook for 10 minutes.

Buttery Veal Chops

Serves: 4 | Ready in about: 60 min

INGREDIENTS

2 lb boneless veal shoulder, cut into pieces
3 large tomatoes, roughly chopped
2 tbsp flour
3 tbsp butter
1 tbsp cayenne pepper

1 tsp salt
1 tbsp parsley, finely chopped
1 cup Greek yogurt for serving
1 pide bread

DIRECTIONS

Grease the bottom of the pot with 1 tbsp of butter. Make a layer with veal pieces and pour water to cover. Season with salt and seal the lid. Cook on High pressure for 45 minutes. Do a quick release.

Meanwhile, melt the remaining butter in a skillet. Add cayenne pepper, flour, and briefly stir-fry - for about 2 minutes. Slice pide bread and arrange on a serving plate. Place the meat and tomato on top. Drizzle with cayenne pepper, top with yogurt and sprinkle with parsley.

Lemony Lamb Stew

Serves: 4 | Ready in about: 60 min

INGREDIENTS

1 lb lamb neck, boneless
2 potatoes, peeled, cut into bite-sized pieces
2 large carrots, chopped
1 tomato, diced
1 small red bell pepper, chopped

1 garlic head, whole
A handful of fresh parsley, chopped
¼ cup lemon juice
½ tsp salt
½ tsp black pepper, ground

DIRECTIONS

Add the meat and season with salt. Add in the remaining ingredients, tuck in one garlic head in the middle of the pot and add 2 cups of water. Add a handful of fresh parsley and seal the lid. Cook on High Pressure for 45 minutes. When ready, do a quick release.

Lamb Chops and Creamy Potato Mash

Serves: 8 | Ready in about: 40 min

INGREDIENTS

8 lamb cutlets
Salt to taste
3 sprigs rosemary leaves, chopped
3 tbsp butter, softened
1 tbsp olive oil
1 tbsp tomato puree

1 green onion, chopped
1 cup beef stock
5 potatoes, peeled and chopped
⅓ cup milk
4 cilantro leaves, for garnish

DIRECTIONS

Rub rosemary leaves and salt to the lamb chops. Warm oil and 2 tbsp of butter on Sauté mode.

Brown lamb chops for 1 minute per each side; set aside on a plate.

In the pot, mix tomato puree and green onion; cook for 2-3 minutes.

Add beef stock into the pot to deglaze, scrape the bottom to get rid of any browned bits of food.

Return lamb cutlets alongside any accumulated juices to the pot. Set a steamer rack on lamb cutlets. Place steamer basket on rack. Arrange potatoes in the steamer basket.

Seal the lid and cook on High Pressure for 4 minutes. Release the pressure quickly.

Remove trivet and steamer basket from pot. In a blender, add potatoes, milk, salt, and remaining butter. Blend well until you obtain a smooth consistency.

Divide the potato mash onto serving dishes. Lay lamb chops on the mash. Drizzle with cooking liquid obtained from the cooker, and sprinkle with cilantro.

Thyme Lamb

Serves: 4 | Ready in about: 40 min

INGREDIENTS

2 lb lamb, cubed
2 garlic cloves, minced
1 cup onions, chopped
1 cup red wine
2 cups beef stock
2 tbsp butter, softened

2 celery stalks, chopped
1 tbsp fresh thyme
1 bay leaf
2 tbsp flour
Salt and ground black pepper to taste

DIRECTIONS

Rub the lamb with salt and pepper. Melt butter on Sauté and cook garlic for a minute. Add lamb and cook until browned, for about 5-6 minutes.

Dust the flour and stir. Pour in stock, seal the lid, and cook on High Pressure for 30 minutes. Do a natural release, for 10 minutes. Serve with sauce and thyme.

Holiday Roast Lamb Leg

Serves: 6 | Ready in about: 35 min

INGREDIENTS

2 lb lamb leg
2 garlic cloves
1 tbsp fresh thyme, chopped
1 lb potatoes
1 lemon, chopped

3 tbsp oil
¼ cup red wine vinegar
1 tsp brown sugar
1 tsp salt

DIRECTIONS

Place the potatoes in the pot, and pour enough water to cover. Season with salt, add garlic and seal the lid. Set on Meat/Stew mode. Cook for 20 minutes on High Pressure. Do a quick release and remove potatoes; reserve the liquid. Rub the meat with oil and thyme. Place in the pot.

Pour in red wine vinegar, sugar, and add lemon. Add 1 cup of the reserved liquid and seal the lid. Cook on High Pressure for 7 minutes. Do a quick release.

Classic Lamb Ragout

Serves: 6 | Ready in about: 25 min

INGREDIENTS

1 lb lamb chops, 1-inch thick
1 cup water
1 cup green peas, rinsed
3 carrots, peeled, chopped
3 onions, peeled, chopped
1 potato, peeled, chopped

1 tomato, peeled, roughly chopped
3 tbsp olive oil
1 tbsp paprika
1 tsp salt
½ tsp freshly ground black pepper

DIRECTIONS

Grease the instant pot with olive oil. Rub salt onto meat and make a bottom layer. Add peas, carrots, onions, potatoes, and tomato. Season with paprika.

Add olive oil, water, salt, and pepper. Give it a good stir and seal the lid. Cook on Meat/Stew mode for 20 minutes on High Pressure. When ready, do a natural pressure release, for about 10 minutes.

Rosemary Roast Lamb

Serves: 4 | Ready in about: 40 min

INGREDIENTS

2 lb lamb leg
1 tbsp garlic powder
3 tbsp extra virgin olive oil

Salt and pepper to taste
4 rosemary sprigs, chopped

DIRECTIONS

Grease the inner pot with oil. Rub the meat with salt, pepper, and garlic powder, and place in the instant pot. Pour enough water to cover and seal the lid. Cook on Meat/Stew for 30 minutes on High. Do a quick release. Make sure the meat is tender and falls off the bones. Top with cooking juices and rosemary.

Garlic & Pancetta Lamb Leg

Serves: 6 | Ready in about: 60 min

INGREDIENTS

2 lb lamb leg
6 garlic cloves
1 large onion, chopped
6 pancetta slices
1 tsp rosemary

½ tsp salt
¼ tsp freshly ground black pepper
2 tbsp oil
3 cups beef broth

INSTRUCTIONS:

Heat oil on Sauté. Add pancetta and onions, making two layers. Season with salt and cook for 3 minutes, until lightly browned. Meanwhile, place the meat in a separate dish.

Using a sharp knife, make 6 incisions into the meat and place garlic clove in each. Rub the meat with spices and transfer to the pot. Press Cancel and pour in beef broth. Seal the lid and cook on High pressure for 25 minutes. When done, do a natural pressure release, for about 10 minutes.

French-Style Sesame Lamb

Serves: 4 | Ready in about: 40 min

INGREDIENTS

1 cup rice
1 cup green peas
12 oz lamb, tender cuts, ½-inch thick
3 tbsp sesame seeds
4 cups beef broth

1 tsp sea salt
1 bay leaf
½ tsp dried thyme
3 tbsp butter

DIRECTIONS

Place the meat in the pot and pour in broth. Seal the lid and cook on High Pressure for 13 minutes. Do a quick release. Remove the meat but keep the liquid. Add rice and green peas.

Season with salt, bay leaf, and thyme. Stir well and top with the meat. Seal the lid and cook on Rice mode for 8 minutes on High. Do a quick release and stir in butter and sesame seeds. Serve immediately.

PORK

Pulled Pork Tacos

Serves: 5 | Ready in about: 1hr 25 min

INGREDIENTS

3 tbsp sugar
3 tsp taco Seasoning
1 tsp ground black pepper
2 lb pork shoulder, trimmed, cut into chunks
1 cup beer
1 cup vegetable broth
¼ cup plus

2 tbsp lemon juice
¼ cup mayonnaise
2 tbsp honey
2 tbsp mustard
3 cups shredded cabbage
5 taco tortillas

DIRECTIONS

In a bowl, combine sugar, taco seasoning, and black pepper. Rub onto pork pieces to coat well. Allow settling for 30 minutes. Into the pot, add ¼ cup lemon juice, broth, pork, and beer.

Seal the lid and cook on High Pressure for 50 minutes. Meanwhile in a bowl, mix mayonnaise, mustard, 2 tablespoons lemon juice, cabbage, and honey until well coated.

Release pressure naturally for 15 minutes before doing a quick release. Transfer the pork to a cutting board and allow to cool before using two forks to shred. Skim and get rid of fat from liquid in the Pressure cooker. Return pork to the pot and mix with the juice. Top the pork with slaw on tacos before serving.

Pork Chops with Broccoli & Gravy

Serves: 6 | Ready in about: 45 min

INGREDIENTS

PORK CHOPS:

1 ½ tsp salt
1 tsp ground black pepper
1 tsp garlic powder
1 tsp onion powder
1 tsp red pepper flakes

6 boneless pork chops
1 broccoli head, broken into florets
1 cup chicken stock
¼ cup butter, melted
¼ cup milk

GRAVY:

3 tbsp flour

½ cup heavy cream

DIRECTIONS

Combine salt, garlic powder, flakes, onion, and black pepper. Rub the mixture onto pork chops. Place stock and broccoli in the instant pot. Lay the pork chops on top.

Seal the lid and cook for 15 minutes on High Pressure. Release the pressure quickly.

Transfer the pork and broccoli to a plate. Press Sauté and simmer the liquid remaining in the pot. Mix cream and flour. Pour into the simmering liquid and cook for 5 minutes until thickened and bubbly. Season with pepper and salt. Top the chops with gravy, drizzle butter over broccoli to serve.

Cuban-Style Pork

Serves: 8 | Ready in about: 2hr 30 min

INGREDIENTS

½ cup orange juice
¼ cup Lime juice
¼ cup canola oil
¼ cup chopped fresh cilantro
1 tsp red pepper flakes
8 cloves garlic, minced

1 tbsp ground cumin
1 tbsp fresh oregano
2 tsp ground black pepper
1 tsp salt
3 pounds pork shoulder

DIRECTIONS

In a bowl, mix orange juice, olive oil, cumin, salt, pepper, oregano, lime juice, and garlic. Add into a large plastic bag alongside the pork. Seal and massage the bag to ensure the marinade covers the pork completely.

Place in the refrigerator for two hours. In the instant pot, set your removed pork from bag.

Add the marinade on top. Seal the lid and cook on High Pressure for 50 minutes. Release pressure naturally for 15 minutes. Transfer the pork to a cutting board and use a fork to break into smaller pieces.

Skim and get rid of the fat from liquid in the cooker. Serve the juice with pork and sprinkle with cilantro.

Baby Back Ribs with BBQ Sauce

Serves: 4 | Ready in about: 45 min

INGREDIENTS

2 pounds baby back pork ribs
4 cups orange juice

Juice from 1 lemon

For BBQ sauce:
2 tbsp honey
½ cup ketchup
Juice from ½ lemon
1 tbsp Worcestershire sauce

1tsp mustard
2 tsp paprika
½ tsp cayenne pepper
Salt to taste

DIRECTIONS

Mix all BBQ ingredients in a bowl, until well incorporated. Set aside.

Place ribs in your instant pot, and add in lemon juice and orange juice.

Seal the lid, press Meat/Stew and cook on High Pressure for 20 minutes. Release pressure naturally for 15 minutes. Meanwhile, preheat oven to 400° F. Line the sheet pan with aluminum foil.

Transfer the ribs to the prepared sheet. Do away with the cooking liquid. Onto both sides of ribs, brush barbecue sauce. Bake ribs in the oven for 10 minutes until sauce is browned and caramelized; set the ribs aside and cut into individual bones to serve.

Holiday Honey-Glazed Ham

Serves: 10 | Ready in about: 30 min

INGREDIENTS

½ cup apple cider
¼ cup honey
1 tbsp Dijon mustard
¼ cup brown sugar
2 tbsp orange juice

2 tbsp pineapple juice (optional)
½ tsp ground cinnamon
¼ tsp grated nutmeg
1 pinch ground cloves
5 pounds ham, bone-in

DIRECTIONS

Set on Sauté. Mix in apple cider, mustard, pineapple juice, cloves, cinnamon, sugar, honey, orange juice, and nutmeg; cook until sauce becomes warm, and the sugar and spices are completely dissolved.

Lay ham into the sauce. Seal the lid and cook on High Pressure for 10 minutes. Release the pressure quickly. As the ham cooks, preheat the oven's broiler. Line aluminum foil to a baking sheet.

Transfer the ham to the prepared baking sheet. On Sauté, cook the remaining liquid for 4 to 6 minutes until you have a thick and syrupy glaze. Brush the glaze onto ham.

Set the glazed ham in the preheated broiler and bake for 3 to 5 minutes until the glaze is caramelized.

Place the ham on a cutting board and slice. Transfer to a serving bowl and drizzle glaze over the ham.

Italian Sausage & Cannellini Stew

Serves: 6 | Ready in about: 45 min

INGREDIENTS

1 tbsp olive oil
1 pound Italian sausages, halved
1 celery stalk, chopped
1 carrot, chopped
1 onion, chopped
1 sprig fresh sage

1 sprig fresh rosemary
1 bay leaf
1 cup Cannellini beans, soaked and rinsed
2 cups vegetable stock
3 cups fresh spinach
1 tsp salt

DIRECTIONS

Warm oil on Sauté. Add in sausage pieces and sear for 5 minutes until browned; set aside on a plate.

To the pot, add celery, onion, bay leaf, sage, carrot, and rosemary; cook for 3 minutes. Stir in vegetable stock and beans. Arrange seared sausage pieces on top of the beans.

Seal the lid, press Bean/Chili and cook on High for 10 minutes. Release pressure naturally for 20 minutes. Get rid of bay leaf, rosemary, and sage. Mix spinach into the mixture to serve.

Red Pork and Chickpea Stew

Serves: 6 | Ready in about: 40 min

INGREDIENTS

1 tbsp olive oil
3 pounds boneless pork shoulder, cubed
1 white onion, chopped
15 ounces canned chickpeas, drained and rinsed
1½ cups water
½ cup sweet paprika

2 tsp salt
1 tbsp chili powder
1 bay leaf
2 red bell peppers, chopped
6 cloves garlic, minced
1 tbsp cornstarch

DIRECTIONS

Set on Sauté, add pork and oil, and cook for 5 minutes until browned. Add in the onion, paprika, bay leaf, salt, water, chickpeas, and chili powder. Seal the lid and cook on High Pressure for 8 minutes.

Do a quick release and discard bay leaf. Remove 1 cup of cooking liquid from the pot; add to a blender alongside garlic, water, cornstarch, and red bell peppers, and blend well until smooth. Add the blended mixture into the stew and mix well.

Beer-Braised Hot Dogs with Peppers

Serves: 6 | Ready in about: 15 min

INGREDIENTS

1 tbsp olive oil
6 sausages pork sausage links
1 green bell pepper, chopped into strips
1 red bell pepper, chopped into strips

1 yellow bell pepper, chopped into strips
2 spring onions, chopped
1 ½ cups beer
6 hot dog rolls

DIRECTIONS

Warm oil on Sauté. Add in sausage links and sear for 5 minutes until browned; set aside on a plate. Into the instant pot, pile peppers. Lay the sausages on top. Add beer into the pot.

Seal the lid and cook for on High Pressure 5 minutes. Release the pressure quickly. Serve sausages in buns topped with onions and peppers.

Pork Chops with Plum Sauce

Serves: 4 | Ready in about: 20 min

INGREDIENTS

4 pork chops
1 tsp cumin seeds
1 tsp salt
1 tsp ground black pepper

2 cups firm plums, pitted and cups
1 tbsp vegetable oil
¾ cup vegetable stock

DIRECTIONS

Sprinkle salt, cumin, and pepper on the chops. Set on Sauté and warm oil. Add the chops and cook for 3 to 5 minutes until browned and set aside. Arrange plum slices at the bottom of the cooker. Top with chops. Add any juice from the plate over the pork and apply stock around the edges.

Seal lid and cook on High Pressure for 8 minutes. Do a quick pressure release. Transfer the pork chops to a serving plate and spoon over the plum sauce before serving.

Jamaican Pulled Pork with Mango Sauce

Serves: 6 | Ready in about: 1hr 15 min

INGREDIENTS

1 ½ tsp onion powder
1 tsp sea salt
1 tsp dried thyme
1 tsp ground black pepper
1 tsp cayenne pepper
1 tsp ground allspice
½ tsp ground nutmeg

½ tsp ground cinnamon
3 pounds pork shoulder
1 mango, cut into chunks
1 tbsp olive oil
½ cup water
2 tbsp fresh cilantro, minced

DIRECTIONS

In a bowl, combine onion, thyme, allspice, cinnamon, sugar, pepper, sea salt, cayenne, and nutmeg.

Coat the pork shoulder with olive oil. Season with seasoning mixture. Warm oil on Sauté. Add in the pork and cook for 5 minutes until browned completely. To the pot, add water and mango chunks.

Seal the lid, press Meat/Stew and cook on High Pressure for 45 minutes. Release the pressure naturally for 15 minutes, then quick release the remaining pressure. Transfer the pork to a cutting board to cool.

To make the sauce, pour the cooking liquid in a food processor and pulse until smooth. Use two forks to shred the pork and arrange on a serving platter. Serve the pork topped with mango salsa and cilantro.

Crispy Pork Fajitas

Serves: 5 | Ready in about: 1hr 30 min

INGREDIENTS

1 tbsp ground cumin
2 tsp dried oregano
1 tsp paprika
1 tsp onion powder
1 tsp salt
1 tsp ground black pepper
½ tsp ground cinnamon
3 pounds boneless pork shoulder

¾ cup vegetable broth
¼ cup pineapple juice
1 Lime, juiced
4 cloves garlic, crushed
2 bay leaves
5 corn tortillas, warmed
½ cup queso Cotija, crumbled

DIRECTIONS

In a bowl, combine cumin, paprika, pepper, onion powder, oregano, salt, and cinnamon; toss in pork to coat. Place the pork in the Pressure cooker and allow settling for 15 to 30 minutes.

Add in broth, garlic, lime juice, bay leaves, and pineapple juice. Seal the lid and cook on High Pressure for 50 minutes. Release pressure naturally for 15 minutes, then release the remaining pressure quickly.

Preheat oven to 450 F. Transfer the pork to a rimmed baking sheet and use two forks to shred the meat. Reserve juices in the instant pot. Bake in the oven for 10 minutes until crispy. Skim and get rid of fat from the liquid remaining in the pot. Dispose of the bay leaves.

Over the pork, pour the liquid and serve alongside warm corn tortillas and queso fresco.

Pork Carnitas Wraps

Serves: 12 | Ready in about: 1hr 15 min

INGREDIENTS

2 tbsp grapeseed oil
1 (4 to 5 pound) boneless pork shoulder
1 onion, chopped
2 garlic cloves, minced
2 oranges, juiced
2 Limes, juiced
2 tbsp sweet smoked paprika

1 tbsp dried oregano
1 tbsp salt
2 jalapeños, chopped
1 avocado, chopped
Fresh cilantro leaves, chopped
2 tsp ground black pepper
12 corn tortillas, warmed

DIRECTIONS

Warm oil on Sauté. Add in pork and cook for 5 minutes until golden brown. Transfer the pork to a plate.

Add garlic and onions to the pot and cook for 2-3 minutes until soft. Add lime and orange juices into pan to deglaze, scrape the bottom to get rid of any browned bits of food.

Stir in pepper, paprika, salt, and oregano. Return the pork to pot; stir to coat in seasoning and liquid.

Seal the lid and cook for 35 minutes on High Pressure. Release the pressure quickly.

Press Sauté. When the liquid starts to simmer, use two forks to shred the pork. Cook for 10 more minutes until liquid is reduced by half. Serve in warmed tortillas topped with jalapeños, avocado and cilantro.

Holiday Apricot-Lemon Ham

Serves: 12 | Ready in about: 1hr

INGREDIENTS

¼ cup water
5 pounds smoked ham
½ cup brown sugar

Juice from 1 Lime
2 tsp mustard
½ tsp ground cardamom

¾ cup apricot jam

¼ tsp ground nutmeg
freshly ground black pepper to taste

DIRECTIONS

Into the pot, add water and ham. In a bowl, mix jam, lemon juice, cardamom, pepper, nutmeg, mustard, and sugar. Pour the mixture over the ham. Seal the lid and cook on High Pressure for 10 minutes. Release the pressure quickly.

Transfer the ham to a cutting board; allow to sit for 10 minutes. Press Sauté.

Simmer the liquid and cook for 4 to 6 minutes until thickened into a sauce. Slice ham and place onto a serving bowl. Drizzle with sauce before serving.

Sausage with Celeriac & Potato Mash

Serves: 4 | Ready in about: 45 min

INGREDIENTS

1 tbsp olive oil
4 pork sausages
1 onion
2 cups vegetable broth
½ cup water
4 potatoes, peeled and diced
1 cup celeriac, chopped

2 tbsp butter
¼ cup milk
Salt and ground black pepper to taste
1 tbsp heavy cream
1 tsp Dijon mustard
½ tsp dry mustard powder
Fresh flat-leaf parsley, chopped

DIRECTIONS

Warm oil on Sauté mode. Add in sausages and cook for 1 to 2 minutes for each side until browned. Set the sausages to a plate. To the same pot, add onion and sauté for 3 minutes until fragrant. Press Cancel.

Add sausages on top of onions and pour water and broth over them. Place a trivet over onions and sausages. Put potatoes and celeriac in a steamer basket and transfer it to the trivet.

Seal the lid and cook for 11 minutes on High Pressure. Release the pressure quickly. Transfer potatoes, and celeriac to a bowl and set sausages on a plate and cover them with aluminum foil.

Using a potato masher, mash potatoes, and celeriac together with black pepper, milk, salt, and butter until mash becomes creamy and fluffy. Adjust the seasonings.

Set on Sauté mode. Add the onion mixture and bring to a boil. Cook for 5 to 10 minutes until the mixture is reduced and thickened. Into the gravy, stir in dry mustard, salt, pepper, mustard, and cream.

Place the mash in 4 bowls in equal parts, top with a sausage or two, and gravy. Garnish with parsley.

Sweet and Sour Pork

Serves: 4 | Ready in about: 40 min

INGREDIENTS

1 pound pork loin, cut into chunks
2 tbsp white wine
15 ounces canned peaches
¼ cup beef stock
2 tbsp sweet chili sauce

2 tbsp honey
2 tbsp soy sauce
2 tbsp cornstarch
¼ cup water

DIRECTIONS

Into the pot, mix soy sauce, beef stock, wine, juice from the canned peaches, and sweet chili sauce. Stir in pork to coat. Seal the lid and cook on High Pressure for 5 minutes.

Release pressure naturally for 10 minutes, then release the remaining pressure quickly. Remove the pork to a serving plate. Chop the peaches into small pieces.

In a bowl, mix water with cornstarch until well dissolved; stir the mixture into the pot. Press Sauté and cook for 5 more minutes until you obtain the desired thick consistency. Add in the chopped peaches and stir well. Serve the pork topped with peach sauce and enjoy.

Pork Chops with Squash Purée & Mushroom Gravy

Serves: 4 | Ready in about: 45 min

INGREDIENTS

3 tbsp olive oil
2 sprigs thyme, leaves removed and chopped
2 sprigs rosemary, leaves removed and chopped
4 pork chops
1 cup mushrooms, chopped
4 cloves garlic, minced

1 cup chicken broth
1 tbsp soy sauce
1 pound butternut squash, cubed
1 tbsp olive oil
1 tsp cornstarch

DIRECTIONS

Set on Sauté and heat rosemary, thyme and 2 tbsp of oil. Add the pork chops and sear for 1 minute for each side until lightly browned.

Sauté garlic and mushrooms in the instant pot for 5-6 minutes until mushrooms are tender. Add soy sauce and broth. Transfer pork chops to a wire trivet and place inside into the pot. Over the chops, place a cake pan. Add butternut squash in the pot and drizzle with 1 tbsp olive oil.

Seal the lid and cook on High Pressure for 10 minutes. Release the pressure quickly. Remove the pan and trivet from the pot. Stir cornstarch into mushroom mixture for 2 to 3 minutes until the sauce thickens.

Transfer the mushroom sauce to an immersion blender and blend until you attain the desired consistency. Scoop sauce into a cup with a pour spout. Smash the squash into a purée. Set pork chops on a plate and ladle squash puree next to them. Top the pork chops with gravy.

Pork & Buckwheat Stew

Serves: 4 | Ready in about: 50 min

INGREDIENTS

8 oz buckwheat porridge, cooked
1 lb pork tenderloin
1 carrot, chopped
1 onion, peeled and finely chopped
3 tbsp vegetable oil
1 tsp dry marjoram

¼ tsp freshly ground black pepper
½ tsp salt
1 garlic clove
½ cup white wine
2 cups chicken broth

DIRECTIONS

Heat oil on Sauté. Add onions, garlic, and stir-fry for 2 minutes, until fragrant and translucent. Add carrot and meat. Cook for 5 minutes, until lightly browned. Add the remaining ingredients. Seal the lid and cook on High pressure for 35 minutes. Do a quick release and stir in the porridge. Serve hot.

Pork Goulash

Serves: 4 | Ready in about: 40 min

INGREDIENTS

12 oz pork neck, cut into bite-sized pieces
2 tbsp flour
4 tbsp vegetable oil
2 onions, peeled, chopped
1 carrot

A handful of chopped celery
10 oz button mushrooms
4 cups beef broth
1 chili pepper, chopped
1 tbsp cayenne pepper

DIRECTIONS

Heat oil on Sauté. Add onions and cook for 2 minutes, until translucent. Add flour, chili pepper, carrot, celery, cayenne pepper, and continue to cook for 2 more minutes, stirring constantly.

Press Cancel and add meat, mushrooms, beef broth, and water. Seal the lid and cook on Manual/Pressure Cook mode for 30 minutes on High Pressure. Do a quick release and serve immediately.

Pork & Mushroom Stew

Serves: 2 | Ready in about: 50 min

INGREDIENTS

2 pork chops, bones removed and cut into pieces
1 cup crimini mushrooms, chopped
2 large carrots, chopped
½ tsp garlic powder
1 tsp salt

½ black pepper
2 tbsp butter
1 cup beef broth
1 tbsp apple cider vinegar
2 tbsp cornstarch

DIRECTIONS

Season the meat with salt, and pepper. Add butter and pork chops to the pot and brown for 10 minutes, stirring occasionally, on Sauté mode. Add mushrooms and cook for 5 minutes. Add the remaining ingredients and seal the lid. Cook on High Pressure for 25 minutes. Do a quick release and serve hot.

Spicy-Sweet Pulled Pork

Serves: 8 | Ready in about: 65 min

INGREDIENTS

3 lb pork shoulder
1 cup onions, finely chopped
2 tbsp butter, unsalted
1 tbsp cayenne pepper
1 tsp salt

1 cup beef broth
3 tbsp maple syrup
2 tbsp soy sauce
⅓ cup Worcestershire sauce
2 bay leaves

DIRECTIONS

On Sauté, stir-fry butter, onions, cayenne, and salt, for 4 minutes. Add maple syrup, soy sauce, Worcestershire sauce, and bay leaves. Cook for 5 minutes. Add meat and pour in the broth.

Seal the lid and cook on High pressure for 40 minutes. When done, do a quick release and serve hot.

Jalapeño Pork

Serves: 4 | Ready in about: 60 min

INGREDIENTS

1 lb pork shoulder
2 tbsp olive oil
3 Jalapeño peppers, seeded and finely chopped
2 Japones chilies
1 tsp ground cumin

3 cups water
1 large onion, roughly chopped
2 garlic cloves, crushed
3 cups beef broth

INSTRUCTIONS:

Heat oil on Sauté and cook the jalapeno peppers for 3 minutes. Add in all the spices, garlic, and onion and stir-fry for another 2 minutes, until soft. Add in the pork shoulder, beef broth and the pureed mixture.

Seal the lid, and cook on Meat/Stew for 30 minutes on High. Release the pressure quickly and serve.

Pork Chops with Apple Sauce

Serves: 4 | Ready in about: 1 hr 15 min

INGREDIENTS

4 pork loin chops, 1-inch thick
2 tbsp oil
1 tbsp butter
3 apples, peeled, cored, chopped

¼ cup soy sauce
1 cup beef broth
2 tbsp honey
¼ tsp cinnamon

DIRECTIONS

Heat oil on Sauté and brown the chops for 3 minutes on each side. Remove and melt the butter.

Add apples, soy sauce, broth, honey, and cinnamon. Cook until apples are half-done and slightly tender. Add the chops back, seal the lid and cook on Meat/Stew for 40 minutes on High. Do a quick release.

Balsamic-Buttery Pork Tenderloin

Serves: 4 | Ready in about: 60 min

INGREDIENTS

2 lb pork tenderloin
2 tbsp butter, unsalted
2 tbsp brown sugar
2 tbsp balsamic vinegar
2 garlic cloves, crushed

1 cup beef broth
1 tsp salt
¼ tsp pepper, freshly ground
1 tbsp cornstarch

DIRECTIONS

Melt butter on Sauté and stir-fry garlic for 1 minute. Add sugar and vinegar, and cook for 1 minute. Rub the meat with salt, and pepper. Place in the instant pot and pour in the broth. Seal the lid.

Cook on High Pressure for 35 minutes. Do a quick release and set the meat aside. Stir in cornstarch in the remaining liquid and cook for 1 minute on Sauté to thicken the sauce. Drizzle over meat and serve.

Honey-Mustard Pork Chops

Serves: 4 | Ready in about: 60 min

INGREDIENTS

2 lb pork chops
1 cup beef broth
2 tbsp oil
¼ cup honey
1 tbsp Dijon mustard

½ tsp cinnamon
1 tsp ginger, grated
1 tsp salt
½ tsp pepper, ground

DIRECTIONS

Season the chops with salt, and pepper. Heat oil on Sauté and brown the chops for 3 minutes per side. In a bowl, mix honey, mustard, cinnamon, and ginger. Whisk together and drizzle over chops.

Pour in broth and seal the lid. Cook on High Pressure for 30 minutes. Do a quick release and serve.

Basil-Flavored Pork Stew

Serves: 4 | Ready in about: 45 min

INGREDIENTS

16 oz pork tenderloin, cut into bite-sized pieces
1 onion, peeled, chopped
2 tbsp vegetable oil
4 tomatoes, peeled, diced
½ tbsp red wine

½ tbsp beef broth
A handful of fresh basil
1 tsp salt
¼ tsp pepper

DIRECTIONS

Heat oil and fry the onions, until translucent. Add the meat, salt, pepper, wine, and basil. Cook for 10 minutes. Pour in broth, seal the lid and cook on High Pressure for 25 minutes. Do a quick release.

Honey & Garlic Pork Shoulder

Serves: 6 | Ready in about: 1 hr 20 min

INGREDIENTS

2 lb pork shoulder, boneless
1 garlic head, Divided into cloves

1 tsp salt
½ tsp black pepper, freshly ground
½ tsp red pepper flakes
1 tbsp butter, unsalted
2 tsp fresh ginger, grated

3 tbsp apple cider vinegar
2 tbsp honey
3 tbsp soy sauce
1 tsp garlic powder

DIRECTIONS

In a bowl, combine apple cider, honey, soy sauce, garlic powder, and ginger. Brush the meat with this mixture and set aside. Brown the pork, evenly on all sides, on Sauté. Then, add 1 cup of water and garlic. Seal the lid and cook on High Pressure for 35 minutes on High.

Do a quick release. Season with salt, pepper, and red pepper flakes. Add butter and cook until the liquid evaporates – for 10 minutes, on Sauté mode.

Pork Roast with Mushrooms Sauce

Serves: 6 | Ready in about: 65 min

INGREDIENTS

2 lb pork shoulder
1 cup button mushrooms, chopped
2 tbsp butter, unsalted
1 tbsp balsamic vinegar
½ tsp garlic powder

1 tsp salt
¼ cup soy sauce
2 bay leaves
1 cup beef broth
2 tbsp cornstarch

DIRECTIONS

Rinse the meat and rub with salt, and garlic powder. Melt butter on Sauté. Brown the meat for 5 minutes on each side. Stir in soy sauce and bay leaves.

Cook for 2 minutes before, add in beef broth and balsamic vinegar. Seal the lid and set on Meat/Stew mode. Cook for 30 minutes on High Pressure.

When done, do a quick release and stir in mushrooms. Cook until tender – for about 5 minutes, on Sauté mode. Stir in cornstarch and cook for 2 minutes.

Maple Pulled Pork

Serves: 6 | Ready in about: 45 min

INGREDIENTS

2 lb pork shoulder
½ cup maple syrup
½ cup sun-dried tomatoes, diced
3 cups beef stock

2 tbsp mustard powder
½ cup brown sugar
2 tbsp sea salt
1 cup fresh cilantro, chopped

DIRECTIONS

Rub the meat with salt, and sugar, and place it in the pot. Add the remaining ingredients except for the cilantro.

Seal the lid and cook on High Pressure for 30 minutes. Allow the Pressure to release naturally, for 10 minutes and serve immediately. Shredd the pork with two forks and top with cilantro to serve.

Bacon & Rice Chowder

Serves: 4 | Ready in about: 20 min

INGREDIENTS

2 cups basmati rice
1 cup bacon, chopped
1 medium onion, finely chopped
½ cup green peas
3 tbsp olive oil

2 garlic cloves, chopped
1 tsp dried thyme
1 tsp salt
4 cups beef broth

DIRECTIONS

Heat oil on Sauté, and stir-fry onions and garlic for 2-3 minutes, or until translucent. Add all the remaining ingredients and seal the lid. Cook on High Pressure for 5 minutes.

When ready, release the pressure naturally for 10 minutes. Stir well, and plate in a serving bowl.

Spicy Bacon & White Peas

Serves: 4 | Ready in about: 30 min

INGREDIENTS

1 lb of white peas
4 slices bacon
1 onion, chopped
1 jalapeno pepper, chopped
2 tbsp flour

2 tbsp butter
1 tbsp cayenne pepper
3 bay leaves, dried
1 tsp salt
½ tsp ground black pepper

DIRECTIONS

Melt 2 tbsp of butter, and stir-fry the onion for 2-3 minutes, until translucent. Add bacon, peas, jalapeno pepper, bay leaves, salt, and pepper.

Gently Stir in 2 tbsp of flour and add 3 cups of water. Seal the lid and cook on High Pressure for 15 minutes. Release the steam naturally, for 10 minutes.

Cinnamon-Orange Braised Pork Belly

Serves: 10 | Ready in about: 30 min

INGREDIENTS

2 lb pork belly slices
2 tbsp oil
½ tsp cinnamon, ground
¼ tsp nutmeg, ground

¼ cup honey
¼ cup red wine
2 cups orange juice
1 cup water

DIRECTIONS

Heat oil on Sauté, and brown the pork for 3 minutes. Add the remaining ingredients, seal the lid and cook on High Pressure for 20 minutes. Do a quick release. Press Sauté and bring to a boil. Let simmer until the excess liquid evaporates. Serve warm.

Winter Minestrone with Pancetta

Serves: 6 | Ready in about: 40 min

INGREDIENTS

2 tbsp olive oil
2 ounces pancetta, chopped
1 onion, diced
1 parsnip, peeled and chopped
2 carrots, peeled and chopped into rounds
2 celery stalks,
2 garlic cloves, minced
1 tbsp dried basil
1 tbsp dried thyme

1 tbsp dried oregano
6 cups chicken broth
2 cups green beans, trimmed and chopped
1 (15 ounces) can diced tomatoes
1 (15 ounces) can chickpeas, rinsed and drained
1 ½ cups small shaped pasta
Salt and ground black pepper to taste
½ cup grated Parmesan Cheese

DIRECTIONS

Heat oil on Sauté. Add onion, carrots, garlic, pancetta, celery, and parsnip, and cook for 5 minutes until they become soft. Stir in basil, oregano, beans, broth, tomatoes, pepper, salt, thyme, chickpeas, and pasta.

Seal the lid and cook for 6 minutes on High Pressure. Release pressure naturally for 10 minutes, then release the remaining pressure quickly. Ladle the soup into bowls and serve garnished with Parmesan.

FISH AND SEAFOOD

Steamed Mediterranean Cod

Serves: 4 | Ready in about: 20 min

INGREDIENTS

1 pound cherry tomatoes, halved
1 bunch fresh thyme sprigs
4 fillets cod
1 tsp olive oil
1 clove garlic, pressed
3 pinches salt

2 cups water
1 cup white rice
1 cup Kalamata olives
2 tbsp pickled capers
1 tbsp olive oil
1 pinch ground black pepper

DIRECTIONS

Line a parchment paper on the basket of your instant pot. Place about half the tomatoes in a single layer on the paper. Sprinkle with thyme, reserving some for garnish.

Arrange cod fillets on top. Sprinkle with a little bit of olive oil.

Spread the garlic, pepper, salt, and remaining tomatoes over the fish. In the pot, mix rice and water.

Lay a trivet over the rice and water. Lower steamer basket onto the trivet.

Seal the lid, and cook for 7 minutes on Low Pressure. Release the pressure quickly.

Remove the steamer basket and trivet from the pot. Use a fork to fluff rice.

Plate the fish fillets and apply a garnish of olives, reserved thyme, pepper, remaining olive oil, and capers. Serve with rice.

Steamed Sea Bass with Turnips

Serves: 4 | Ready in about: 15 min

INGREDIENTS

1½ cups water
1 lemon, chopped
4 sea bass fillets
4 sprigs thyme
1 white onion, sliced into thin rings

2 turnips, chopped
2 pinches salt
1 pinch ground black pepper
2 tbs olive oil

DIRECTIONS

Add water and set a rack into the pot.

Line a parchment paper to the bottom of steamer basket. Place lemon slices in a single layer on the rack.

Arrange fillets on the top of the lemons, cover with onion and thyme sprigs. Top with turnip slices.

Drizzle pepper, salt, and olive oil over the mixture. Put steamer basket onto the rack.

Seal lid and cook on Low pressure for 8 minutes. Release the pressure quickly.

Serve over the delicate onion rings and turnips.

Cod on Millet

Serves: 4 | Ready in about: 20 min

INGREDIENTS

1 tbsp olive oil
1 cup millet
1 yellow bell pepper, diced
1 red bell pepper, diced
2 cups chicken broth

1 cup breadcrumbs
4 tbsp melted butter
¼ cup minced fresh cilantro
1 tsp salt
4 cod fillets

DIRECTIONS

Combine oil, millet, yellow and red bell peppers in the pot, and cook for 1 minute on Sauté. Mix in the broth. Place a trivet on top. In a bowl, mix crumbs, butter, cilantro, lemon zest, juice, and salt.

Spoon the breadcrumb mixture evenly on the cod fillet. Lay the fish on the trivet. Seal the lid and cook on High for 6 minutes. Do a quick release and serve immediately.

Chorizo and Shrimp Boil

Serves: 4 | Ready in about: 30 min

INGREDIENTS

3 red potatoes
3 ears corn, cut into rounds
2 cups water
1 cup white wine
4 chorizo sausages, sliced

1 pound shrimp, peeled and deveined
2 tbsp seafood Seasoning
Salt to taste
1 lemon, cut into wedges
¼ cup butter, melted

DIRECTIONS

Add all ingredients, except butter and lemon wedges. Do not stir.

Seal the lid and cook for 2 minutes on High Pressure. Release the pressure quickly.

Drain the mixture through a colander. Transfer to a serving platter. Serve with melted butter and lemon wedges.

White Wine Mussels

Serves: 5 | Ready in about: 15 min

INGREDIENTS

1 cup white wine
½ cup water
1 tsp garlic powder

2 pounds mussels, cleaned and debearded
Juice from 1 lemon

DIRECTIONS

In the pot, mix garlic powder, water, and wine.

Put the mussels into the steamer basket, rounded-side should be placed facing upwards to fit as many as possible. Insert rack into the cooker and lower steamer basket onto the rack. Seal the lid and cook on Low Pressure for 1 minute. Release the pressure quickly.

Remove unopened mussels. Coat the mussels with the wine mixture. Serve with a side of French fries or slices of toasted bread.

Paella Señorito

Serves: 5 | Ready in about: 25 min

INGREDIENTS

¼ cup olive oil
1 onion, chopped
1 red bell pepper, diced
2 garlic cloves, minced
1 tsp paprika
1 tsp turmeric
Salt and ground white pepper to taste

1 cup bomba rice
¼ cup frozen green peas
2 cups fish broth
1 pound frozen shrimp, peeled and deveined
chopped fresh parsley
1 lemon, cut into wedges

DIRECTIONS

Warm oil on Sauté mode. Add in bell pepper and onions, and cook for 5 minutes until fragrant. Mix in garlic and cook for one more minute until soft.

Add paprika, pepper, salt, and turmeric to the vegetables with paprika and cook for 1 minute.

Stir in fish broth and rice. Add shrimp to the rice mixture. Seal the lid and cook on High Pressure for 5 minutes.

Release the pressure quickly. Stir in green peas and let sit for 5 minutes until green peas are heated through. Serve warm garnished with parsley and lemon wedges.

Spicy Tangy Salmon with Rice

Serves: 4 | Ready in about: 20 min

INGREDIENTS

1 cup rice
2 cups vegetable stock
4 skinless salmon fillets
1 cup green peas
3 tbsp olive oil
1 tsp salt
1tsp freshly ground black pepper

2 limes, juiced
2 tbsp honey
1 tsp sweet paprika
2 jalapeño peppers, seeded and diced
4 garlic cloves, minced
½ cup canned corn kernels, drained
2 tbsp chopped fresh dill

DIRECTIONS

Add in rice, stock, and salt. Place a trivet over the rice. In a bowl, mix oil, lime juice, honey, paprika, jalapeño, garlic, and dill. Coat the fish with the honey sauce while reserving a little for garnishing.

Lay the salmon fillets on the trivet. Seal the lid and cook on High Pressure for 8 minutes. Do a quick release. Fluff the rice with a fork and mix in the green peas and corn kernels. Transfer to a serving plate and top with the salmon. Drizzle with the remaining honey sauce and enjoy.

Salmon with Dill Chutney

Serves: 2 | Ready in about: 15 min

INGREDIENTS

2 salmon fillets
Juice from ½ lemon
¼ tsp paprika

Salt and freshly ground pepper to taste
2 cups water

For Chutney:

¼ cup fresh dill
Juice from ½ lemon

Sea salt to taste
¼ cup extra virgin olive oil

DIRECTIONS

In a food processor, blend all the chutney ingredients until creamy. Set aside.

To your cooker, add the water and place a steamer basket.

Arrange salmon fillets skin-side down on the steamer basket. Drizzle lemon juice over salmon and sprinkle with paprika. Seal the lid and cook for 3 minutes on High Pressure. Release the pressure quickly.

Season the fillets with pepper and salt, Transfer to a serving plate and top with the dill chutney.

Buttery Herb Trout with Green Beans

Serves: 4 | Ready in about: 20 min

INGREDIENTS

1 cup farro
2 cups water
4 skinless trout fillets
8 ounces green beans
1 tbsp olive oil
1 tsp freshly ground black pepper
1 tsp salt

4 tbsp melted butter
½ tbsp sugar
½ tbsp freshly squeezed lemon juice
½ tsp dried rosemary
2 garlic cloves, minced
½ tsp dried thyme

DIRECTIONS

Pour the farro and water in the pot and mix. Season with salt. In a bowl, toss the green beans with olive oil, ½ tsp of black pepper, and ½ tsp of salt. In another bowl, mix together the remaining ½ tsp of black pepper and salt, butter, sugar, lemon juice, rosemary, garlic, and rosemary.

Coat the trout with the buttery herb sauce. Insert a trivet in the pot and lay the trout fillets on the trivet. Seal the lid and cook on High Pressure for 12 minutes. Do a quick release and serve immediately.

Potato Chowder with Hot Shrimp

Serves: 4 | Ready in about: 20 min

INGREDIENTS

4 slices pancetta, chopped
4 tbsp minced garlic
1 onion, chopped
2 potatoes, chopped
16 ounces canned corn kernels
4 cups vegetable stock
1 tsp dried rosemary

1 tsp salt
1 tsp black pepper
1 pound jumbo shrimp, peeled, deveined
1 tbsp olive oil
½ tsp red chili flakes
¾ cup heavy cream

DIRECTIONS

Fry the pancetta for 5 minutes until crispy, on Sauté mode, and set aside. Add in 2 tbsp of garlic and onion, and stir-fry for 3 minutes. Add in potatoes, corn, stock, rosemary, half of the salt, and pepper.

Seal the lid and cook on High Pressure for 10 minutes. Do a quick pressure release. Remove to a serving bowl. In a bowl, toss the shrimp in the remaining garlic, salt, black pepper, olive oil, and flakes.

Wipe the pot clean and fry shrimp for 3-4 minutes per side, until pink. Mix in the heavy cream and cook for 2 minutes. Add shrimp to chowder, garnish with the reserved pancetta and serve immediately.

Prawn & Clam Paella

Serves: 4 | Ready in about: 30 min

INGREDIENTS

2 tbsp olive oil
1 onion, chopped
4 garlic cloves, minced
½ cup dry white wine
2 cups bomba (Spanish) rice
4 cups chicken stock
1 ½ tsp sweet paprika

1 tsp turmeric powder
½ tsp freshly ground black pepper
½ tsp salt
1 pound small clams, scrubbed
1 pound fresh prawns, peeled and deveined
1 red bell pepper, diced
1 lemon, cut in wedges

DIRECTIONS

Stir-fry onion and garlic in a tbsp of oil on Sauté mode for 3 minutes. Pour in wine to deglaze, scraping the bottom of the pot of any brown. Cook for 2 minutes, until the wine is reduced by half.

Add in rice and water. Season with the paprika, turmeric, salt, and pepper. Seal the lid and cook on High Pressure for 10 minutes. Do a quick release. Remove to a plate and wipe the pot clean.

Heat the remaining oil on Sauté. Cook clams and prawns for 6 minutes, until the clams have opened and the shrimp are pink. Discard unopened clams. Arrange seafood and lemon wedges over paella, to serve.

Haddock Fillets with Crushed Potatoes

Serves: 4 | Ready in about: 25 min

INGREDIENTS

8 ounces beer
2 eggs
1 cup flour
½ tbsp cayenne powder
1 tbsp cumin powder

Salt and pepper to taste
4 haddock fillets
Nonstick cooking spray
4 potatoes, cut into ½-inch matchsticks
2 tbsp olive oil

DIRECTIONS

In a bowl, whisk beer and eggs. In another bowl, combine flour, cayenne, cumin, black pepper, and salt. Coat each fish piece in the egg mixture, then dredge in the flour mixture, coating all sides well.

Spray a baking dish with nonstick cooking spray. Place in the fish fillets, pour ¼ cup of water and grease with cooking spray. Place the potatoes in the pot and cover with water and place a trivet over the potatoes.

Lay the baking dish on top and seal the lid. Cook on High Pressure for 15 minutes. Do a quick release. Drain and crush the potatoes with olive oil and serve with the fish.

Seafood Spicy Penne

Serves: 4 | Ready in about: 20 min

INGREDIENTS

1 tbsp olive oil
1 onion, diced
16 ounces penne
24 ounces Arrabbiata sauce
3 cups chicken broth

½ tsp freshly ground black pepper
½ tsp salt
16 ounces scallops
¼ cup parmesan cheese, grated
Basil leaves for garnish

DIRECTIONS

Heat oil on Sauté and stir-fry onion for 5 minutes. Add the garlic and cook until fragrant, for about 1 minute. Stir in penne, arrabbiata sauce, and 2 cups of broth. Season with the black pepper and.

Seal the lid and cook for 6 minutes on High Pressure. Do a quick release. Remove to a plate. Pour the remaining broth and add scallops. Stir to coat, seal the lid and cook on High Pressure for 4 minutes.

Do a quick release. Mix in the pasta and serve topped with parmesan cheese and basil leaves.

Shrimp Farfalle with Spinach

Serves: 4 | Ready in about: 20 min

INGREDIENTS

1¼ pounds shrimp, peeled and deveined
1½ tsp salt
1 tbsp melted butter
2 garlic cloves, minced
¼ cup white wine
10 ounces farfalle

2½ cups water
⅓ cup tomato puree
½ tsp red chili flakes or to taste
1 tsp grated lemon zest
1 tbsp lemon juice
6 cups spinach

DIRECTIONS

On Sauté, pour white wine, bring to simmer for 2 minutes to reduce the liquid by half. Stir in the farfalle, water, salt, garlic, puréed tomato, shrimp, melted butter, and chili flakes. Seal the lid. Cook for 5 minutes on High pressure. Do a quick release. Stir in lemon zest, juice, and spinach until wilted and soft.

Mussel Chowder with Oyster Crackers

Serves: 4 | Ready in about: 20 min

INGREDIENTS

2 cups low carb oyster crackers
2 tbsp olive oil
¼ cup finely grated Pecorino Romano cheese
½ tsp garlic powder
Salt and pepper to taste
2 pancetta slices
2 celery stalks, chopped
1 medium onion, chopped
1 tbsp flour

¼ cup white wine
1 cup water
20 ounces canned mussels, drained, liquid reserved
1 pound potatoes, peeled and cut chunks
1 tsp dried rosemary
1 bay leaf
1½ cups heavy cream
2 tbsp chopped fresh chervil

DIRECTIONS

Fry pancetta on Sauté for 5 minutes, until crispy. Remove to a paper towel–lined plate and set aside. Sauté the celery, and onion in the same fat for 1 minute, stirring, until the vegetables soften.

Mix in the flour to coat the vegetables. Pour in the wine simmer. Cook for about 1 minute or until reduced by about one-third. Pour in the water, the reserved mussel liquid, potatoes, salt, rosemary, and bay leaf.

Seal the lid and cook on High Pressure for 4 minutes. Do a natural pressure release for 5 minutes. Stir in the mussels and heavy cream. Press Sauté and bring the soup to a simmer to heat the mussels through.

Discard the bay leaf. Spoon the soup into bowls and crumble the pancetta over the top. Garnish with the chervil and crackers, on side.

Crabmeat with Asparagus & Broccoli Pilaf

Serves: 4 | Ready in about: 20 min

INGREDIENTS

½ pound asparagus, trimmed and cut into pieces
½ pound broccoli florets
Salt to taste
2 tbsp olive oil
1 small onion, chopped (about ½ cup)

1 cup rice
⅓ cup white wine
3 cups vegetable stock
8 ounces lump crabmeat

DIRECTIONS

Heat oil on Sauté and cook onions for 3 minutes, until soft. Stir in rice and cook for 1 minute. Pour in the wine. Cook for 2 to 3 minutes, stirring until the liquid has almost evaporated.

Add vegetable stock and salt; stir to combine. Place a trivet atop. Arrange the broccoli and asparagus on the trivet. Seal the lid and cook on High Pressure for 8 minutes. Do a quick release.

Remove the vegetables to a bowl. Fluff the rice with a fork and add in the crabmeat, heat for a minute. Taste and adjust the seasoning. Serve immediately topped with broccoli and asparagus.

Cajun Salmon with Creamy Polenta

Serves: 4 | Ready in about: 20 min

INGREDIENTS

1 cup corn grits polenta
½ cup coconut milk
3 cups chicken stock
3 tbsp butter
Salt to taste

3 tbsp Cajun Seasoning
1 tbsp sugar
4 salmon fillets, skin removed
Nonstick cooking spray

DIRECTIONS

Combine polenta, milk, chicken stock, butter, and salt in the pot. Stir and bring mixture to boil on Sauté.

In a bowl mix Cajun seasoning, sugar, and salt. Oil the fillets with cooking spray and add the spice mixture. Insert a trivet and arrange the fillets on top. Seal the lid and cook on High Pressure for 9 minutes.

Do a natural pressure release for 10 minutes. Stir and serve immediately with the salmon.

Shrimp Andouille Sausage Gumbo

Serves: 4 | Ready in about: 25 min

INGREDIENTS

1 pound jumbo shrimp
1½ tsp salt
¼ cup olive oil, plus 2 tbsp
⅓ cup flour
1½ tsp Cajun Seasoning
1 medium onion, chopped
1 cup red bell pepper, chopped

2 celery stalks, chopped
2 garlic cloves, minced
1 small serrano pepper, seeded and minced
2½ cups chicken broth
6 ounces andouille sausage, sliced
¾ cup water
2 green onions, finely sliced

DIRECTIONS

Heat olive oil on Sauté. Whisk in the flour with a wooden spoon and cook 3 minutes, stirring constantly. Stir in Cajun, onion, bell pepper, celery, garlic, and serrano pepper for about 5 minutes.

Pour in the chicken broth, water, and andouille sausage. Seal and cook for 6 minutes on High Pressure.

Do a natural pressure for 5 minutes. Stir the shrimp into the gumbo to eat it up for 3 minutes. Adjust the seasoning. Ladle the gumbo into bowls and garnish with the green onions.

Garlic-Lemon Salmon Steak

Serves: 3 | Ready in about: 65 min

INGREDIENTS

1 lb salmon steaks
1 tsp garlic powder
½ tsp rosemary powder
1 cup olive oil

½ cup apple cider vinegar
1 tsp salt
¼ cup lemon juice
½ tsp white pepper

DIRECTIONS

In a bowl, mix garlic, rosemary, olive oil, apple cider vinegar, salt, lemon juice, and pepper. Pour the mixture into a Ziploc bag along with the salmon.

Seal the bag and shake to coat well. Refrigerate for 30 minutes. Pour in 3 cups of water in the instant pot and insert the trivet. Remove the fish from the Ziploc bag and place on top. Reserve the marinade.

Seal lid and cook on Steam mode for 15 minutes on High Pressure. When ready, do a quick release and remove the steaks.

Discard the liquid and wipe clean the pot. Grease with some of the marinade and hit Sauté. Add salmon steaks and brown on both sides for 3-4 minutes.

Crispy Herbed Trout

Serves: 2 | Ready in about: 30 min

INGREDIENTS

1 lb fresh trout, (2 pieces)
2 cups fish stock
1 tbsp fresh mint, chopped
¼ tsp dried thyme, ground
1 tbsp fresh parsley, chopped

3 garlic cloves, chopped
3 tbsp olive oil
2 tbsp fresh lemon juice
1 tsp sea salt

DIRECTIONS

In a bowl, mix mint, thyme, parsley, garlic, olive oil, lemon juice, chili, and salt.

Stir to combine. Spread the abdominal cavity of the fish and brush with the marinade. Then, brush the fish from the outside and set aside.

Insert the trivet in instant pot. Pour in the stock and place the fish on top. Seal the lid and cook on Steam mode for 15 minutes on High Pressure.

Do a quick release and serve immediately.

Green Mackerel with Potatoes

Serves: 4 | Ready in about: 32 min

INGREDIENTS

4 mackerels, skin on
1 lb of fresh spinach, torn
5 potatoes, peeled and chopped
¼ cup of olive oil,
2 garlic cloves, crushed

1 tsp dried rosemary, chopped
2 sprigs of fresh mint leaves, chopped
1 lemon, juiced
Sea salt to taste

DIRECTIONS

Grease the pot with 4 tbsp olive oil. Stir-fry garlic, and rosemary on Sauté, for 1 minute. Stir in spinach, a pinch of salt, and cook for 4-5 minutes, until soft. Remove the spinach from the cooker and set aside.

Add the remaining oil to and make a layer of potatoes. Top with fish and drizzle with lemon juice, olive oil, and sea salt. Pour in 1 cup of water, seal the lid and cook on Steam mode for 7 minutes on High.

When ready, do a quick release. Plate the fish and potatoes with spinach, and serve immediately.

Herbs & Lemon Stuffed Tench

Serves: 2 | Ready in about: 20 min

INGREDIENTS

1 tench, cleaned and gutted
1 lemon, quartered
2 tbsp olive oil
1 tsp fresh rosemary, chopped

¼ tsp dried thyme, ground
2 garlic cloves, crushed
½ tsp sea salt

DIRECTIONS

In a bowl, mix olive oil, rosemary, thyme, garlic, and salt. Stir to combine. Brush the fish with the previously prepared mixture and stuff with lemon slices.

Pour 4 cups of water into the instant pot, set the steamer tray and place the fish on top. If the fish is too big and can't fit in, cut in half.

Seal the lid and cook on Steam mode for 15 minutes on High Pressure. Do a quick release. For a crispier taste, briefly brown the fish in a grill pan.

Quick Salmon Fillets

Serves: 4 | Ready in about: 15 min

INGREDIENTS

4 salmon fillets
1 cup lemon juice
2 tbsp butter, softened

2 tbsp dill
¼ tsp salt
¼ tsp pepper, freshly ground

DIRECTIONS

Sprinkle the fillets with salt, and pepper. Insert the steamer tray and place the salmon on top. Pour in the lemon juice and 2 cups of water. Seal the lid.

Cook on Steam mode for 5 minutes on High. When done, release the pressure naturally, for 10 minutes. Set aside the salmon and discard the liquid.

Wipe the pot clean and Press Sauté. Add butter and briefly brown the fillets on both sides – for 3-4 minutes. Sprinkle with dill, to serve.

Fish Stew

Serves: 6 | Ready in about: 30 min

INGREDIENTS

2 lb of different fish and seafood
¼ tbsp olive oil
2 onions, peeled, chopped
2 carrots, grated

A handful of fresh parsley, finely chopped
2 garlic cloves, crushed
3 cups water
1 tsp sea salt

DIRECTIONS

Heat 3 tbsp olive oil on Sauté. Stir-fry onion and garlic, for 3-4 minutes, or until translucent. Add the remaining ingredients. Seal the lid, and cook on High Pressure for 10 minutes. Do a quick release.

Orange Salmon Fillets

Serves: 3 | Ready in about: 17 min

INGREDIENTS

1 lb salmon fillets
1 cup orange juice, freshly squeezed
2 tbsp cornstarch
1 tsp himalayan pink salt

½ tsp black pepper, freshly ground
½ tsp garlic, minced
1 tsp orange zest, freshly grated

DIRECTIONS

Add all ingredients and seal the lid. Cook on High pressure for 10 minutes. Do a quick pressure release.

Garlicky Seafood Pasta

Serves: 4 | Ready in about: 30 min

INGREDIENTS

1 lb fresh seafood mix
¼ cup olive oil
4 garlic cloves, crushed
1 tbsp fresh parsley, chopped

1 tsp fresh rosemary, chopped
½ tbsp white wine
1 tsp salt
1 lb squid ink pasta

DIRECTIONS

Heat 3 tbsp olive oil on Sauté and stir-fry the garlic, for 1-2 minutes, until fragrant. Add seafood, parsley, rosemary, and salt, and stir. Add the remaining oil, wine, and ½ cup of water.

Seal the lid and cook on High Pressure for 4 minutes. Do a quick release and set aside. Follow the instructions to prepare the pasta. Open the instant pot, add the pasta, give it a final stir, and serve hot.

Lemon & Dill Salmon with Greens

Serves: 4 | Ready in about: 30 min

INGREDIENTS

1 lb salmon filets, boneless
1 lb fresh spinach, torn
4 tbsp olive oil
2 garlic cloves, chopped

2 tbsp lemon juice
1 tbsp fresh dill, chopped
1 tsp sea salt
¼ tsp black pepper, ground

DIRECTIONS

Place spinach in the pot, cover with water and lay the trivet on top. Rub the salmon filets with half of the olive oil, dill, salt, pepper, and garlic. Lay on the trivet. Seal the lid and cook on Steam for 5 minutes on High.

Do a quick release. Remove salmon to a serving plate. Drain the spinach in a colander. Serve the fish on a bed of spinach. Season with salt and drizzle with lemon juice.

Cod in Lemon-Sweet Sauce

Serves: 3 | Ready in about: 20 min

INGREDIENTS

1 lb cod fillets, skinless and boneless
1 cup maple syrup
½ cup soy sauce
3 garlic cloves, finely chopped

1 lemon, juiced
1 tsp black pepper, ground
1 tsp sea salt
1 tbsp butter

DIRECTIONS

In a bowl, mix maple syrup, soy sauce, garlic, lemon juice, pepper, and salt. Stir until combined and set aside. Grease the pot with butter. Place the fillets at the bottom and pour over the maple sauce.

Seal the lid and cook on Steam for 8 minutes on High. Release the pressure naturally.

Marinated Squid in White Wine Sauce

Serves: 3 | Ready in about: 45 min

INGREDIENTS

1 lb fresh squid rings
1 cup dry white wine
1 cup olive oil
2 garlic cloves, crushed
1 lemon, juiced

2 cups fish stock
¼ tsp red pepper flakes
¼ tsp dried oregano
1 tbsp fresh rosemary, chopped
1 tsp sea salt

DIRECTIONS

In a bowl, mix wine, olive oil, lemon juice, garlic, flakes, oregano, rosemary, and salt. Submerge squid rings in this mixture and cover with a lid.

Refrigerate for 1 hour. Remove the squid from the fridge and place them in the pot along with stock and half of the marinade. Seal the lid.

Cook on High Pressure for 6 minutes. Release the pressure naturally, for 10 minutes. Transfer the rings to a plate and drizzle with some marinade to serve.

Octopus & Shrimp with Collard Greens

Serves: 4 | Ready in about: 35 min

INGREDIENTS

1 lb collard greens, chopped
1 lb shrimp, whole
6 oz octopus, cut into bite-sized pieces
1 large tomato, peeled, chopped
3 cups fish stock

4 tbsp olive oil
3 garlic cloves
2 tbsp fresh parsley, chopped
1 tsp sea salt

DIRECTIONS

Place shrimp and octopus in the pot. Add tomato and fish stock. Seal the lid and cook on High Pressure for 15 minutes. Do a quick release. Remove shrimp and octopus, drain the liquid.

Heat olive oil on Sauté, add garlic, parsley, and cook until translucent. Add collard greens and simmer for 10 minutes. Season with salt and remove from the cooker. Serve with shrimp and octopus.

Shrimp with Brussels Sprouts

Serves: 8 | Ready in about: 45 min

INGREDIENTS

1 lb large shrimp, cleaned, rinsed
6 oz Brussels sprouts, outer leaves removed
4 oz of okra, whole
2 carrots, chopped
2 cups chicken broth
2 tomatoes, diced
2 tbsp tomato paste
½ tsp cayenne pepper, ground

¼ tsp black pepper, freshly ground
1 tsp sea salt
1 cup olive oil, plus 2 tbsp
¼ cup balsamic vinegar
1 tbsp fresh rosemary, chopped
1 small celery stalk, for decoration
2 tbsp sour cream, optionally

DIRECTIONS

Mix oil, vinegar, rosemary, salt, and pepper in a large bowl. Stir and submerge the shrimp into the mixture. Toss well to coat and refrigerate for 20 minutes. Add tomatoes, paste, 2 tbsp olive oil, and cayenne pepper.

Cook on Sauté for 5 minutes, stirring constantly. Remove to a bowl, cover and set aside. Pour in broth, and add Brussels sprouts, carrots, and okra. Sprinkle with salt, black pepper and seal the lid.

Cook on High pressure for 15 minutes. Then, do a quick release. Remove the vegetables and add shrimp in the remaining broth. Seal the lid again and cook on Steam for 3 minutes on High.

Do a quick release and set aside. Add the remaining oil, and cooked vegetables. Cook for 2-3 minutes, stirring constantly, on Sauté. Remove to a bowl. Top with sour cream and drizzle with shrimp marinade.

Anchovy and Mussel Rice

Serves: 4 | Ready in about: 40 min

INGREDIENTS

1 cup rice
6 oz mussels
1 onion, finely chopped
1 garlic clove, crushed
1 tbsp dried rosemary, finely chopped

¼ cup salted capers
1 tsp chili pepper, ground
½ tsp salt
3 tbsp olive oil
4 salted anchovies

DIRECTIONS

Add rice to the pot, and pour 2 cups of water. Seal the lid and cook on Rice mode for 8 minutes on High.

Do a quick release. Remove the rice and set aside. Grease the pot with oil, and stir-fry garlic and onions, for 2 minutes, on Sauté. Add mussels and rosemary. Cook for 10 more minutes. Stir in rice and season with salt, and chili pepper. Serve with anchovies and capers.

Steamed Sea Bream

Serves: 4 | Ready in about: 50 min

INGREDIENTS

2 pieces sea bream (2 lb), cleaned
¼ cup olive oil
¼ cup freshly squeezed lemon juice
1 tbsp fresh thyme sprigs

1 tbsp Italian Seasoning mix
½ tsp sea salt
1 tsp garlic powder
4 cups fish stock

DIRECTIONS

In a bowl, mix oil, lemon juice, thyme, Italian seasoning, sea salt, and garlic powder. Brush onto fish and wrap tightly with a plastic foil. Refrigerate for 30 minutes before cooking. Pour fish stock in the pot.

Set the steamer rack and place the fish on top. Seal the lid. Cook on Steam mode for 8 minutes on High. Do a quick release, open the lid, and unwrap the fish. Serve immediately with steam vegetables.

Marinated Smelt with Mustard Rice

Serves: 4 | Ready in about: 35 min

INGREDIENTS

1 lb fresh smelt, cleaned, heads removed
1 cup extra virgin olive oil
½ cup freshly squeezed lemon juice
¼ cup freshly squeezed orange juice
1 tbsp Dijon mustard
1 tsp fresh rosemary, finely chopped
2 garlic cloves, crushed
1 tsp sea salt

½ tbsp rice
5 oz okra
1 carrot, chopped
¼ cup green peas, soaked overnight
5 oz cherry tomatoes, halved
4 tbsp vegetable oil
2 cups fish stock

DIRECTIONS

In a bowl, mix oil, juices, dijon, garlic, salt, and rosemary. Stir well and submerge fish in this mixture.

Refrigerate for 1 hour. Meanwhile, heat oil on Sauté and stir-fry carrot, peas, cherry tomatoes, and okra, for 10 minutes. Add rice and fish stock. Seal the lid and cook on Rice for 8 minutes on High.

Do a quick release and add in the fish along with half of the marinade. Seal the lid again and cook on Steam for 4 minutes on High. Release the pressure naturally, for 10 minutes. Serve immediately.

Rosemary & Dill Trout Fillet

Serves: 6 | Ready in about: 1 hr 20 min

INGREDIENTS

2 lb trout fillets, skin on
½ cup olive oil
¼ cup apple cider vinegar
1 red onion, chopped
1 lemon, sliced
2 garlic cloves, crushed

1 tbsp fresh rosemary, chopped
1 tbsp dill sprigs, chopped
½ sea salt
¼ tsp freshly ground black pepper
3 cups fish stock

DIRECTIONS

In a bowl, mix oil, apple cider, onions, garlic, rosemary, dill, sea salt, and pepper. Submerge the fillets into this mixture and refrigerate for 1 hour. Grease the bottom of the pot with 4 tbsp of the marinade and pour in the stock. Add the fish, seal the lid and cook on High pressure for 4 minutes. Do a quick release.

Red Pollock & Tomato Stew

Serves: 4 | Ready in about: 50 min

INGREDIENTS

1 lb pollock fillet
4 cloves, crushed
1 lb tomatoes, peeled and chopped
2 bay leaves, whole
2 cups fish stock

1 tsp freshly ground black pepper
1 onion, peeled and finely chopped
½ cup olive oil
1 tsp sea salt

DIRECTIONS

Heat 2 tbsp olive oil on Sauté. Add onion and sauté until translucent, stirring constantly, for about 3-4 minutes. Add tomatoes and cook until soft. Press Cancel. Add the remaining ingredients and seal the lid. Cook on High pressure for 15 minutes. When ready, do a quick release and serve warm.

Thick Fish Soup

Serves: 4 | Ready in about: 45 min

INGREDIENTS

6 oz mackerel fillets
½ cup wheat groats, soaked
½ cup kidney beans, soaked
¼ cup sweet corn
1 lb tomatoes, peeled, roughly chopped

4 cups fish stock
4 tbsp olive oil
1 tsp sea salt
1 tsp fresh rosemary, finely chopped
2 garlic cloves, crushed

DIRECTIONS

Heat olive oil on Sauté, and stir-fry tomatoes and garlic for 5 minutes. Add rosemary, stock, salt, corn, kidney beans, and wheat groats. Seal the lid and cook on High Pressure for 25 minutes.

Do a quick release and add mackerel fillets. Seal the lid and cook on Steam for 8 minutes on High. Do a quick release, open the lid and serve immediately drizzled with freshly squeezed lemon juice.

Squid Ink Pasta with Trout Fillets

Serves: 5 | Ready in about: 25 min

INGREDIENTS

1 lb squid ink pasta
6 oz trout fillet
1 cup olive oil
½ cup lemon juice
1 tsp fresh rosemary, chopped

3 garlic cloves, crushed, halved
2 tsp sea salt
2 tbsp fresh parsley, finely chopped
A handful of olives and capers for serving

DIRECTIONS

In a bowl, mix oil, lemon juice, rosemary, 2 garlic cloves, and 1 teaspoon of salt. Stir well and submerge fillets in this mixture. Refrigerate for 30 minutes. Remove from the fridge and drain, reserving the liquid.

Grease the pot with some of the marinade. Add fillets, 1 cup of water, and 3 tablespoons of the marinade. Seal the lid and cook on High pressure for 4 minutes. Do a quick release, add the pasta and 1 cup of water.

Seal the lid and cook for 3 minutes on High pressure. Do a quick release. Serve with capers and olives.

Trout & Spinach with Tomato Sauce

Serves: 3 | Ready in about: 55 min

INGREDIENTS

1 lb trout fillets
6 oz fresh spinach, torn
2 tomatoes, peeled, diced
3 cups fish stock
1 tsp dried thyme

½ tsp fresh rosemary
¼ cup olive oil
¼ cup freshly squeezed Lime juice
1 tsp sea salt
2 garlic cloves, crushed

DIRECTIONS

Rinse the fillets and sprinkle them with sea salt. In a bowl, mix olive oil, thyme, rosemary, and lime juice. Stir well and submerge fillets in this mixture. Refrigerate for 30 minutes; then drain the fillets.

Reserve the marinade, grease the pot with 3 tbsp of the marinade and add the fillets and stock.

Seal the lid and cook on Steam for 8 minutes on High Pressure. Do a quick release, remove the fish and set aside. Add the remaining marinade to the pot. Hit Sauté and add the tomatoes and spinach. Cook until soft. Give it a good stir and remove to a plate. Add fish, drizzle with tomato sauce and serve warm.

Citrusy Marinated Grilled Catfish

Serves: 4 | Ready in about: 60 min

INGREDIENTS

1 lb flathead catfish
1 cup orange juice
¼ cup lemon juice
½ cup olive oil
1 tbsp dried thyme

1 tbsp dried rosemary
1 tsp chili flakes
1 tsp sea salt
3 cups fish stock

DIRECTIONS

In a bowl, mix orange juice, lemon juice, olive oil, thyme, rosemary, chili flakes, and salt. Brush the fish with this mixture and refrigerate for 30 minutes. Remove from the fridge, drain; reserve the marinade.

Insert the trivet in the pot. Pour in stock and marinade, and place the fish onto the top. Seal the lid and cook on High Pressure for 10 minutes. Do a quick release and serve immediately.

Chili & Oregano Salmon Fillet

Serves: 4 | Ready in about: 60 min

INGREDIENTS

1 lb fresh salmon fillets, skin on
¼ cup olive oil
½ cup freshly squeezed lemon juice
2 garlic cloves, crushed

1 tbsp fresh oregano leaves, chopped
1 tsp sea salt
¼ tsp chili flakes
2 cups fish stock

DIRECTIONS

In a bowl, mix oil, lemon juice, garlic, oregano leaves, salt, and chili flakes. Brush the fillets with the mixture and refrigerate for 30 minutes. Pour the stock in, and insert the trivet. Pat-dry the salmon and place on the steamer rack. Seal the lid, and cook on Steam for 10 minutes on High. Do a quick release and serve.

Garlic Seafood with Brown Rice

Serves: 4 | Ready in about: 30 min

INGREDIENTS

1 lb frozen seafood mix
1 cup brown rice
1 tbsp calamari ink
2 tbsp extra virgin olive oil
2 garlic cloves, crushed

1 tbsp finely chopped rosemary
½ tsp salt
3 cups fish stock
Freshly squeezed lemon juice

DIRECTIONS

Add in all ingredients, seal the lid and cook on Rice mode for 10 minutes on High. Release the pressure naturally, for 10 minutes. Squeeze lemon juice and serve.

White Wine Catfish Fillets

Serves: 3 | Ready in about: 50 min

INGREDIENTS

1 lb catfish fillet
1 lemon, juiced
½ cup parsley leaves, chopped
2 garlic cloves, crushed
1 onion, finely chopped
1 tbsp fresh dill, chopped

1 tbsp fresh rosemary
2 cups white wine
2 tbsp Dijon mustard
1 cup extra virgin olive oil
3 cups fish stock

DIRECTIONS

In a bowl, mix lemon juice, parsley, garlic, onion, fresh dill, rosemary, wine, mustard, and oil. Stir well to combine. Submerge fillets in this mixture and cover with a tight lid. Refrigerate for 1 hour.

Insert the trivet, remove the fish from the fridge and place it on the rack. Pour in stock along with the marinade and seal the lid. Cook on Steam for 8 minutes on High. Release the pressure quickly and serve.

Tuna & Rosemary Pizza

Serves: 4 | Ready in about: 25 min

INGREDIENTS

1 cup canned tuna, oil-free
½ cup mozzarella cheese, shredded
¼ cup goat's cheese
3 tbsp olive oil

1 tbsp tomato paste
½ tsp dried rosemary
14 oz pizza crust
1 cup olives, optional

DIRECTIONS

Grease the bottom of a baking dish with one tablespoon of olive oil. Line some parchment paper. Flour the working surface and roll out the pizza dough to the approximate size of your instant pot. Gently fit the dough in the previously prepared baking dish.

In a bowl, combine olive oil, tomato paste, and rosemary. Whisk together and Spread the mixture over the crust.

Sprinkle with goat cheese, mozzarella, and tuna. Place a trivet inside the pot and pour in 1 cup of water.

Seal the lid, and cook for 15 minutes on High Pressure. Do a quick release. Remove the pizza from the pot. Cut and serve.

SNACKS AND APPETIZERS

Hot Chicken Wings

Serves: 4 | Ready in about: 30 minutes

INGREDIENTS

½ cup sriracha sauce
1 cup water
¼ cup ranch salad dressing mix
2 tbsp butter, melted

Juice from ½ lemon
2 pounds chicken vignettes
½ tsp paprika
Non-stick cooking spray

DIRECTIONS

Mix chicken, water, sriracha, butter and lemon in the inner pot. Seal the lid and cook on High Pressure for 5 min minutes. Do a quick pressure release. Serve with the paprika and ranch dressing.

Tangy Cheesy Arancini

Serves: 6 | Ready in about: 60 minutes

INGREDIENTS

½ cup olive oil, plus 1 tbsp
1 white onion, diced
2 garlic cloves, minced
5 cups chicken stock
½ cup apple cider vinegar
2 cups short grain rice
1½ cups grated Cheddar cheese,

¼ cup grated Parmesan cheese for garnish
1 cup canned Kernel sweet corn, drained
1 tsp salt
1 tsp ground black pepper
2 cups fresh breadcrumbs
2 eggs

DIRECTIONS

On Sauté, heat 1 tbsp of oil and sauté onion for 2 minutes until translucent. Add the garlic and cook for a minute. Stir in the stock and rice. Seal the lid and cook on High Pressure for 7 minutes.

Do a natural pressure release for 10 minutes. Stir in cheddar cheese, corn, salt, and pepper. Spoon into a bowl and let cool completely. Wipe clean the pot.

In a bowl, pour the breadcrumbs. In a separate bowl, beat the eggs. Form balls out of the rice mixture, dip each into the beaten eggs, and coat in the breadcrumb mixture.

Heat the remaining oil on Sauté and fry in batches arancini until crispy and golden brown. Sprinkle with Parmesan cheese and serve.

Hot Turkey Meatballs with Tomato Sauce

Serves: 6 | Ready in about: 50 minutes

INGREDIENTS

1 pound ground turkey
1 carrot, shredded
2 celery stalks, minced
¼ cup Cotija queso, crumbled
¼ cup hot sauce
¼ cup breadcrumbs

1 egg, beaten
2 tbsp olive oil
½ cup water
4 tomatoes, chopped
Salt and pepper to taste
2 tsp fresh basil, chopped

DIRECTIONS

In a bowl, combine turkey, carrot, celery, cotija cheese, hot sauce, breadcrumbs, and egg. Season with salt and pepper. Shape the mixture into 12 meatballs.

Heat oil on Sauté and fry the meatballs in batches until lightly golden. Pour in water, tomatoes, and salt. Seal the lid and cook on High Pressure for 5 minutes. Do a quick release. Sprinkle with basil and serve.

Savoy Cabbage and Beef Dumplings

Serves: 8 | Ready in about: 30 min

INGREDIENTS

8 ounces ground beef
½ cup savoy cabbage, shredded
1 carrot, grated
1 large egg, beaten
1 garlic clove, minced
2 tbsp coconut aminos
½ tbsp melted ghee

½ tbsp ginger powder
½ tsp salt
½ tsp freshly ground black pepper
20 dumpling wrappers
2 tbsp olive oil
1 cup water

DIRECTIONS

In a bowl, mix beef, cabbage, carrot, egg, garlic, coconut aminos, ghee, ginger, salt, and pepper. Put the dumpling wrappers on a flat surface and spoon 1 tbsp of the beef filling into the middle of each wrapper.

Run the edges of the wrapper with a little water. Fold the dough to cover filling and create a semi-circle shape, pinching the edges to Seal. Then, brush the dumplings with the olive oil.

Arrange the dumplings in the pot. Pour in water, seal the lid and cook on High Pressure for 15 minutes. Do a quick release. Drain the dumplings and place under the broiler for about 4-5 minutes.

Cheesy Green Bites

Serves: 8 | Ready in about: 45 minutes

INGREDIENTS

¼ cup frozen chopped kale
¼ cup finely chopped artichoke hearts
¼ cup ricotta cheese
2 tbsp grated Parmesan cheese
¼ cup goat cheese
1 large egg white

1 tsp dried basil
1 lemon, zested
½ tsp salt
½ tsp freshly ground black pepper
4 frozen filo dough, thawed
1 tbsp extra-virgin olive oil

DIRECTIONS

In a bowl, combine kale, artichoke, ricotta, parmesan, goat cheese, egg white, basil, lemon zest, salt, and pepper. Place a filo dough on a clean flat surface. Brush with olive oil.

Place a second filo sheet on the first and brush with more oil. Continue layering to form a pile of four oiled sheets. Working from the short side, cut the phyllo sheets into 8 strips and half them.

Spoon 1 tablespoon of filling onto one short end of every strip. Fold a corner to cover the filling and a triangle; continue folding over and over to the end of the strip, creating a triangle-shaped filo packet.

Repeat the process with the other filo bites. Place a trivet into the pot. Pour in 1 cup of water. Place the bites on top of the trivet. Seal the lid and cook on High Pressure for 15 minutes. Do a quick release.

Teriyaki Chicken Wings

Serves: 6 | Ready in about: 30 min

INGREDIENTS

1 tbsp honey
1 cup teriyaki sauce
1 tsp finely ground black pepper
2 lb chicken wings

2 tbsp cornstarch
2 tbsp cold water
1 tsp sesame seeds

DIRECTIONS

In the pot, combine honey, teriyaki sauce, and black pepper until the honey dissolves completely. Toss in chicken to coat. Seal the lid, press Poultry and cook for 10 minutes on High. Release the pressure quickly.

Transfer chicken wings to a platter. Mix cold water with the cornstarch. Press Sauté and stir in cornstarch slurry into the sauce and cook for 4 to 6 minutes until thickened. Top the chicken with thickened sauce. Add a garnish of sesame seeds, and serve.

Green Vegan Dip

Serves: 4 | Ready in about: 20 min

INGREDIENTS

2 cups broccoli florets
¾ cup green bell pepper, chopped
¼ cup raw cashews
10 oz canned green chiles, drained, liquid reserved

¼ cup soy sauce
½ tsp sea salt
¼ tsp chili powder
¼ tsp garlic powder

DIRECTIONS

In the pot, add cashews, broccoli, green bell pepper, and 1 cup of water. Seal the lid and cook for 5 minutes on High Pressure. Release the pressure quickly. Drain water from the pot.

Add reserved liquid from canned green chilies, salt, garlic powder, chili powder, soy sauce, and cumin. Use an immersion blender to blend the mixture until smooth. Set aside in a mixing bowl. Stir green chilies through the dip.

Homemade Spinach Hummus

Serves: 12 | Ready in about: 1hr 10 min

INGREDIENTS

8 cups water
2 cups dried chickpeas
5 tbsp grapeseed oil
2 tsp salt

½ cup tahini
5 tbsp lemon juice
2 cups spinach, chopped
5 garlic cloves, crushed

DIRECTIONS

In the instant pot, mix 2 tbsp oil, water, 1 tsp salt, and chickpeas. Seal the lid and cook on High Pressure for 35 minutes. Release the pressure quickly. In a small bowl, reserve ½ cup of the cooking liquid and drain chickpeas.

Mix half the reserved cooking liquid and chickpeas in a food processor and puree until no large chickpeas remain. Add remaining cooking liquid, spinach, lemon juice, a tsp salt, garlic, and tahini. Process hummus for 8 minutes until smooth. Stir in the remaining olive oil before serving.

Sweet-Heat Pickled Cucumbers

Serves: 6 | Ready in about: 5 min

INGREDIENTS

1 pound cucumbers, sliced
2 cups white vinegar
1 cup water
1 cup sugar

¼ cup green garlic, minced
2 tbsp Dill Pickle Seasoning
2 tsp salt
1 tsp cumin

DIRECTIONS

Into the pot, add cucumber, vinegar, water, sugar, cumin, dill pickle seasoning, and salt. Stir well to dissolve the sugar. Seal the lid and cook for 4 minutes on High Pressure. Release the pressure quickly.

Ladle cucumbers into a large storage container and pour cooking liquid over. Chill for one hour.

Cheesy Spinach Tarts

Serves: 4 | Ready in about: 45 minutes

INGREDIENTS

2 tbsp butter
1 small white onion, sliced
2 cups spinach, chopped
¼ tsp salt
¼ tsp freshly ground black pepper

¼ cup dry white wine
1 pie pastry, thawed
1 cup Camembert cheese, cubed
1 tbsp thinly sliced fresh green onions

DIRECTIONS

Melt 1 tsp of butter on Sauté and cook onion and spinach for 5 minutes, or until tender. Season with salt and black pepper, then pour in white wine and cook until evaporated, about 2 minutes. Set aside.

Unwrap the pie pastry and cut into 4 squares. Prink the dough with a fork and brush both sides with the remaining butter. Share half of the cheese over the pie pastry squares.

Cover with the spinach and top with the remaining cheese. Arrange the tarts in a buttered baking dish, pour 1 cup of water in the pot. Insert a trivet and lower the baking dish on top.

Seal the lid and cook on High Pressure for 30 minutes. Do a quick release. Serve with green onions.

Italian Baked Turnips

Serves: 4 | Ready in about: 20 minutes

INGREDIENTS

4 small turnips, scrubbed clean
¼ cup whipping cream
¼ cup sour cream
½ cup chopped roasted red bell pepper

1 tsp Italian Seasoning mix
1½ cups shredded Monterey Jack cheese
4 green onions, chopped
⅓ cup grated Parmesan cheese

DIRECTIONS

Pour 1 cup of water into the pot and insert a trivet. Place the turnips on top. Seal the lid and cook on High and for 10 minutes. Do a quick pressure release. Remove the turnips to a cutting board and allow cooling.

Cut the turnips in half. Scoop out the pulp into a bowl, mix in the whipping cream and sour cream using a potato mash until smooth. Stir in the roasted bell pepper, Cajun seasoning, and Monterey Jack cheese.

Fetch out 2 tablespoons of green onions and stir the remaining into the turnips. Fill the turnip skins with the mashed mixture and sprinkle with the Parmesan. Arrange on a greased baking dish and place on the trivet. Seal the lid and cook on High pressure for 3 minutes. Do a quick pressure release.

Let cool for a few minutes and garnish with the remaining onions.

Turkey Stuffed Potatoes

Serves: 4 | Ready in about: 30 min

INGREDIENTS

2 cups vegetable broth
1 tsp chili powder
1 tsp ground cumin
½ tsp onion powder
½ tsp garlic powder

1 pound turkey breasts
4 potatoes
2 tbsp fresh cilantro, chopped
1 Fresno chili pepper, chopped

DIRECTIONS

In the pot, combine broth, cumin, garlic powder, onion powder, and chili powder. Toss in turkey to coat. Place a steamer rack over the turkey. On top of the rack, set the steamer basket.

Use a fork to pierce the potatoes and set them into the steamer basket. Seal the lid and cook for 20 minutes on High Pressure. Release the pressure quickly. Remove steamer basket from the cooker. Place the potatoes on a plate. Place turkey in a mixing bowl and use two forks to shred.

Cut in half each potato lengthwise. Stuff with shredded turkey. Top with cilantro, onion, and chili pepper.

Chorizo Mac and Cheese

Serves: 6 | Ready in about: 30 min

INGREDIENTS

1 pound macaroni
3 ounces chorizo, chopped
3 cups water
1 tbsp garlic powder

2 tbsp minced garlic
2 cups milk
2 cups Cheddar cheese, shredded
Salt to taste

DIRECTIONS

On Sauté and stir-fry chorizo until crispy, for about 6 minutes. Set aside. Wipe the pot with kitchen paper. Add in water, macaroni, and salt to taste. Seal lid and cook on for 5 minutes High Pressure.

Release the pressure quickly. Stir in cheese and milk until the cheese melts. Divide the mac and cheese between serving bowls. Top with chorizo and serve.

Beef Meatballs with Dilled Yogurt Dip

Serves: 4 | Ready in about: 35 min

INGREDIENTS

1 lb lean ground beef
2 garlic cloves, crushed
¼ cup flour
1 tbsp fresh rosemary, crushed

1 large egg, beaten
½ tsp salt
3 tbsp olive oil

FOR SERVING:

1 cup Greek yogurt, full-fat
2 tbsp fresh dill

1 garlic clove, crushed

DIRECTIONS

In a bowl, mix with hands ground beef, garlic, rosemary, 1 egg, and salt. Lightly dampen hands and shape 1 ½-inch balls. Grease the instant pot with oil.

Transfer the balls to the pot. Add 1 cup of water. Seal the lid and cook on High Pressure for 13 minutes. Do a quick release.

For the sauce, mix Greek yogurt, dill, and garlic. Stir well and drizzle over meatballs.

Spinach & Two-Cheese Pie

Serves: 5 | Ready in about: 30 min

INGREDIENTS

1 lb spinach, chopped
½ cup mascarpone cheese
½ cup feta cheese, shredded
3 eggs, beaten
½ cup goat's cheese

3 tbsp butter
½ cup milk
1 pack (6 sheets) pie dough
Oil for greasing

DIRECTIONS

In a bowl, mix spinach, eggs, mascarpone, feta, and goat cheese. Dust a clean surface with flour and unfold the pie sheets onto it. Using a rolling pin, roll the dough to fit your instant pot. Repeat with the other five sheets.

Combine milk and butter in a skillet. Bring it to a boil and melt the butter completely. Remove from the heat.

Grease a baking pan with oil. Place in 2 pie sheets and brush with milk mixture. Make the first layer of spinach mixture and cover with another two pie sheets. Again, brush with butter and milk mixture, and repeat until you have used all ingredients. Pour 1 ½ cups water in your instant pot and insert the trivet. Lower the pan on the trivet and seal the lid.

Cook on High pressure for 6 minutes. Do a quick release. Place parchment paper under the pie to use it as a lifting method, to remove the cake. Serve cold.

Yummy Beef Meatballs

Serves: 4 | Ready in about: 20 min

INGREDIENTS

1 lb ground beef
2 tbsp milk
3 tbsp oil
1 tbsp Italian Seasoning mix

1 onion, chopped
2 eggs
2 slices wheat bread
Salt and black pepper to taste

DIRECTIONS

Place two slices of bread in a bowl. Add ¼ cup water and let soak for 5 minutes.

Meanwhile, mix beef, milk, oil, Italian seasoning mix, onion, eggs, salt, and pepper. Add soaked bread and shape balls with an approximately ¼ cup of the mixture. Flatten each ball with hand and place on a lightly floured surface. Grease the stainless steel insert with oil.

Add the meatballs to the pot and fry for 3 minutes per side, on Sauté. Serve with garlic sauce.

Garlic Shrimp with Herbs

Serves: 4 | Ready in about: 15 min

INGREDIENTS

1 lb shrimp, whole
½ cup olive oil
1 tsp garlic powder
1 tsp dried rosemary, crushed
1 tsp dried thyme

½ tsp dried basil
½ tsp dried sage
½ tsp salt
1 tsp chili pepper

DIRECTIONS

Pour 1 ½ cups of water in the inner pot. In a bowl, mix oil, garlic, rosemary, thyme, basil, sage, salt, and chili. Brush the marinade over shrimp.

Insert the steamer rack, and arrange the shrimp on top. Seal the lid and cook on Steam for 3 minutes on High. Release the steam naturally, for 10 minutes. Press Sauté and stir-fry for 2 more minutes, or until golden brown.

Garlic Leek with Parmesan

Serves: 2 | Ready in about: 15 min

INGREDIENTS

3 leeks, cut into 2-inches long pieces
3 garlic cloves, crushed
1 tsp sea salt

¼ cup extra virgin olive oil
3 tbsp freshly squeezed lemon juice
½ cup Parmesan Cheese, grated

DIRECTIONS

Pour 1 ½ cups of water in your instant pot and insert the trivet. In a baking pan combine leeks, oil, garlic, and salt. Lower the pan on the trivet. Cook on High Pressure for 3 minutes.

Do a quick pressure release. Transfer to a plate and sprinkle with freshly squeezed lemon juice and Parmesan Cheese.

Tip: Add some dried herbs to the olive oil mixture for some extra taste.

Yogurt Beef Pie

Serves: 6 | Ready in about: 35 min

INGREDIENTS

2 lb lean ground beef
4 garlic cloves, crushed
1 tsp salt
½ tsp freshly ground black pepper

1 (16 oz) pack pie dough
½ tbsp butter, melted
1 tbsp sour cream
3 cups liquid yogurt

DIRECTIONS

In a bowl, mix beef, garlic, salt, and pepper, until fully incorporated. Lay a sheet of dough on a flat surface and brush with melted butter.

Line with the meat mixture and roll up. Repeat the process until you have used all the ingredients. Grease a baking dish and carefully place the rolls inside. In your instant pot, pour in 1 ½ cups of water and put the trivet. Lay the baking dish on the trivet. Seal the lid and cook on High Pressure for 15 minutes.

Do a quick pressure release, and transfer the pie to a serving plate. Mix sour cream and yogurt. Spread the mixture over cake and serve cold.

Gingery Chicken Wings

Serves: 4 | Ready in about: 15 min

INGREDIENTS

2 lb chicken wings
¼ cup olive oil
4 garlic cloves, crushed
1 tbsp rosemary leaves
1 tsp white pepper

1 tsp paprika
1 tbsp fresh thyme, chopped
1 tbsp freshly grated ginger
¼ cup Lime juice
½ cup apple cider vinegar

DIRECTIONS

In a bowl, mix oil, garlic, rosemary, white pepper, paprika, thyme, ginger, lime juice, and apple cider vinegar. Submerge wings into the mixture and cover.

Refrigerate for one hour. Remove the wings from the marinade and pat dry. Insert the steaming rack, 1 cup of water, and place the chicken on the rack.

Seal the lid and cook on High Pressure for 8 minutes. Release the steam naturally, for about 10 minutes. Serve with fresh vegetable salad.

Quatro Formaggi Pizza

Serves: 4 | Ready in about: 25 min

INGREDIENTS

1 pizza crust
½ cup tomato paste
¼ cup water
1 tsp dried oregano
1 oz cheddar cheese

5-6 slices mozzarella
¼ cup grated gouda
¼ cup grated parmesan
½ cup grated gouda cheese
2 tbsp extra virgin olive oil

DIRECTIONS

Grease the bottom of a baking dish with one tablespoon of olive oil. Line some parchment paper. Flour the working surface and roll out the pizza dough to the approximate size of your instant pot. Gently fit the dough in the previously prepared baking dish.

In a small bowl, combine tomato paste with water, and dry oregano. Spread the mixture over dough and finish with cheeses.

Add a trivet inside your the pot and pour in 1 cup of water. Seal the lid, and cook for 15 minutes on High Pressure. Do a quick release. Remove the pizza from the pot using a parchment paper. Cut and serve.

Tasty Hot Chicken Wings

Serves: 3 | Ready in about: 25 min

INGREDIENTS

6 chicken wings
¼ cup cayenne hot pepper sauce
2 tbsp oil
4 tbsp butter

2 tbsp Worcestershire sauce
1 tsp Tabasco
½ tsp salt
4 cups chicken broth

DIRECTIONS

Grease the pot with oil and place the chicken wings. Pour in broth and cayenne hot pepper sauce. Seal the lid and cook on Poultry for 15 minutes on High.

Do a quick release and remove the wings from broth; set aside. In the pot, melt the butter on Sauté on High.

Brown the wings for 3-4 minutes, turning once. Add the Worcestershire sauce and tabasco. Stir and remove from heat. Serve hot.

Beef Prosciutto with Horseradish Sauce

Serves: 6 | Ready in about: 40 min

INGREDIENTS

2 lb beef fillet, center cut
1 onion, finely chopped
¼ cup horseradish sauce
3 tbsp butter

1 cup red wine
3 cups beef stock
6 oz prosciutto

DIRECTIONS

Melt butter on Sauté, and stir-fry the onions for 2 minutes. Add fillets, one at the time and briefly brown them on both sides, for a few minutes.

Pour the wine and stock. Seal the lid and cook on High Pressure for 30 minutes. Do a quick release and remove the fillets on a serving platter. In a saucepan, mix horseradish sauce with prosciutto. Warm up and drizzle over the meat.

Aglio & Funghi Pizza

Serves: 2 | Ready in about: 25 min

INGREDIENTS

¾ cup all-purpose flour
1 cup whole wheat flour
½ tsp brown sugar
1 tsp garlic powder
2 tsp dried yeast
¼ tsp salt
1 tbsp olive oil

1 cup lukewarm water
1 cup button mushrooms, chopped
¼ cup Gouda, grated
2 tbsp tomato paste, sugar-free
½ tsp dried oregano
¼ cup lukewarm water

DIRECTIONS

In a bowl fitted with a dough hook attachment, combine all-purpose flour with whole wheat flour, brown sugar, dried yeast, and salt. Mix well and gradually add lukewarm water and oil. Continue to beat until smooth dough.

Transfer to a lightly floured surface and knead until completely smooth. Form into a tight ball and wrap tightly in plastic foil. Set aside for one hr.

Line a baking dish with some parchment paper and set aside.

Roll out the dough with a rolling pin and transfer to the baking dish. Brush with tomato paste and sprinkle with oregano, gouda, and button mushroom.

Add a trivet inside your Instant Pot and pour in 1 cup of water. Seal the lid, and cook for 15 minutes on High Pressure. Do a quick release. Remove the pizza from the pot using a parchment paper. Cut and serve.

Sweet Carrots with Crumbled Bacon

Serves: 8 | Ready in about: 30 min

INGREDIENTS

3 slices bacon, crumbled
4 pounds carrots, peeled and chopped
½ cup fresh orange juice
¼ cup olive oil

3 tbsp honey
1 tsp salt
2 tsp cornstarch
1 tbsp cold water

DIRECTIONS

Fry the bacon on Sauté mode until crispy, for about 5 minutes. Set aside. In a bowl, mix salt, olive oil, orange juice, and maple syrup; add the mixture and carrots to the pot and mix well to coat.

Seal the lid, and cook for 6 minutes on High Pressure. Release the pressure quickly. Transfer carrots to a serving dish. Press Cancel, then press Sauté. In a bowl, mix cold water and cornstarch until dissolved.

Add to the liquid remaining in the cooker. Simmer sauce as you stir for 2 minutes to obtain a thick and smooth consistency. Ladle sauce over the carrots and scatter over the crumbled bacon.

EGGS AND SALADS

Kale-Egg Frittata

Serves: 6 | Ready in about: 20 min

INGREDIENTS

6 large eggs
2 tbsp heavy cream
½ tsp freshly grated nutmeg
Salt and ground black pepper to taste

1 ½ cups kale, chopped
¼ cup grated Parmesan Cheese
cooking spray
1 cup water

DIRECTIONS

In a bowl, beat eggs, nutmeg, pepper, salt, and cream until smooth. Stir in Parmesan Cheese and kale. Apply a cooking spray to a cake pan. Wrap aluminum foil around outside of the pan to cover completely.

Place egg mixture into the prepared pan. Pour in water, set a steamer rack over the water. Gently lay the pan onto the rack. Seal the lid and cook for 10 minutes on High Pressure. Release the pressure quickly.

Spicy Deviled Eggs

Serves: 6 | Ready in about: 20 min

INGREDIENTS

1 cup water
10 large eggs
¼ cup cream cheese

¼ cup mayonnaise
Salt and ground black pepper to taste
¼ tsp chili powder

DIRECTIONS

Add water, insert the steamer basket and lay the eggs inside. Seal the lid and cook on High Pressure for 5 minutes. Release the pressure quickly.

Drop eggs into an ice bath to cool for 5 minutes. Peel eggs and halve them.

Transfer yolks to a bowl and use a fork to mash; Stir in cream cheese, and mayonnaise. Add pepper and salt for seasoning. Ladle yolk mixture into egg white halves.

Quick Soft-Boiled Eggs

Serves: 4 | Ready in about: 15 min

INGREDIENTS

4 large eggs
1 cups water

Salt and ground black pepper, to taste

DIRECTIONS

To the pressure cooker, add water and place a wire rack. Carefully put eggs on it. Seal the lid, press Steam and cook for 3 minutes on High Pressure. Do a quick release.

Allow cooling completely in an ice bath. Peel the eggs and Season with salt and pepper to serve.

Perfect Hard-Boiled Eggs

Serves: 6 | Ready in about: 20 min

INGREDIENTS

1 ½ cups water

6 large eggs

DIRECTIONS

In the pot, add water and place a trivet. Lay your eggs on top. Seal the lid and cook for 5 minutes on High Pressure. Do a natural release for 10 minutes. Transfer the eggs to cold water to cool completely.

Sweet Potato & Egg Salad

Serves: 8 | Ready in about: 20 min

INGREDIENTS

1 ½ cups water
6 sweet potatoes, peeled and diced
4 large eggs
2 ½ cups mayonnaise

¼ cup dill, chopped
⅓ cup Greek yogurt
Salt and ground black pepper to taste
½ cup Arugula

DIRECTIONS

Pour water. Place eggs and potatoes into the steamer basket; Transfer to the pot and seal the lid.

Cook for 4 minutes on High Pressure. Do a quick release.

Take out the eggs and place in a bowl of ice-cold water for purposes of cooling. In a bowl, combine yogurt, mayonnaise, and dill.

In a separate bowl, mash potatoes using a potato masher; mix with mayonnaise mixture to coat.

Skin and dice the eggs. Transfer to the potato salad and mix. Season to taste and serve.

Nordic Tuna Salad with Olives

Serves: 4 | Ready in about: 15 min

INGREDIENTS

1½ pounds potatoes, quartered
2 eggs
3 tbsp melted butter
Salt and pepper to taste
6 pickles, chopped

2 tbsp red wine vinegar
½ cup pimento stuffed green olives
½ cup chopped roasted red peppers
2 tbsp chopped fresh parsley
10 ounces canned tuna, drained

DIRECTIONS

Pour 2 cups of water into the pot and add potatoes. Place a trivet over the potatoes. Lay the eggs on the trivet. Seal the lid and cook for 8 minutes on High Pressure. Do a quick release.

Drain and remove potatoes to a bowl. Transfer the eggs infilled with an ice water bowl. Drizzle melted butter over the potatoes and season with salt and pepper. Peel and chop the chilled eggs.

Add pickles, eggs, peppers, tuna, vinegar to the potatoes and mix to coat. Serve topped with olives.

Picnic Potato Salad

Serves: 12 | Ready in about: 30 min

INGREDIENTS

3 pounds potatoes, peeled and chopped
3 cups water
1 tsp salt
1 cup Dijon mayonnaise
¼ cup mustard

¼ cup pickle
¼ cup diced white onion, chopped
2 tbsp salt
2 tbsp sweet paprika
Salt to taste

DIRECTIONS

In the pot, mix 1 teaspoon salt, water, and potatoes. Seal the lid and cook for 6 minutes on High Pressure. Once ready, do a natural release for 10 minutes. Drain the potatoes and allow to cool. Chop into smaller pieces.

In a bowl, mix salt, pickles, mayonnaise, paprika, potatoes, mustard, and onion to get the desired consistency. Chill for one hour while covered.

Curried Egg Salad

Serves: 6 | Ready in about: 30 min

INGREDIENTS

2 cups water
cooking spray
6 eggs
¼ cup crème frâiche
2 large spring onions, minced

1 tbsp dill, minced
1 tbsp curry paste
2 tbsp mustard
Salt and black pepper to taste

DIRECTIONS

Spray cooking spray to a cake pan. To the inner pot, add water. Set eggs on a trivet.

Seal the lid and cook for 5 minutes on High Pressure. Do a quick release. Drain any water from the eggs in the pan. Loosen the eggs on the edges with a knife. Transfer to a cutting board and chop into smaller sizes.

Transfer the chopped eggs to a bowl. Add in onion, mustard, salt, dill, crème frâiche, curry powder, and black pepper.

Cold Cauliflower & Broccoli Salad

Serves: 4 | Ready in about: 15 min

INGREDIENTS

1 lb cauliflower florets
1 lb broccoli, into florets
3 garlic cloves, crushed

¼ tbsp olive oil
1 tsp salt
1 tbsp dry rosemary, crushed

DIRECTIONS

Cut the veggies into bite-sized pieces and place them in the pot. Add olive oil and 1 cup of water. Season with salt, garlic, and rosemary. Seal the lid.

Cook on High Pressure for 3 minutes. When ready, do a quick release.

Hot German Potato Salad

Serves: 6 | Ready in about: 19min

INGREDIENTS

6 smoked bacon, chopped
½ cup apple cider vinegar
½ cup water
3 tbsp sugar
2 tbsp mustard
1 tsp fresh flat-leaf parsley, chopped

1 tsp salt
⅓ tsp black pepper
6 red potatoes, peeled and quartered
2 onions, chopped
A handful of parsley for garnishing

DIRECTIONS

On Sauté, briefly brown the bacon for 2 minutes per side. In a bowl, mix sugar, salt, mustard, vinegar, water, and black pepper. In the inner pot, add potatoes, chopped bacon, and onions, and top with the vinegar mixture.

Seal the lid and cook for 6 minutes on High Pressure. Release pressure naturally for 10 minutes. Place on serving plate and add fresh parsley for garnishing.

Beef Steak Salad with Nuts

Serves: 4 | Ready in about: 60 min

INGREDIENTS

1 lb rib-eye steaks, boneless
4 oz fresh arugula
1 large tomato, chopped
¼ cup fresh goat's cheese
4 almonds
4 walnuts

4 hazelnuts
3 tbsp olive oil
2 cups beef broth
2 tbsp red wine vinegar
1 tbsp Italian Seasoning mix

DIRECTIONS

Whisk together vinegar, Italian mix, and olive oil. Brush each steak with this mixture and place in your instant pot. Pour in the broth and seal the lid.

Cook on Meat/Stew for 25 minutes on High Pressure. Release the pressure naturally, for about 10 minutes, and remove the steaks along with the broth.

Grease the inner pot with oil and hit Sauté. Brown the steaks on both sides for 5-6 minutes. Remove from the pot and let cool for 5 minutes before slicing.

In a bowl, mix arugula, tomato, cheese, almonds, walnuts, and hazelnuts. Top with steaks and drizzle with red wine mixture.

Bell Pepper Omelet

Serves: 2 | Ready in about: 20 min

INGREDIENTS

2 red bell peppers, chopped
4 eggs
2 tbsp olive oil

2 garlic cloves, crushed
1 tsp Italian Seasoning mix

DIRECTIONS

Grease the pot with oil. Stir-fry the peppers for 2-3 minutes on each side, or until lightly charred. Set aside. Add garlic, and stir-fry for 2-3 minutes, until soft.

Whisk the eggs and Season with Italian seasoning. Pour the mixture into the pot and cook for 2-3 minutes, or until set. Using a spatula, loosen the edges and Gently slide onto a plate. Add grilled peppers and fold over. Serve hot.

Beef & Goat Cheese Scrambled Eggs

Serves: 3 | Ready in about: 25 min

INGREDIENTS

6 oz lean ground beef
1 onion, chopped
6 eggs
¼ cup skim milk
¼ cup goat cheese

¼ tsp garlic powder
¼ tsp rosemary powder
1 tbsp tomato paste
½ tsp sea salt
2 tbsp olive oil

DIRECTIONS

Grease the inner pot with olive oil. Stir-fry the onions, for 4 minutes, until translucent, on Sauté. Add beef and tomato paste. Cook for 5 minutes, stirring twice.

Meanwhile, Whisk the eggs, milk, goat cheese, rosemary, garlic, and salt. Pour the mixture into the pot and stir slowly with a wooden spatula. Cook until slightly underdone. Remove from the heat and serve.

Green Omelet

Serves: 2 | Ready in about: 25 min

INGREDIENTS

1 cup spinach, chopped
1 cup Swiss chard, chopped
4 eggs
2 tbsp olive oil

1 tsp garlic powder
½ tsp sea salt
¼ tsp red pepper flakes

DIRECTIONS

Grease the inner pot with 2 tbsp of olive oil. Stir-fry the greens for 5 minutes on Sauté. Set aside. Whisk the eggs, garlic, salt, and red pepper flakes.

Pour the mixture in the pot. Spread the eggs evenly with a wooden spatula and cook for 3-4 minutes on Sauté. With a spatula, ease around the edges and slide to a serving plate. Add greens and fold it over in half.

Cheesy Mushroom Omelet

Serves: 2 | Ready in about: 25 min

INGREDIENTS

4 eggs
½ cup fresh goat's cheese
¼ cup milk
1 cup button mushrooms
1 large onion, finely chopped

1 tsp dried oregano
¼ tsp sea salt
2 tbsp olive oil
Fresh parsley, to garnish

DIRECTIONS

Grease the pot with oil. Stir-fry onions for a few minutes, until translucent. Stir in oregano and button mushrooms. Cook for 5-6 minutes, stirring occasionally.

Crack the eggs into a bowl, and mix with goat cheese and milk. Remove the mushrooms from the pot and set aside.

Pour the egg mixture in the pot and cook for 2 minutes, stirring continually, on Sauté. Serve with button mushrooms and topped with fresh parsley.

Caprese Scrambled Eggs

Serves: 2 | Ready in about: 25 min

INGREDIENTS

4 eggs
½ cup fresh mozzarella cheese
1 cup button mushrooms, chopped
1 large tomato, chopped

2 spring onions, chopped
¼ cup milk
2 tbsp olive oil
½ tsp salt

DIRECTIONS

Grease the pot with oil and set on Sauté. Stir-fry the onions for 3 minutes, or until translucent. Add tomatoes and mushrooms.

Cook until liquid evaporates, for 5-6 minutes. Meanwhile, Whisk eggs, cheese, milk, and salt. Pour into the pot and stir. Cook for 2 minutes, or until set.

Italian Tomato Omelet

Serves: 4 | Ready in about: 30 min

INGREDIENTS

1 lb tomatoes, peeled, roughly diced
1 tbsp tomato paste
1 tsp brown sugar
1 cup cottage cheese
4 eggs

3 tbsp olive oil
1 tbsp Italian Seasoning mix
¼ cup fresh parsley, chopped
¼ tsp salt

DIRECTIONS

Grease the inner pot with oil. Press Sauté and add tomatoes, sugar, Italian seasoning, parsley, and salt. Give it a good stir and cook for 15 minutes or until the tomatoes soften. Stir occasionally.

Meanwhile, whisk eggs and cheese. Pour the mixture into the pot stir well. Cook for 3 more minutes.

Eggs Baked in Avocado

Serves: 2 | Ready in about: 30 min

INGREDIENTS

1 avocado, halved
2 eggs
3 tbsp butter, melted

1 tsp dry oregano
½ tsp pink salt

DIRECTIONS

Grease a baking dish with butter, and place the avocado halves in it. Crack an egg into each avocado half. Season with salt, and oregano.

Add 1 ½ cups of water and place the trivet inside the pot. Lower the baking dish on top. Seal the lid and cook on High Pressure for 10 minutes.

When done, do a quick release and plate. Serve immediately.

Hard-Boiled Eggs with Spinach and Nuts

Serves: 4 | Ready in about: 25 min

INGREDIENTS

1 lb spinach, rinsed, chopped
3 tbsp olive oil
1 tbsp butter
1 tbsp almonds, crushed

1 tbsp peanuts, crushed
4 eggs
½ tsp chili flakes
½ tsp sea salt

DIRECTIONS

Pour 1 ½ cups of water into the inner pot and insert a steamer basket. Place the eggs onto the basket. Seal the lid and cook on High Pressure for 5 minutes.

Do a quick release. Remove the eggs to an ice bath. Wipe the pot clean, and heat oil on Sauté. Add spinach and cook for 2-3 minutes, stirring occasionally.

Stir in 1 tbsp of butter and Season with salt, and chili flakes. Mix well and cook for 1 more minute. Press Cancel and sprinkle with nuts. Peel and slice each egg in half, lengthwise. Transfer to a serving plate and pour over spinach mixture.

Chili Poached Eggs with Mushrooms

Serves: 1 | Ready in about: 25 min

INGREDIENTS

3 oz button mushrooms, cut half lengthwise
2 oz fresh arugula
1 egg

2 tbsp olive oil
Chili flakes, for Seasoning

DIRECTIONS

Melt butter on Sauté, add mushrooms and cook for 4-5 minutes, until soft. Stir in arugula. Cook for one minute. Crack the egg and cook until set – for 2 minutes.

Season with chili flakes. Press Cancel and remove the omelet to a serving plate.

Poached Egg Leeks

Serves: 3 | Ready in about: 15 min

INGREDIENTS

1 cup leeks, chopped into 1-inch pieces
6 eggs
2 tbsp oil
1 tbsp butter

1 tsp mustard seeds
1 tbsp dried rosemary
¼ tsp chili flakes
¼ tsp salt

DIRECTIONS

Heat oil on Sauté and add mustard seeds. Stir-fry for 2-3 minutes. Add leeks and butter. Cook for 5 minutes, stirring occasionally.

Crack eggs and season with dried rosemary, chili flakes, and salt. Cook until set, for about 4 minutes. Press Cancel and serve immediately.

Chessy Vegetable Frittata

Serves: 4 | Ready in about: 30 min

INGREDIENTS

4 eggs
8 oz spinach, finely chopped
½ cup cheddar cheese
½ cup fresh ricotta cheese
3 cherry tomatoes, halved
¼ cup red bell pepper, chopped

1 cup chopped broccoli, pre-cooked
4 tbsp olive oil
½ tsp salt
¼ tsp freshly ground black pepper
¼ tsp dried oregano
½ cup fresh celery leaves, finely chopped

DIRECTIONS

Heat olive oil on Sauté. Add spinach and cook for 5 minutes, stirring occasionally. Add tomatoes, peppers, and broccoli. Cook for more 3-4 minutes.

In a bowl, Whisk 2 eggs, cheddar, and ricotta. Pour in the pot and cook for 2 more minutes. Then, crack the remaining 2 eggs and cook for another 5 minutes.

When done, press Cancel and serve immediately with chopped celery leaves.

Cranberry Scramble

Serves: 2 | Ready in about: 10 min

INGREDIENTS

4 large eggs, beaten
¼ tsp cranberry extract, sugar-free
2 tbsp butter
¼ tsp salt

1 tbsp milk
4-5 cranberries, to garnish
Fresh mint, to garnish

DIRECTIONS

In a bowl, whisk eggs, cranberry extract, salt, and milk. Melt butter on Sauté. Pour the egg mixture and pull the eggs across the pot with a spatula.

Do not stir continually. Cook for 2 minutes, or until thickened and no visible liquid egg lumps. When done, press Cancel and transfer to a serving plate. Top with cranberries and fresh mint.

Spinach Poached Egg Pancake

Serves: 2 | Ready in about: 20 min

INGREDIENTS

6 oz spinach, chopped
2 eggs
3 tbsp oil
½ tsp garlic powder

¼ tsp dried oregano
¼ tsp dried rosemary
½ tsp sea salt, Divided
Kalamata olives and red bell peppers, for garnishing

DIRECTIONS

Heat the oil on Sauté and add chopped spinach. Season with salt, and garlic powder. Give it a good stir and cook for 5 minutes, until soft.

Crack eggs and season with oregano, rosemary, and salt. Cook until completely set, for about 5 more minutes. Transfer to a serving plate and serve with kalamata olives or chopped red bell peppers.

Kale & Cheese Omelet Cups

Serves: 3 | Ready in about: 10 min

INGREDIENTS

6 eggs
½ cup cheddar cheese, crumbled
1 small onion, finely chopped
½ tsp Italian Seasoning mix

1 tsp salt
½ tsp black pepper, ground
2 tbsp heavy cream

DIRECTIONS

In a bowl, mix eggs, salt, pepper, and heavy cream. Whisk until well combined and add the remaining ingredients.

Add 1 ½ cups of water and lay the steam rack. Lower the ramekins on the steam rack and seal the lid. Cook on High Pressure for 6 minutes.

When ready, do a quick release. Serve hot.

Steamed Eggs with Spring Onions

Serves: 1 | Ready in about: 10 min

INGREDIENTS

2 eggs
1 tbsp spring onions, chopped
½ cup water

¼ tsp garlic powder
½ tsp salt
¼ tsp black pepper

DIRECTIONS

In a bowl, whisk eggs and water. Add the remaining ingredients and stir well. Transfer the mixture to a heat-proof bowl, that fits in your instant pot.

Add 1 cup of water in the pot. Set the steamer tray and place the bowl on top. Seal the lid and cook on High Pressure for 5 minutes. Do a quick release.

GRAINS AND PASTA

Indian-Style Beef with Rice

Serves: 5 | Ready in about: 40 min

INGREDIENTS

¼ cup yogurt
2 cloves garlic, smashed
1 tbsp olive oil
1 Lime, juiced
Salt and ground black pepper to taste
2 pounds beef stew meat, cut into cubes
1 tbsp garam masala
1 tbsp fresh ginger, grated
1 ½ tsp smoked paprika
1 tsp ground cumin

¼ tsp cayenne pepper
3 tbsp butter
1 onion, chopped
1 (14-ounces) can puréed tomatoes
½ cup beef broth
2 cups basmati rice, rinsed
2 cups water
½ cup heavy cream
½ bunch fresh cilantro, chopped

DIRECTIONS

In a bowl, mix garlic, lime juice, olive oil, pepper, salt, and yogurt. Stir in the beef to coat.

In a different bowl, thoroughly mix paprika, garam masala, cumin, ginger, and cayenne pepper.

Melt butter on Sauté and stir-fry the onion for 7 to 9 minutes, until translucent. Sprinkle spice mixture over onion; cook for about 30 seconds until soft.

To the onion, add in the beef-yogurt mixture; Sauté for 3 to 4 minutes until meat is slightly cooked. Mix in broth and puréed tomatoes. Set trivet over beef in the Pressure cooker's inner pot.

In an oven-proof bowl, mix water and rice. Set the bowl onto the trivet.

Seal the lid and cook on High Pressure for 10 minutes. Release pressure quickly.

Remove the bowl with rice and trivet. Add pepper, salt, and cream into beef and stir. Use a fork to fluff rice and Divide into serving plates; apply a topping of beef. Use cilantro to garnish.

Creamed Kale Parmesan Farro

Serves: 2 | Ready in about: 35 min

INGREDIENTS

1 tbsp butter
1 small onion, diced
1 cup pearl barley, rinsed and drained
2 garlic cloves, smashed
2 cups vegetable broth

½ cup grated Parmesan Cheese, + 1 tbsp for topping
1 cup kale, chopped
juice of ½ lemon, juiced
Salt and freshly ground black pepper to taste

DIRECTIONS

Warm butter on Sauté. Add in onion and cook for 3 minutes until soft.

Stir in garlic and barley and continue cooking for 1 to 2 minutes until barley is toasted. Mix in broth.

Seal the lid and cook for 9 minutes on High Pressure. Release pressure naturally for 10 minutes, then quick-release the remaining Pressure. Add Parmesan Cheese into barley mixture and stir until melted. Add lemon juice and kale into barley mixture. Add pepper and salt for seasoning.

Veggie Quinoa Bowls with Pesto

Serves: 2 | Ready in about: 30 min

INGREDIENTS

1 cup quinoa, rinsed and drained
2 cups vegetable broth
Salt and ground black pepper to taste
1 potato, peeled, cubed
1 head broccoli, cut into small florets
1 bunch baby heirloom carrots, peeled

¼ cabbage, sliced
2 eggs
1 avocado, chopped
¼ cup pesto sauce
Lemon wedges, for serving

DIRECTIONS

In the pot, mix broth, pepper, quinoa, and salt. Set trivet to the inner pot on top of quinoa and add a steamer basket to the top of the trivet. Mix carrots, potato, eggs, and broccoli in the steamer basket. Add pepper and salt for seasoning.

Seal the lid and cook for 1 minute on High Pressure. Quick-release the pressure.

Take away the trivet and steamer basket from pot. Set the eggs in a bowl of ice water. Then peel and halve the eggs. Use a fork to fluff quinoa. Adjust the seasonings.

In two bowls, equally divide avocado, quinoa, broccoli, eggs, carrots, sweet potatoes, and a dollop of pesto. Serve alongside a lemon wedge.

Shrimp Risotto with Vegetables

Serves: 4 | Ready in about: 1hr 15 min

INGREDIENTS

1 tbsp avocado oil
1 pound asparagus, trimmed and chopped
1 cup spinach, chopped
1½ cups mushrooms, chopped
1 cup rice, rinsed and drained
1¼ cups chicken broth

¾ cup coconut milk
1 tbsp coconut oil
16 shrimp, cleaned and deveined
Salt and ground black pepper to taste
¾ cup Parmesan Cheese, shredded

DIRECTIONS

Warm the oil on Sauté. Add spinach, mushrooms, and asparagus and sauté for 10 minutes until cooked through. Press Cancel. Add rice, coconut milk, and chicken broth to the pot as you stir.

Seal the lid, press Multigrain and cook for 40 minutes on High Pressure. Do a quick release, open the lid and put the rice on a serving plate.

Take back the empty pot to the pressure cooker, add coconut oil and press Sauté. Add shrimp and cook each side taking 4 minutes until cooked through and turns pink. Set shrimp over rice, add pepper and salt for seasoning. Serve topped with shredded Parmesan cheese.

Baked Garbanzo Beans and Pancetta

Serves: 6 | Ready in about: 50 min

INGREDIENTS

3 strips pancetta
1 onion, diced
15 oz canned garbanzo beans
2 cups water
1 cup apple cider
2 garlic cloves, minced
Fresh parsley to garnish

½ cup ketchup
¼ cup sugar
1 tsp ground mustard powder
1 tsp salt
1 tsp ground black pepper

DIRECTIONS

Cook pancetta for 5 minutes, until crispy, on Sauté mode. Add onion and garlic, and cook for 3 minutes until soft. Mix in garbanzo beans, ketchup, sugar, salt, apple cider, mustard powder, water, and pepper.

Seal the lid, press Bean/Chili and cook on High Pressure for 30 minutes. Release pressure naturally for 10 minutes. Serve in bowls garnished with parsley.

Red Lentil and Spinach Dhal

Serves: 6 | Ready in about: 35 min

INGREDIENTS

2 tbsp olive oil
1 red jalapeño, seeded and minced
1 cup spinach, chopped
4 cloves garlic, minced
1 tsp fresh ginger, peeled and grated
1 tbsp cumin seeds
1 tbsp coriander seeds
1 tsp ground turmeric

¼ tsp cayenne pepper
3 cups water
1½ cups red lentils
1 tomato, diced
¼ cup lemon juice
Salt to taste
Fresh Cilantro, chopped for garnish
Natural yogurt for garnish

DIRECTIONS

Heat oil on Sauté, add cayenne, jalapeño pepper, ginger, turmeric, cumin, and garlic, and coriander and cook for 2 to 3 minutes until seeds become fragrant and begin to pop.

Pour in water, tomato, and lentils into pot and stir. Seal the lid and cook on High Pressure for 10 minutes.

Release pressure naturally for 10 minutes, then release the remaining pressure quickly. Stir in spinach until wilted. Add lemon juice and Season to taste. Divide lentils between bowls and garnish with yogurt and cilantro.

Black Beans Tacos

Serves: 6 | Ready in about: 1hr 30 min

INGREDIENTS

2 cups black beans, soaked overnight
1 cup shallots, chopped
4 cups water
1 tbsp dried oregano
1 tsp chili powder

6 soft Taco tortillas
1 avocado, chopped
Salt to taste
Fresh Cilantro for garnish

DIRECTIONS

Drain the beans and add to the cooker. Mix in the onion, oregano and chili powder. Top with water.

Seal the lid and cook on High Pressure for 60 minutes. Do a quick release, and allow to cool for a few minutes. Serve with taco tortillas, avocado slices, and cilantro.

Parsley-Lime Bulgur Bowl

Serves: 4 | Ready in about: 30 min

INGREDIENTS

1 tbsp olive oil
1small onion, chopped
2 cloves garlic, minced
1 cup bulgur
1 pinch salt

2 ½ cups vegetable broth
1 tbsp Lime juice, or more to taste
1 handful fresh parsley, roughly chopped
10 black olives to garnish
Salt and freshly ground black pepper to taste

DIRECTIONS

Heat oil on Sauté. Stir in garlic and onion and cook for 10 to 13 minutes until golden brown. Add in cilantro, bulgur, and salt. Place lime juice and broth into the cooker. Seal the lid and cook on High Pressure for 1 minute. Do a quick release.

Use a fork to fluff bulgur. Add fresh parsley as you stir. Season with additional lime juice, salt, and pepper if desired. Serve in bowls topped with black olives.

Tri-Color Quinoa and Pinto Bean Bowl

Serves: 5 | Ready in about: 30 min

INGREDIENTS

1 tsp extra-virgin olive oil
1 green bell pepper, diced
1 onion, diced
1 tsp ground cumin
½ tsp salt

14 ounces canned pinto beans, drained and rinsed
1 cup organic Tri-Color Quinoa, rinsed
1 cup red salsa
1 cup vegetable broth

DIRECTIONS

Warm oil on Sauté mode. Add red onion and green bell pepper as you stir. Add salt and cumin, and cook for 7-8 minutes until fragrant. To the vegetable mixture, add quinoa, broth, salsa, and pinto beans. Seal the lid and cook on High Pressure for 12 minutes. Do a quick pressure release.

Use a fork to fluff quinoa and Divide between serving bowls to serve.

Spinach and Kidney Bean Stew

Serves: 4 | Ready in about: 45 min

INGREDIENTS

2 tbsp olive oil
1 onion, chopped
2 cloves garlic, minced
2 carrots, peeled and chopped
1 cup celery, chopped
4 cups vegetable broth
1 cup white kidney beans, soaked, drained, rinsed

1 tsp dried thyme
1 tsp dried rosemary
1 bay leaf
A pinch of salt
1 cup spinach, torn into pieces
Salt and freshly ground black pepper to taste

DIRECTIONS

Warm olive oil on Sauté. Stir in garlic and onion, and cook for 3 minutes until tender and fragrant. Mix in celery and carrots and cook for 2 to 3 minutes more until they start to soften. Add broth, bay leaf, thyme, rosemary, kidney beans, and salt.

Seal the lid and cook for 30 minutes on High Pressure. Quick release the pressure and stir in spinach. Allow sitting for 2 to 4 minutes until the spinach wilts, and season with pepper and salt.

Spicy Lentils with Chorizo

Serves: 10 | Ready in about: 50 min

INGREDIENTS

2 cups lentils, drained and rinsed
7 ounces chorizo, chopped
1 onion, diced
2 garlic cloves, crushed
2 cups tomato sauce
2 cups vegetable broth
½ cup mustard
½ cup cider vinegar
3 tbsp Worcestershire sauce

2 tbsp maple syrup
2 tbsp liquid smoke
1 tbsp Lime juice
2 cups brown sugar
1 tbsp salt
1 tbsp ground black pepper
1 tsp chili powder
1 tsp paprika
¼ tsp cayenne pepper

DIRECTIONS

Set on Sauté mode, add in chorizo and cook for 3 minutes as you stir until crisp. Add garlic and onion and cook for 2 minutes until translucent.

Mix tomato sauce, broth, cider vinegar, liquid smoke, Worcestershire sauce, lime juice, mustard, and maple syrup in a mixing bowl. Pour the mixture in the Pressure cooker to deglaze the pan, scrape the bottom of the pan to do away with any browned bits of food. Add pepper, chili, sugar, paprika, salt, and cayenne into the sauce mixture as you stir to mix.

Stir in lentils to coat. Seal the lid and cook on High Pressure for 30 minutes.

Release pressure naturally for 10 minutes.

Herby Millet with Cherry Tomatoes

Serves: 8 | Ready in about: 1hr 15 min

INGREDIENTS

2 cups millet, rinsed and drained
4 cups vegetable stock
½ sweet onion, chopped
1 cup cherry tomatoes, cut into halves

1 tbsp fresh sage, chopped
1 tsp fresh thyme, chopped
1 tsp fresh parsley, chopped
Salt and ground black pepper to taste

DIRECTIONS

Add millet, onion, and vegetable stock. Seal the lid and cook for 10 minutes on High Pressure. Release pressure quickly. Fluff the millet with a fork, add in herbs and tomatoes and season with pepper and salt.

Simple Brown Rice

Serves: 6 | Ready in about: 30 min

INGREDIENTS

1 ½ cups brown rice
3 cups chicken broth
2 tbsp lemon juice

2 tbsp sesame olive oil
1 tbsp toasted sunflower seeds

DIRECTIONS

Add broth and brown riceç Seal the lid, press Multigrain and cook on High for 15 minutes. Release the pressure quickly. Do not open the lid for an additional 5 minutes. Use a fork to fluff rice. Add lemon juice, sunflower seeds, and oil.

Creamy Grana Padano Risotto

Serves: 6 | Ready in about: 25 min

INGREDIENTS

1 tbsp olive oil
1 white onion, chopped
1 tbsp butter
2 cups Carnaroli rice, rinsed
¼ cup dry white wine

4 cups chicken stock
1 tsp salt
½ tsp ground white pepper
2 tbsp Grana Padano cheese, grated
¼ tbsp Grana Padano cheese, flakes

DIRECTIONS

Warm oil on Sauté. Stir-fry onion for 3 minutes until soft and translucent. Add in butter and rice and cook for 5 minutes stirring occasionally.

Pour wine into the pot to deglaze, scrape away any browned bits of food from the pan.

Stir in stock, pepper, and salt to the pot. Seal the lid, press Rice and cook on High for 15 minutes. Release the pressure quickly.

Sprinkle with grated Parmesan cheese and stir well. Top with flaked cheese for garnish before serving.

Lemony Wild Rice Pilaf

Serves: 6 | Ready in about: 25 min

INGREDIENTS

4 cups vegetable broth
2 cups wild rice, rinsed and drained
1 tbsp butter

Zest and juice from 1 lemon
½ tsp salt
½ tsp ground black pepper

DIRECTIONS

Add rice, lemon zest, butter, and water. Stir, seal the lid and cook on High Pressure for 3 minutes.

Release pressure naturally for 10 minutes. Sprinkle salt, lemon juice, and pepper over the pilaf and use a fork to Gently fluff.

White Rice Pilaf with Mushrooms

Serves: 6 | Ready in about: 35 min

INGREDIENTS

1 tbsp olive oil
2 cloves garlic, minced
1 yellow onion, finely chopped
2 cups button mushrooms, chopped

4 cups vegetable stock
2 cups white rice
1 tsp salt
2 sprigs parsley, chopped

DIRECTIONS

Select Sauté mode and heat oil. Add mushrooms, onion, and garlic, and stir-fry for 5 minutes until tender. Mix in rice, stock, and salt. Seal the lid and cook on High Pressure for 20 minutes. Release pressure naturally for 10 minutes.

Use a fork to fluff the rice and add parsley for garnishing before serving.

Quinoa with Carrots and Onion

Serves: 6 | Ready in about: 15 min

INGREDIENTS

1 cup quinoa, rinsed until the water runs clear
2 cups water
2 carrots, cut into sticks
1 large onion, chopped

2 tbsp olive oil
Salt to taste
Fresh cilantro, chopped for garnish

DIRECTIONS

Heat oil on Sauté. Add in onion and carrots and stir-fry for about 10 minutes until tender and crispy. Remove to a plate and set aside. Add water, salt, and quinoa in the instant pot.

Seal the lid and cook on High Pressure for 1 minute. Do a quick release. Fluff the cooked quinoa with a fork. Transfer to a serving plate and top with the carrots and onion. Serve scattered with cilantro.

Three-Bean Veggie Chili

Serves: 8 | Ready in about: 1hr

INGREDIENTS

1 tbsp canola oil
1 onion, chopped
3 stalks of celery, chopped
1 green bell pepper, chopped
1 head broccoli, chopped into florets
2 tbsp minced garlic
2 tbsp chili powder
2 tsp ground cumin
4 cups vegetable broth

1 (28 ounces) can tomatoes, crushed
½ cup dried pinto beans, soaked, drained and rinsed
½ cup dried black beans, soaked, drained and rinsed
½ cup dried cannellini beans, soaked, drained and rinsed
1 bay leaf
Salt to taste
Fresh parsley, chopped for garnish

DIRECTIONS

Warm oil on Sauté. Add onion and bell pepper, broccoli, and celery, and cook for about 8 minutes until softened. Mix in cumin, chili powder, and garlic and cook for another 1 minute.

Add vegetable broth, tomatoes, black beans, salt, cannellini beans, pinto beans, and bay leaf to the pot.

Seal the lid and cook for 25 minutes on High Pressure. Do a quick pressure release.

Dispose of the bay leaf. Taste and adjust the seasonings. Sprinkle with fresh parsley and serve.

Black-Eyed Peas with Kale

Serves: 6 | Ready in about: 30 min

INGREDIENTS

1 tsp olive oil
1 onion, chopped
2 garlic cloves, minced
1 cup fire-roasted red peppers, diced
½ tsp ground allspice
½ tsp red pepper, crushed

Salt to taste
1 ½ cups dried black-eyed peas, soaked and rinsed
1 ½ cups vegetable broth
1 bay leaf
1 (15 ounces) can fire roasted tomatoes
2 cups chopped kale

DIRECTIONS

Warm oil on Sauté mode. Add onion and cook for 5 minutes until fragrant; add garlic and fire roasted red peppers and cook for 1 more minute until softened. Season with salt, crushed red pepper, and allspice.

Add broth, bay leaf, and black-eyed peas to the pot.

Seal the lid and cook on High Pressure for 5 minutes. Do a quick pressure release.

Remove the bay leaf, and discard. Mix the peas with kale and tomatoes.

Seal the lid and cook on High Pressure for 1 minute. Release the pressure quickly.

Adjust the seasoning and serve.

South American Black Bean Chili

Serves: 8 | Ready in about: 1hr 10 min

INGREDIENTS

1 tsp olive oil
1 onion, chopped
3 cloves garlic, minced
6 cups vegetable broth
2 cups dried black beans, soaked
1 jalapeño pepper, deseeded and diced

1 tsp dried oregano
1 tsp dried chili flakes
Salt to taste
Cotija Cheese, crumbled for garnish
Fresh cilantro for garnish

DIRECTIONS

Warm oil on Sauté. Add in garlic and onion and cook for 3 to 4 minutes until fragrant. Add beans, vegetable broth, oregano, chili flakes, salt, and jalapeño pepper.

Seal the lid and cook for 35 minutes on High Pressure. quick release the pressure.

Divide into serving plates. Top with cilantro and cotija cheese, to serve.

Spicy Pinto Bean and Corn Stew

Serves: 6 | Ready in about: 1hr 5 min

INGREDIENTS

2 tbsp olive oil
1 onion, chopped
1 red bell pepper, chopped
1 tbsp dried oregano
1 tbsp ground cumin
1 tsp red pepper flakes
3 cups vegetable stock

2 cups dried pinto beans, rinsed
14 ounces canned tomatoes, chopped
1 tsp sea salt
1 tbsp white wine vinegar
½ cup fresh chives, chopped
¼ cup fresh corn kernels

DIRECTIONS

Set on Sauté, stir in oil, bell pepper, pepper flakes, oregano, onion, and cumin. Cook for 3 minutes until soft. Mix in pinto beans, vegetable stock, and tomatoes.

Seal the lid, select Bean/Chili and cook for 30 minutes on High Pressure. Release the pressure naturally for 20 minutes. Add in salt and vinegar. Divide in serving plates and top with corn and fresh chives.

Simple Jasmine Rice

Serves: 4 | Ready in about: 25 min

INGREDIENTS

2 cups jasmine rice
3 ½ cups water

Salt and black pepper to taste

DIRECTIONS

Stir rice and water together in the cooker. Season with salt to taste.

Seal the lid and cook for 15 minutes on High Pressure.

Release pressure naturally for 10 minutes. Use a fork to fluff rice. Add black pepper before serving.

Easy Vegan Sloppy Joes

Serves: 6 | Ready in about: 45 min

INGREDIENTS

2 cups water
1 cup pearl barley, rinsed
1 cup green onion, chopped
1 clove garlic, minced
2 cups tomato sauce
2 tbsp brown sugar

2 tbsp Worcestershire sauce
1 tsp Dijon mustard
1 tsp smoked paprika
1 tsp chili powder
6 brioche buns
Dill Pickles for garnish

DIRECTIONS

In the pot, mix Worcestershire sauce, water, onion, garlic, brown sugar, barley, tomato sauce, and spices.

Seal the lid and cook for 25 minutes on High Pressure. Release the pressure quickly.

Press Sauté and cook until the mixture becomes thick. Transfer the sloppy joe mixture to the brioche buns and top with dill pickles.

Indian Yellow Lentils

Serves: 6 | Ready in about: 30 min

INGREDIENTS

1 tbsp ghee
2 tsp cumin seeds
1 onion, chopped
4 garlic cloves, minced
1-inch piece of ginger, peeled, minced
Sea salt salt
1 tomato, chopped

2 cups split yellow lentils, soaked and drained
2 tbsp garam masala
½ tsp ground turmeric
½ tsp cayenne pepper
6 cups water
1tbsp fresh cilantro, finely chopped

DIRECTIONS

Warm ghee on Sauté. Add cumin seeds and cook for 10 seconds until they begin to pop. Stir in onion and cook for 2 to 3 minutes until softened. Mix in ginger,salt, and garlic and cook for 1 minute as you stir.

Mix in tomato and cook for 3 to 5 minutes until the mixture breaks down. Stir in turmeric, lentils, garam masala, and cayenne and cover with water. Seal the lid and cook for 8 minutes on High Pressure. Release the pressure quickly. Serve in bowls sprinkled with fresh cilantro.

Chicken and Chickpea Stew

Serves: 6 | Ready in about: 40 min

INGREDIENTS

1 pound boneless, skinless chicken legs
2 tsp ground cumin
1 tsp salt
½ tsp cayenne pepper
2 tbsp olive oil
1 onion, minced
2 jalapeño peppers, deseeded and minced
3 garlic cloves, crushed

2 tsp freshly grated ginger
¼ cup chicken stock
1 (24 ounces) can crushed tomatoes
2 (14 ounces) cans chickpeas, drained and rinsed
Salt to taste
½ cup coconut milk
¼ cup fresh parsley, chopped
2 cups hot cooked basmati rice

DIRECTIONS

Season the chicken with 1 tsp salt, cayenne pepper, and cumin. Set on Sauté and warm the oil.

Add in jalapeño peppers, and onion, and cook for 5 minutes until soft. Mix in ginger and garlic, and cook for 3 minutes until tender.

Add ¼ cup chicken stock into the cooker to ensure the pan is deglazed, from the pan's bottom scrape any browned bits of food.

Mix the onion mixture with, chickpeas, tomatoes, and salt. Stir in seasoned chicken to coat in sauce.

Seal the lid and cook on High Pressure for 20 minutes. Release the pressure quickly.

Remove the chicken and slice into chunks. Into the remaining sauce, mix in coconut milk; simmer for 5 minutes on Keep Warm. Split rice into 4 bowls. Top with chicken, then sauce and add cilantro for garnish.

Rice & Olives Stuffed Mushrooms

Serves: 4 | Ready in about: 45 min

INGREDIENTS

4 portobello mushrooms, stems and gills removed
2 tbsp melted butter
½ cup brown rice, cooked
1 tomato, seed removed and chopped
¼ cup black olives, pitted and chopped
1 green bell pepper, seeded and diced

½ cup feta cheese, crumbled
Juice of 1 lemon
½ tsp salt
½ tsp ground black pepper
Minced fresh cilantro, for garnish
1 cup vegetable broth

DIRECTIONS

Brush the mushrooms with butter. Arrange the mushrooms in a single layer in an oiled baking pan. In a bowl, mix the rice, tomato, olives, bell pepper, feta cheese, lemon juice, salt, and black pepper.

Spoon the rice mixture into the mushrooms. Pour in the broth, seal the lid and cook on High Pressure for 10 minutes. Do a quick release. Garnish with fresh cilantro and serve immediately.

Roasted Bell Peppers and Tangy Pilaf

Serves: 4 | Ready in about: 25 minutes

INGREDIENTS

2 tbsp olive oil
1 garlic clove, minced
4 cups vegetable stock
¼ cup freshly squeezed lemon juice
1 tsp grated lemon zest

2 cups rice
2 tsp salt,
6 ounces roasted Bell Peppers
1 tsp freshly ground black pepper

DIRECTIONS

Warm half of the oil on Sauté and cook garlic until soft, about 1 minute. Stir in stock, lemon juice, lemon zest, 1 tsp of salt, and rice. Seal the lid and cook on High Pressure for 7 minutes.

In a bowl, toss peppers with the remaining oil, salt, and black pepper. To the cooker, do a natural pressure release for 10 minutes. Fluff the rice with a fork and transfer to a plate. Top with roasted peppers to serve.

Crispy Feta with Roasted Butternut Squash and Rice

Serves: 4 | Ready in about: 30 minutes

INGREDIENTS

½ cup water
2 cups vegetable broth
1 small butternut squash, peeled and sliced
2 tablespoons melted butter, Divided
1 tsp salt

1 tsp freshly ground black pepper
1 cup feta cheese, cubed
1 tbsp coconut aminos
2 tsp arrowroot starch
1 cup jasmine rice, cooked

DIRECTIONS

Pour the rice and broth in the pot and stir to combine. In a bowl, toss butternut squash with 1 tbsp of melted butter and season with salt and black pepper.

In another bowl, mix the remaining butter, water, and coconut aminos. Toss feta in the mixture, add the arrowroot starch and toss again to combine well. Transfer to a greased baking dish.

Lay a trivet over the rice and place the baking dish on the trivet. Seal the lid and cook on High for 15 minutes. Do a quick pressure release. Fluff the rice with a fork and serve with squash and feta.

Rice Stuffing Zucchini Boats

Serves: 4 | Ready in about: 20 minutes

INGREDIENTS

2 small zucchini, halved lengthwise
½ cup cooked rice
½ cup canned white beans, drained and rinsed
½ cup chopped tomatoes
½ cup chopped toasted cashew nuts

½ cup grated Parmesan cheese
2 tbsp melted butter
½ tsp salt
½ tsp freshly ground black pepper

DIRECTIONS

Pour 1 cup of water in the instant pot and insert a trivet. Scoop out the pulp of zucchini and chop roughly.

In a bowl, mix the zucchini pulp, rice, tomatoes, cashew nuts, ¼ cup of Parmesan, 1 tbsp of melted butter, salt, and black pepper. Fill the zucchini boats with the mixture, and arrange the stuffed boats in a single layer on the trivet. Seal the lid and cook for 15 minutes on Steam on High. Do a quick release and serve.

Easy Mexican Rice

Serves: 4 | Ready in about: 30 minutes

INGREDIENTS

3 tbsp olive oil
1 small onion, chopped
2 garlic cloves, minced
1 serrano pepper, seeded and chopped
1 cup bomba rice
⅓ cup red salsa

¼ cup tomato sauce
½ cup vegetable broth
1 tsp Mexican Seasoning Mix
16 ounces canned pinto beans, drained and rinsed
1 tsp salt
1 tbsp chopped fresh parsley

DIRECTIONS

Warm oil on Sauté and cook onion, garlic, and serrano pepper for 2 minutes, stirring occasionally until fragrant. Stir in rice, salsa, tomato sauce, vegetable broth, Mexican seasoning, beans, and salt.

Seal the lid and cook on High Pressure for 10 minutes. Do a natural pressure release for 10 minutes. Sprinkle with fresh parsley and serve.

Chard & Mushroom Risotto with Pumpkin Seeds

Serves: 4 | Ready in about: 30 minutes

INGREDIENTS

3 tbsp olive oil
1 onion, chopped
2 swiss chard, stemmed and chopped
1 cup risotto rice
⅓ cup white wine

3 cups vegetable stock
½ tsp salt
½ cup mushrooms
4 tbsp pumpkin seeds, toasted
⅓ cup grated Pecorino Romano cheese

DIRECTIONS

Heat oil on Sauté, and cook onion and mushrooms for 5 minutes, stirring, until tender. Add the rice and cook for a minute. Stir in wine and cook for 2 to 3 minutes until almost evaporated.

Pour in stock and season with salt. Seal the lid and cook on High Pressure for 10 minutes. Do a quick release. Stir in chard until wilted, mix in cheese to melt, and serve scattered with pumpkin seeds.

Chili-Garlic Rice Noodles with Tofu

Serves: 6 | Ready in about: 20 min

INGREDIENTS

2 cups water
½ cup soy sauce
2 tbsp brown sugar
2 tbsp rice vinegar
1 tbsp sweet chili sauce

1 tbsp sesame oil
1 tsp fresh minced garlic
20 ounces extra firm tofu, Pressed and cubed
8 ounces rice noodles
¼ cup chopped fresh chives, for garnish

DIRECTIONS

Heat the oil on Sauté and fry the tofu for 5 minutes until golden brown. Set aside.

To the pot, add water, garlic, olive oil, vinegar, sugar, soy sauce, and chili sauce and mix well until smooth. Stir in rice noodles. Seal the lid and cook on High Pressure for 3 minutes. Release the pressure quickly. Split the noodles between bowls. Top with fried tofu and sprinkle with fresh chives.

Rigatoni with Sausage and Spinach

Serves: 4 | Ready in about: 45 min PREP TIME: 10 min COOK TIME: 15 min

INGREDIENTS

1 tbsp butter
½ cup diced red bell pepper
1 onion, chopped
3 cups vegetable broth
¼ cup tomato purée
4 sausage links, chopped

½ cup milk
2 tsp chili powder
Salt and ground black pepper to taste
12 ounces rigatoni pasta
1 cup baby spinach
½ cup Parmesan Cheese

DIRECTIONS

Warm butter on Sauté. Add red bell pepper, onion, and sausage, and cook for 5 minutes. Mix in broth, chili, tomato paste, salt, and pepper. Stir in rigatoni pasta.

Seal the lid and cook on High Pressure for 12 minutes. Naturally release pressure for 20 minutes.Stir in spinach and let simmer until wilted. Sprinkle with Parmesan and serve.

Shrimp Lo Mein

Serves: 2 | Ready in about: 20 min

INGREDIENTS

1 tbsp sesame oil
1 lb shrimp, peeled and deveined
½ cup diced onion
2 cloves garlic, minced
1 cup carrots, cut into strips
1 cup green beans, washed

2 cups vegetable stock
3 tbsp soy sauce
2 tbsp rice wine vinegar
10 ounces lo mein egg noodles
½ tsp toasted sesame seeds
Sea salt and ground black pepper to taste

DIRECTIONS

Warm oil on Sauté. Stir-fry the shrimp for 5 minutes. Remove to a plate and set aside.

Add in garlic and onion, and cook for 3 minutes until fragrant. Mix in soy sauce, carrots, stock, beans, and rice wine vinegar. Add noodles into the mixture and ensure they are covered. Season with pepper and salt. Seal the lid and cook on High Pressure for 5 minutes. Release the pressure quickly.

Place the lo mein in 2 plates, add the reserved shrimp, sprinkle with sesame seeds, and serve.

Cherry Tomato-Basil Linguine

Serves: 4 | Ready in about: 22 min

INGREDIENTS

2 tbsp olive oil
1 small onion, diced
2 garlic cloves, minced
1 cup cherry tomatoes, halved
1 ½ cups vegetable stock
¼ cup julienned basil leaves

1 tsp salt
½ tsp ground black pepper
¼ tsp red chili flakes
1 pound Linguine noodles, halved
Fresh basil leaves for garnish
½ cup Parmigiano-Reggiano cheese, grated

DIRECTIONS

Warm oil on Sauté. Add onion and sauté for 2 minutes until soft. Mix garlic and tomatoes and sauté for 4 minutes. To the pot, add vegetable stock, salt, julienned basil, red chili flakes, and pepper.

Add linguine to the tomato mixture until covered. Seal the lid and cook on High Pressure for 5 minutes.

Naturally release the pressure for 5 minutes. Stir the mixture to ensure it is broken down.

Divide into plates. Top with basil and Parmigiano-Reggiano cheese and serve.

Beef-Stuffed Pasta Shells

Serves: 4 | Ready in about: 35 min

INGREDIENTS

2 tbsp olive oil
1 pound ground beef
16 ounces pasta shells
2 cups water
15 ounces tomato sauce
15-ounce can black beans, drained and rinsed
15-ounces canned corn, drained

10 ounces red enchilada sauce
4 ounces diced green chiles
1 cup shredded mozzarella cheese
Salt and ground black pepper to taste
additional cheese for topping
Finely chopped parsley for garnish

DIRECTIONS

Heat oil on Sauté. Add ground beef and cook for 7 minutes until it starts to brown.

Mix in pasta, tomato sauce, enchilada sauce, black beans, water, corn, and green chiles and stir to coat well. Add more water if desired.

Seal the lid and cook on High Pressure for 10 minutes. Do a quick pressure release. Into the pasta mixture, mix in mozzarella cheese until melted; add black pepper and salt. Garnish with parsley to serve.

Turkey Fajita Tortellini

Serves: 6 | Ready in about: 35 min

INGREDIENTS

2 tsp chili powder
1 tsp salt
1 tsp cumin
1 tsp onion powder
1 tsp garlic powder
½ tsp thyme
1 ½ pounds chicken turkey breast, cut into strips
1 tbsp olive oil
1 red onion, cut into wedges
4 garlic cloves, minced

3 cups chicken broth
1 cup salsa
16 ounces tortellini
1 red bell pepper, chopped diagonally
1 yellow bell pepper, chopped diagonally
1 green bell pepper, chopped diagonally
1 cup shredded Gouda cheese
½ cup sour cream
½ cup chopped parsley

DIRECTIONS

In a bowl, mix chili powder, cumin, garlic powder, onion powder, salt, and oregano. Reserve 1 tsp of seasoning. Coat turkey with the remaining seasoning.

Warm oil on Sauté. Add in turkey strips and sauté for 4 to 5 minutes until browned. Place the turkey in a bowl. Sauté the onion and garlic for 1 minute in the cooker until soft. Press Cancel.

Mix in salsa, broth, and scrape the bottom of any brown bits. Into the broth mixture, stir in tortellini pasta and cover with bell peppers and chicken.

Seal the lid and cook for 5 minutes on High Pressure. Do a quick pressure release.

Open the lid and sprinkle with shredded gouda cheese and reserved seasoning, and stir well. Divide into plates and top with sour cream. Add parsley for garnishing and serve.

Chipotle Mac and Cheese

Serves: 6 | Ready in about: 15 min

INGREDIENTS

12 ounces macaroni
4 cups cold water
1 tsp salt
2 eggs
1 tbsp chipotle chili powder
½ tsp ground black pepper

4 tbsp butter
1½ cup milk
4 cups sharp Cheddar cheese, grated
2 cups Pecorino Romano cheese, grated
kosher Salt and ground black pepper to taste

DIRECTIONS

Add salt, water, and macaroni. Seal the lid and cook for 4 minutes on High Pressure.

As the pasta cooks, take a bowl and beat eggs, chipotle chili powder, and black pepper, to mix well.

Release the pressure quickly. Add butter to the pasta and stir until melts. Stir in milk and egg mixture.

Pour in Pecorino Romano and cheddar cheeses until melted. Cook in batches, if needed. Season to taste.

Chicken Ragù Bolognese

Serves: 8 | Ready in about: 50 min

INGREDIENTS

2 tbsp olive oil
6 ounces bacon, cubed
1 onion, minced
1 carrot, minced
1 celery stalk, minced
2 garlic cloves, crushed
¼ cup tomato paste

¼ tsp crushed red pepper flakes
1 ½ pounds ground chicken
½ cup white wine
1 cup milk
1 cup chicken broth
Salt to taste
1 pound spaghetti

DIRECTIONS

Warm oil on Sauté. Add in bacon and fry for 5 minutes until crispy.

Add celery, carrot, garlic, and onion and cook for 5 minutes until fragrant. Mix in red pepper flakes and tomato paste, and cook for 2 minutes. Break chicken into small pieces and place in the pot.

Cook for 10 minutes, as you stir, until browned. Pour in wine and simmer for 2 minutes. Add in chicken broth and milk. Seal the lid and cook for 15 minutes on High Pressure. Release the pressure quickly.

Add in the spaghetti and stir. Seal the lid, and cook on High Pressure for another 5 minutes.

Release the pressure quickly. Check the pasta for doneness. Taste, adjust the seasoning and serve hot.

Pasta Caprese Ricotta-Basil Fusilli

Serves: 3 | Ready in about: 15 min

INGREDIENTS

1 tbsp olive oil
1 onion, chopped
6 garlic cloves, minced
1 tsp red pepper flakes
2 ½ cups dried fusilli
1 (15 ounces) can tomato sauce

1 cup tomatoes, halved
1 cup water
¼ cup basil leaves
1 tsp salt
1 cup Ricotta cheese, crumbled
2 tbsp chopped fresh basil

DIRECTIONS

Warm oil on Sauté. Add in red pepper flakes, garlic, and onion and cook for 3 minutes until soft.

Mix in fusilli, tomatoes, half of the basil leaves, water, tomato sauce, and salt. Seal the lid, and cook on High Pressure for 4 minutes. Release the pressure quickly.

Transfer the pasta to a serving platter and top with the crumbled ricotta and remaining chopped basil.

Cheese and Spinach Stuffed Conchiglioni

Serves: 6 | Ready in about: 1hr s

INGREDIENTS

2 cups onion, chopped
1 cup carrot, chopped
3 garlic cloves, minced
Salt to taste
3 ½ tbsp olive oil,
1 (28 ounces) canned tomatoes, crushed
12 ounces conchiglioni pasta
1 tbsp olive oil

2 cups ricotta cheese, crumbled
1 ½ cup feta cheese, crumbled
2 cups spinach, chopped
¾ cup grated Pecorino Romano cheese
2 tbsp chopped fresh chives
1 tbsp chopped fresh dill
Salt and ground black pepper to taste
1 cup shredded cheddar cheese

DIRECTIONS

Warm olive oil on Sauté. Add in onion, carrot, and garlic, and cook for 5 minutes until tender. Stir in tomatoes and cook for another 10 minutes. Remove to a bowl and set aside.

Wipe the pot with a damp cloth, add pasta and cover with enough water. Seal the lid and cook for 5 minutes on High Pressure. Do a quick release and drain the pasta. Lightly Grease olive oil to a baking sheet.

In a bowl, combine feta and ricotta cheese. Add in spinach, Pecorino Romano cheese, dill, and chives, and stir well. Adjust the seasonings. Using a spoon, fill the shells with the mixture.

Spread 4 tomato sauce on the baking sheet. Place the stuffed shells over with seam-sides down and sprinkle cheddar cheese atop. Use aluminum foil to the cover the baking dish.

Pour 1 cup of water in the pot of the Pressure cooker and insert the trivet. Lower the baking dish onto the trivet. Seal the lid, and cook for 15 minutes on High Pressure. Do a quick release. Take away the foil.

Place the stuffed shells to serving plates and top with tomato sauce before serving.

Pomodoro Sauce with Rigatoni and Kale

Serves: 6 | Ready in about: 15 min

INGREDIENTS

1 pound rigatoni pasta
15 ounces canned tomato sauce
3 garlic cloves, minced
1 tsp chili flakes
2 tsp salt

2 tbsp extra-virgin olive oil
1 handful fresh basil, minced
1 cup kale, chopped
¼ cup Parmesan Cheese

DIRECTIONS

Add tomato sauce, salt, pasta, chili flakes, and garlic powder and mix well. Cover with water.

Seal lid and cook for 5 minutes on Low Pressure. Release the pressure quickly. Stir in kale until wilted.

Plate the pasta and top with the parmesan and basil. Drizzle olive oil over the pasta.

Pork Spaghetti with Spinach and Tomatoes

Serves: 4 | Ready in about: 35 min

INGREDIENTS

2 tbsp olive oil
½ cup onion, chopped
1 garlic clove, minced
1 pound pork sausage meat
1 teaspoon Italian seasoning

1 fresh jalapeño chile, stemmed, seeded, and minced
1 tsp salt

2 cups water
1 (14 ounces) can diced tomatoes, drained
½ cup sun-dried tomatoes
1 tbsp dried oregano

8 ounces dried spaghetti, halved
1 cup spinach

DIRECTIONS

Warm oil on Sauté. Add in onion and garlic and cook for 2 minutes until softened.

Stir in sausage meat and cook for 5 minutes. Stir in jalapeño, water, sun-dried tomatoes, Italian seasoning, oregano, diced tomatoes, and salt with the chicken; mix spaghetti and press to submerge into the sauce.

Seal the lid and cook on High Pressure for 9 minutes. Release the pressure quickly.

Stir in spinach, close lid again, and simmer on Keep Warm for 5 minutes until spinach is wilted.

Squash Parmesan and Linguine

Serves: 4 | Ready in about: 45 min

INGREDIENTS

1 cup flour
2 tsp salt
2 eggs
4 cups water
1 cup Seasoned breadcrumbs
½ cup grated Parmesan cheese, + more for garnish

1 yellow squash, peeled and sliced
1 pound linguine
24 ounces canned Seasoned tomato sauce
2 tbsp olive oil
1 cup shredded mozzarella cheese
Minced fresh basil, for garnish

DIRECTIONS

Break the linguine in half. Put it in the pot and add water and salt. Seal the lid and cook on High Pressure for 5 minutes. Combine the flour and 1 teaspoon of salt in a bowl. In another bowl, whisk the eggs and 2 tbsp of water. In a third bowl, mix the breadcrumbs and mozzarella cheese.

Coat each squash slices in the flour. Shake off excess flour, dip in the egg wash, and dredge in the breadcrumbs. Set aside. Quickly release the pressure. Remove linguine to a serving bowl and mix in the tomato sauce and sprinkle with fresh basil. Heat oil on Sauté and fry breaded squash until crispy.

Serve the squash topped mozzarella cheese with the linguine on side.

Gruyère Garganelli with Mushrooms

Serves: 4 | Ready in about: 10 minutes

INGREDIENTS

8 ounces garganelli
2 cups water
1½ tsp salt
1 large egg
8 ounces Gruyère cheese, shredded

1 recipe sautéed mushrooms
2 tbsp chopped fresh cilantro
3 tbsp sour cream
3 tbsp melted butter
3 tbsp grated Cheddar cheese

DIRECTIONS

Put the garganelli with water, butter, and salt into the inner pot. Seal the lid and cook on High Pressure for 4 minutes. Do a quick pressure release. In a bowl, Whisk egg, Gruyère cheese, and sour cream.

Stir in garganelli to melt the cheese and add the mushrooms. Serve hot sprinkled with cheddar cheese.

Minestrone with Pesto and Rigatoni

Serves: 4 | Ready in about: 15 minutes

INGREDIENTS

3 tbsp olive oil
1 onion, diced
1 celery stalk, diced
1 large carrot, peeled and diced
14 ounces canned chopped tomatoes
4 ounces rigatoni
3 cups water
1 cup chopped zucchini

1 bay leaf
1 tsp mixed herbs
¼ tsp cayenne pepper
½ tsp salt
¼ cup shredded Pecorino Romano cheese
1 garlic clove, minced
⅓ cup olive oil based pesto

DIRECTIONS

Heat oil on Sauté and cook onion, celery, garlic, and carrot for 3 minutes, stirring occasionally until the vegetables are softened. Stir in rigatoni, tomatoes, water, zucchini, bay leaf, herbs, cayenne, and salt.

Seal the lid and cook on High for 4 minutes. Do a natural pressure release for 5 minutes. Adjust the taste of the soup with salt and black pepper, and remove the bay leaf.

Ladle the soup into serving bowls and drizzle the pesto over. Serve with the garlic toasts.

Creamy Farfalle Primavera Creamy Spring Noodles

Serves: 4 | Ready in about: 20 minutes

INGREDIENTS

1 bunch asparagus, trimmed, cut into 1-inch pieces
2 cups broccoli florets
3 tbsp olive oil
3 tsp salt
10 ounces egg noodles
3 garlic cloves, minced

2 ½ cups vegetable stock
½ cup heavy cream
1 cup small tomatoes, halved
¼ cup chopped basil
½ cup grated Parmesan cheese

DIRECTIONS

Pour 2 cups of water, add the noodles, 2 tbsp of olive oil, garlic, and salt. Place a trivet over the water. Combine asparagus, broccoli, remaining olive oil and salt in a bowl. Place the vegetables on the trivet.

Seal the lid and cook on Steam for 12 minutes on High. Do a quick release. Remove the vegetables to a plate. Stir the heavy cream and tomatoes in the pasta. Press Sauté and simmer the cream until desired consistency. Gently mix in the asparagus and broccoli. Garnish with basil and Parmesan, to serve.

Quattro Formaggi Tagliatelle

Serves: 6 | Ready in about: 15 min

INGREDIENTS

¼ cup goat's cheese, chevre
¼ cup grated Pecorino cheese
½ cup grated Parmesan
1 cup heavy cream
½ cup grated Gouda

¼ cup butter, softened
1 tbsp Italian Seasoning mix
1 cup vegetable broth
1 lb tagliatelle

DIRECTIONS

In a bowl, mix goat cheese, pecorino, parmesan, and heavy cream. Stir in Italian seasoning. Transfer to your instant pot. Stir in the broth and butter.

Seal the lid and cook on High Pressure for 4 minutes. Do a quick release. Meanwhile, drop the tagliatelle in boiling water and cook for 6 minutes.

Remove the instant pot's lid and stir in the tagliatelle. Top with grated gouda and let simmer for about 10 minutes on Sauté mode.

Cheddar Beef Fettuccine

Serves: 6 | Ready in about: 20 min

INGREDIENTS

10 oz ground beef
1 lb fettuccine pasta
1 cup cheddar cheese, shredded
1 cup fresh spinach, torn
1 medium onion, chopped

2 cups tomatoes, diced
1 tbsp butter
1 tsp salt
½ tsp ground black pepper

DIRECTIONS

Melt butter on Sauté. Stir-fry the beef and onion for 5 minutes. Add the pasta. Pour water enough to cover and Season with salt and pepper. Cook on High Pressure for 5 minutes.

Do a quick release. Press Sauté and stir in the tomato and spinach. Cook for 5 minutes. Top with shredded cheddar and serve.

VEGETABLES AND VEGAN

Green Minestrone

Serves: 4 | Ready in about: 30 min

INGREDIENTS

2 tbsp olive oil
1 head broccoli, cut into florets
4 celery stalks, chopped thinly
1 leek, chopped thinly
1 zucchini, chopped
1 cup green beans

2 cups vegetable broth
3 whole black peppercorns
Salt to taste
water to cover
2 cups chopped kale

DIRECTIONS

Add broccoli, leek, beans, salt, peppercorns, zucchini, and celery. Mix in vegetable broth, oil, and water. Seal the lid and cook on High Pressure for 4 minutes. Release pressure naturally for 5 minutes, then release the remaining pressure quickly. Stir in kale; set on Sauté, and cook until tender.

Pesto Quinoa Bowls with Veggies

Serves: 2 | Ready in about: 30 min

INGREDIENTS

1 cup quinoa, rinsed
2 cups water
Salt and ground black pepper to taste
1 small beet, peeled and cubed
1 cup broccoli florets
1 carrot, peeled and chopped

½ pound Brussels sprouts
2 eggs
1 avocado, chopped
¼ cup pesto sauce
Lemon wedges, for serving

DIRECTIONS

In the pot, mix water, salt, quinoa, and pepper. Set trivet over quinoa and set steamer basket on top. To the steamer basket, add eggs, Brussels sprouts, broccoli, beet cubes, carrots, pepper, and salt.

Seal the lid and cook for 1 minute on High Pressure. Release pressure naturally for 10 minutes, then release any remaining pressure quickly. Remove steamer basket and trivet from the pot and set the eggs to a bowl of ice water. Peel and halve the eggs. Use a fork to fluff quinoa.

Separate quinoa, broccoli, avocado, carrots, beet, Brussels sprouts, eggs, and a dollop of pesto into two bowls. Serve alongside a lemon wedge.

Vegan Carrot Gazpacho

Serves: 4 | Ready in about: 2hr 30 min

INGREDIENTS

1 pound trimmed carrots
1 pinch salt
1 pound tomatoes, chopped
1 cucumber, peeled and chopped
¼ cup olive oil

2 tbsp lemon juice
1 red onion, chopped
2 cloves garlic
2 tbsp white wine vinegar
Salt and freshly ground black pepper to taste

DIRECTIONS

Add carrots, salt, and enough water. Seal the lid and cook for 20 minutes on High Pressure. Do a quick release. Set the beets to a bowl and place in the refrigerator to cool. In a blender, add carrots, cucumber, red onion, pepper, garlic, oil, tomatoes, lemon juice, vinegar, and salt. Blend until very smooth. Place gazpacho to a serving bowl, chill while covered for 2 hours.

Creamy Mashed Potatoes with Spinach

Serves: 6 | Ready in about: 30 min

INGREDIENTS

3 pounds potatoes, peeled and quartered
1½ cups water
½ tsp salt
½ cup milk

⅓ cup butter
2 tbsp chopped fresh chives
fresh black pepper to taste
2 cups spinach, chopped

DIRECTIONS

In the cooker, mix water, salt, and potatoes. Seal the lid and cook on High Pressure for 8 minutes. Release the pressure quickly. Drain the potatoes, and reserve the liquid in a bowl. In a bowl, mash the potatoes. Mix with butter and milk; season with pepper, and salt.

With reserved cooking liquid, thin the potatoes to attain the desired consistency. Put the spinach in the remaining potato liquid and stir until wilted; Season to taste. Drain and serve with potato mash. Garnish with cracked black pepper and chives.

Herby-Garlic Potatoes

Serves: 4 | Ready in about: 30 min

INGREDIENTS

1½ pounds potatoes
3 tbsp butter
3 cloves garlic, chopped
2 tbsp fresh rosemary, chopped

½ tsp fresh thyme, chopped
½ tsp fresh parsley, chopped
¼ tsp ground black pepper
½ cup vegetable broth

DIRECTIONS

Use a small knife to pierce each potato to ensure there are no blowouts when placed under pressure. Melt butter on Sauté. Add in potatoes, rosemary, parsley, pepper, thyme, and garlic, and cook for 10 minutes until potatoes are browned, and the mixture is aromatic.

In a bowl, mix miso paste and vegetable stock. Stir into the mixture in the instant pot. Seal the lid and cook for 5 minutes on High Pressure. Release the pressure quickly.

Punjabi Palak Paneer

Serves: 4 | Ready in about: 20 min

INGREDIENTS

¼ cup milk
2 tbsp butter
1 tsp cumin seeds
1 tsp coriander seeds
1 tomato, chopped
1 tsp minced fresh ginger
1 tsp minced fresh garlic

1 red onion, chopped
1 pound spinach, chopped
1 cup water
1 tsp salt, or to taste
2 cups paneer, cubed
1 tsp chilli powder

DIRECTIONS

Warm butter on Sauté. Add in garlic, cumin seeds, coriander, chilli powder, ginger, and garlic and fry for 1 minute until fragrant. Add onion and cook for 2 minutes until crispy. Add in salt, water, and spinach.

Seal the lid and cook for 1 minute on High Pressure. Release the pressure quickly. Add spinach mixture to a blender and blend to obtain a smooth paste. Mix paneer and tomato with spinach mixture.

Indian Vegan Curry

Serves: 3 | Ready in about: 25 min

INGREDIENTS

1 tbsp butter
1 onion, chopped
2 cloves garlic, minced
1 tsp ginger, grated
1 tsp ground cumin
1 tsp red chilli powder
1 tsp salt

½ tsp ground turmeric
1 (15 ounces) can chickpeas, drained and rinsed
1 tomato, diced
⅓ cup water
5 cups collard greens, chopped
½ tsp garam masala
1 tsp lemon juice

DIRECTIONS

Melt butter on Sauté. Toss in the onion to coat. Close the lid and cook for 2 minutes until soft. Mix in ginger, cumin powder, turmeric, red chili powder, garlic, and salt and cook for 30 seconds until crispy. Stir in tomatoes. Into the cooker, mix in ⅓ water, tomato, and chickpeas.

Seal the lid and cook on High Pressure for 4 minutes. Release the pressure quickly. Press Sauté.

Into the chickpea mixture, stir in lemon juice, collard greens, and garam masala, until well coated. Cook for 2 to 3 minutes until collard greens wilt, on Sauté. Serve over rice or naan.

Sticky Noodles with Tofu and Peanuts

Serves: 4 | Ready in about: 20 min

INGREDIENTS

1 package tofu, cubed
8 ounces egg noodles
2 bell peppers, chopped
¼ cup soy sauce
¼ cup orange juice
1 tbsp fresh ginger, peeled and minced

2 tbsp vinegar
1 tbsp sesame oil
1 tbsp sriracha
¼ cup roasted peanuts
3 scallions, chopped

DIRECTIONS

In the instant pot, mix tofu, bell peppers, orange juice, sesame oil, ginger, egg noodles, soy sauce, vinegar, and sriracha. Cover with enough water. Seal the lid and cook for 2 minutes on High Pressure.

Release the pressure quickly. Place the mixture into 4 plates; top with scallions and peanuts to serve.

Pilau Rice with Veggies

Serves: 4 | Ready in about: 30 min

INGREDIENTS

3 tbsp olive oil
1 tbsp ginger, minced
1 cup onion, chopped
1 cup green peas
1 cup carrot, chopped
1 cup mushroom, chopped
1 cup broccoli, chopped
1 tbsp chili powder

½ tbsp ground cumin
1 tsp garam masala
½ tsp turmeric powder
1 cup basmati rice, rinsed and drained
2 cups vegetable broth
1 tbsp lemon juice
2 tbsp chopped fresh cilantro

DIRECTIONS

Warm 1 tbsp olive oil on Sauté. Add in onion and ginger and cook for 3 minutes until soft. Stir in broccoli, green peas, mushrooms, and carrots; cook for 1 more minute. Add turmeric powder, chili powder, garam masala, and cumin; cook for 1 minute until soft.

Add ¼ cup water to deglaze; scrape the bottom to get rid of any browned bits. To the vegetables, add the remaining water and rice. Seal the lid and cook for 1 minute on High Pressure. Release the pressure quickly. Use a fork to fluff rice, sprinkle with lemon juice. Divide into plates and garnish with cilantro.

Carrot and Lentil Chili

Serves: 4 | Ready in about: 30 min

INGREDIENTS

1 tbsp olive oil
1 onion, chopped
1 cup celery, chopped
2 garlic cloves, chopped
1 onion, chopped
3 cups vegetable stock

1½ cups dried lentils, rinsed
4 carrots, halved lengthwise
1 tbsp harissa, or more to taste
½ tsp sea salt
A handful of fresh parsley, chopped

DIRECTIONS

Warm olive oil on Sauté. Add in onion, garlic, and celery, and sauté for 5 minutes until onion is soft. Mix in lentils, carrots, and vegetable stock. Seal the lid and cook on High Pressure for 10 minutes. Release the pressure quickly. Mix lentils with salt and harissa and serve topped with parsley.

Steamed Artichokes with Lemon Aioli

Serves: 4 | Ready in about: 20 min

INGREDIENTS

4 artichokes, trimmed
1 lemon, halved
1 tsp lemon zest
1 tbsp lemon juice
3 cloves garlic, crushed

½ cup mayonnaise
1 cup water
Salt
1 handful parsley, chopped

DIRECTIONS

On artichokes' cut ends, rub with lemon. Add water into the pot. Set steamer rack over water and set steamer basket on top. Place artichokes into the basket with the points upwards; sprinkle with salt.

Seal lid and cook on high Pressure for 10 minutes. Release the pressure quickly. In a mixing bowl, combine mayonnaise, garlic, lemon juice, and lemon zest. Season to taste with salt. Serve with warm steamed artichokes sprinkled with parsley.

Garlic Veggie Mash with Parmesan

Serves: 6 | Ready in about: 15 min

INGREDIENTS

3 pounds Yukon Gold potatoes, chopped
1 ½ cups cauliflower, broken into florets
1 carrot, chopped
1 cup Parmesan Cheese, shredded
¼ cup butter, melted

¼ cup milk
1 tsp salt
1 garlic clove, minced
Fresh parsley for garnish

DIRECTIONS

Into the pot, add veggies, salt, and cover with enough water. Seal the lid and cook on High Pressure for 10 minutes. Release the pressure quickly. Drain the vegetables and mash with a potato masher.

Add garlic, butter, and milk, and Whisk until everything is well incorporated. Serve topped with Parmesan cheese and chopped parsley.

Green Beans with Feta and Nuts

Serves: 6 | Ready in about: 15 min

INGREDIENTS

Juice from 1 lemon
1½ cups water
2 pounds green beans, trimmed
1 cup chopped toasted pine nuts

1 cup feta cheese, crumbled
6 tbsp olive oil
½ tsp salt
Freshly ground black pepper to taste

DIRECTIONS

Add water and set the rack over the water and the steamer basket on the rack. Loosely heap green beans into the steamer basket. Seal lid and cook on High Pressure for 5 minutes. Release pressure quickly.

Drop green beans into a salad bowl. Top with the olive oil, feta cheese, pepper, and pine nuts.

Mashed Parsnips and Cauliflower

Serves: 8 | Ready in about: 15 min

INGREDIENTS

1 ½ pounds parsnips, peeled and cubed
1 head cauliflower, cut into florets
2 garlic cloves
¾ tsp salt
¼ tsp pepper

2 cups water
¼ cup sour cream
¼ cup grated Parmesan Cheese
1 tbsp butter
2 tbsp minced chives

DIRECTIONS

In the pot, mix parsnips, garlic, water, salt, cauliflower, and pepper. Seal the lid and cook on High Pressure for 4 minutes. Release the pressure quickly. Drain the veggies and return to pot.

Add Parmesan, butter, and sour cream. Use a potato masher to mash until desired consistency is attained. Into the mashed parsnip, add 1 tbsp chives; place to a serving plate and garnish with remaining chives.

Tahini Sweet Potato Mash

Serves: 4 | Ready in about: 25 min

INGREDIENTS

1 cup water
2 pounds sweet potatoes, peeled and cubed
2 tbsp tahini
1 tbsp sugar

¼ tsp ground nutmeg
Chopped fresh chives, for garnish
sea salt to taste

DIRECTIONS

Into the cooker, add 1 cup cold water and insert a steamer basket. Add sweet potato cubes into the steamer basket. Seal the lid and cook for 8 minutes at High Pressure. Release the pressure quickly.

In a bowl, add cooked sweet potatoes and slightly mash. Using a hand mixer, whip in nutmeg, sugar, and tahini until the sweet potatoes attain desired consistency. Add salt to taste and top with chives to serve.

Aloo Gobi with Cilantro

Serves: 4 | Ready in about: 40 min

INGREDIENTS

1 tbsp vegetable oil
1 head cauliflower, cored and cut into florets
1 potato, peeled and diced
1 tbsp ghee
2 tsp cumin seeds
1 onion, minced
4 garlic cloves, minced
1 tomato, cored and chopped

1 jalapeño pepper, deseeded and minced
1 tbsp curry paste
1 tsp ground turmeric
½ tsp chili pepper
1 cup water
Salt to taste
A handful of cilantro leaves, chopped

DIRECTIONS

Warm oil on Sauté mode. Add in potato and cauliflower and cook for 8 to 10 minutes until lightly browned; season with salt. Set the vegetables to a bowl. Add ghee to the pot.

Mix in cumin seeds and cook for 10 seconds until they start to pop; add onion and cook for 3 minutes until softened. Mix in garlic; cook for 30 seconds.

Add in tomato, curry paste, chili pepper, jalapeño pepper, and turmeric; cook for 4 to 6 minutes until the tomato starts to break down. Return potato and cauliflower to the pot. Stir water over the vegetables.

Seal the lid and cook on High Pressure for 4 minutes. Quick release the pressure. Top with cilantro.

Spicy Cauliflower Rice with Peas

Serves: 2 | Ready in about: 15 min

INGREDIENTS

1 head cauliflower, cut into florets
1 cup water
2 tbsp olive oil
Salt to taste

1 tsp chili powder
¼ cup green peas
1 tbsp chopped fresh parsley

DIRECTIONS

Add water, set rack over water and place the steamer basket onto the rack. Add cauliflower into the steamer basket. Seal the lid and cook on High Pressure for 1 minute. Release the pressure quickly.

Remove rack and steamer basket. Drain water from the pot, pat dry, and return to pressure cooker base.

Set on Sauté mode and warm oil. Add in cauliflower and stir to break into smaller pieces like rice. Stir in chili powder, peas, and salt. Place the cauliflower rice into plates and add parsley for garnishing.

Chipotle Vegetarian Chili

Serves: 12 | Ready in about: 45 min

INGREDIENTS

1 (28 ounces) can diced tomatoes
2 cups cashews, chopped
1 cup onion, chopped
1 cup red lentils
1 cup red quinoa
3 chipotle peppers, chopped
3 garlic cloves, minced

2 tbsp chili powder
1 tsp salt
4 ½ cups water
2 cups carrots, chopped
1 (15 ounces) can black beans, rinsed and drained
¼ cup fresh parsley, chopped

DIRECTIONS

In the pot, mix tomatoes, onion, chipotle peppers, chili powder, lentils, walnuts, carrots, quinoa, garlic, and salt. Stir in more water. Seal the lid, press Soup/Stew and cook for 30 minutes on High Pressure.

Release the pressure quickly. Into the chili, add black beans; simmer on Sauté until heated through. Add ¼ cup to 1 cup water if you want a thinner consistency. Top with a garnish of parsley.

Thai Vegetable Stew

Serves: 4 | Ready in about: 30 min

INGREDIENTS

1 tbsp coconut oil
1 cup onion, chopped
1 tbsp fresh ginger, minced
2 garlic cloves, minced
3 carrots, peeled and chopped
1 red bell pepper, chopped

1 orange bell pepper, chopped
1 (14 ounces) can coconut milk
1 cup bok choy, chopped
½ cup water
2 tbsp red curry paste

DIRECTIONS

Melt coconut oil on Sauté. Add in onion and cook for 3 to 4 minutes until soft; add garlic and ginger and cook for 30 more seconds until soft. Mix in orange bell pepper, red bell pepper, and carrots; cook for 3 to 4 minutes until the peppers become soft and tender.

Add curry paste, bok choy, coconut milk, and water and stir well to obtain a consistent color of the sauce.

Press Cancel and seal lid. Cook for 1 minute on High Pressure. Release the pressure quickly. Serve hot!

Honey-Glazed Acorn Squash

Serves: 4 | Ready in about: 30 min

INGREDIENTS

½ cup water
3 tablespoons honey
1 lb acorn squash, cut into 2-inch chunks
2 tbsp butter

1 tbsp dark brown sugar
1 tbsp cinnamon
Salt and ground black pepper to taste

DIRECTIONS

In a small bowl, mix 1 tablespoon honey and water. Pour into the pot. Add in squash, seal the lid and cook on High Pressure for 4 minutes. Release the pressure quickly.

Transfer the squash to a serving dish. Set on Sauté. Mix sugar, cinnamon, the remaining honey and the liquid in the pot. Cook as you stir for 4 minutes to obtain a thick consistency and starts to turn caramelized and golden. Spread honey glaze over squash; add pepper and salt to taste.

Coconut Milk and Lime Yogurt

Serves: 6 | Ready in about: 10hr 30 min

INGREDIENTS

2 cans coconut milk
1 tbsp gelatin
1 tbsp honey

1 tsp probiotic powder
Zest from 1 Lime

DIRECTIONS

Into the pot, stir in gelatin and coconut milk until well dissolved. Seal the lid, press Yogurt button until the display is reading "Boil". Once complete, the screen will then display "Yogurt". Ensure milk temperature is at 180° F. Remove steel pot from Pressure cooker's base and place into a large ice bath to cool milk for 5 minutes to reach 112° F.

Remove pot from ice bath and wipe the outside dry. Into the coconut milk mixture, add probiotic powder, honey, and lime zest, and stir to combine. Return steel pot to the base of the instant pot. Seal the lid, press Yogurt and cook for 10 hours. Once complete, spoon yogurt into clean glass canning jars with rings and lids; place in the refrigerator to chill for 4 hrs to thicken.

Artichoke with Garlic Mayo

Serves: 4 | Ready in about: 20 min

INGREDIENTS

2 large artichokes
2 cups water
2 garlic cloves, smashed

½ cup mayonnaise
Salt and black pepper to taste
Juice of 1 Lime

DIRECTIONS

Using a serrated knife, trim about 1 inch from the artichokes' top. Into the pot, add water and set trivet over. Lay the artichokes on the trivet. Seal lid and cook for 14 minutes on High Pressure.

Release the pressure quickly. Mix the mayonnaise with garlic and lime juice. Season with salt and pepper. Serve artichokes in a platter with garlic mayo on side.

Asparagus with Feta

Serves: 4 | Ready in about: 15 min

INGREDIENTS

1 cup water
1 pound asparagus spears, ends trimmed
1 tbsp olive oil

Salt and ground black pepper to taste
1 lemon, cut into wedges
1 cup feta cheese, cubed

DIRECTIONS

Into the pot, add water and set trivet over the water. Place steamer basket on the trivet. Place the asparagus into the steamer basket. Seal the lid and cook on High Pressure for 1 minute.

Release the pressure quickly. Add olive oil in a bowl and toss in asparagus until well coated. Season with pepper and salt. Serve alongside feta cheese and lemon wedges.

Parsley Mashed Cauliflower

Serves: 4 | Ready in about: 15 min

INGREDIENTS

2 cups water
1 head cauliflower
1 tbsp butter
¼ tsp celery salt

¼ cup heavy cream
1 tbsp fresh parsley, finely chopped
½ tsp freshly ground black pepper

DIRECTIONS

Into the pot, add water and set trivet on top. Lay cauliflower head onto the trivet. Seal the lid and cook for 8 minutes on High Pressure. Release the pressure quickly. Drain liquid from the pot.

Take back the cauliflower to the pot alongside the pepper, heavy cream, salt, and butter. Use an immersion blender to blend until smooth. Top with parsley and serve.

Garlic Potato Mash with Chives

Serves: 6 | Ready in about: 30 min

INGREDIENTS

1 ½ cups water
1 tbsp olive oil
2 garlic cloves, smashed
4 large potatoes, peeled and cut into chunks

⅓ cup butter, melted
¼ cup milk
Salt and ground black pepper to taste
1 tbsp chopped chives

DIRECTIONS

Select Sauté and heat olive oil. Cook for 8-10 minutes, turning periodically until browned. Set aside. Wipe the pot with paper towels. Add in water and set steamer rack over water and steamer basket onto the rack. Place potatoes to the steamer basket. Seal the lid and cook on High Pressure for 12 minutes.

Release the pressure quickly. Remove basket and rack from the pot. Drain water from the pot. Return potatoes to pot. Add in salt, butter, pepper, garlic, and milk and use a hand masher to mash until no large lumps remain. Using an immersion blender, blend potatoes on Low for 1 minute until fluffy and light.

Avoid over-blending to ensure the potatoes do not become gluey! Transfer the mash to a serving plate and scatter chopped chives over to serve.

Breakfast Burrito Bowls

Serves: 4 | Ready in about: 30 min

INGREDIENTS

2 tbsp olive oil
1 onion
2 garlic cloves, minced
1 tbsp chili powder
2 tsp ground cumin
2 tsp paprika
1 tsp salt
½ tsp black pepper
¼ tsp cayenne pepper

1 cup quinoa, rinsed
1 (14.5 ounces) can diced tomatoes
1 (14.5 ounces) can black beans
1 ½ cups vegetable stock
1 cup frozen corn kernels
2 tbsp chopped cilantro
1 tbsp roughly chopped fresh coriander
Cheddar cheese, grated for garnish
1 avocado, chopped

DIRECTIONS

Warm oil on Sauté. Add in onion and stir-fry for 3 to 5 minutes, until fragrant. Add garlic and sauté for 2 more minutes until soft and golden brown. Add in chili powder, paprika, cayenne pepper, salt, cumin, and black pepper and cook for 1 minute until spices are soft.

Pour quinoa into onion and spice mixture and stir to coat quinoa completely in spices. Add diced tomatoes, black beans, vegetable stock, and corn; stir to combine.

Seal the lid and cook for 7 minutes on High Pressure. Release the pressure quickly. Open the lid and let sit for 6 minutes until flavors combine. Use a fork to fluff quinoa and season with pepper and salt.

Into quinoa and beans mixture, stir in cilantro and divide into plates. Top with cheese and avocado slices.

Green Lasagna Soup

Serves: 4 | Ready in about: 30 min

INGREDIENTS

1 tsp olive oil
1 cup leeks, chopped
2 garlic cloves minced
1 cup tomato paste
1 cup tomatoes, chopped
1 carrot, chopped

½ pound broccoli, chopped
¼ cup dried green lentils
2 tsp Italian Seasoning
Salt to taste
2 cups vegetable broth
3 lasagna noodles

DIRECTIONS

Warm oil on Sauté mode. Add garlic and leeks and cook for 2 minutes until soft; add tomato paste, carrot, Italian seasoning, broccoli, tomatoes, lentils, and salt. Stir in vegetable broth and lasagna pieces.

Seal the lid and cook on High Pressure for 3 minutes. Release pressure naturally for 10 minutes, then release the remaining pressure quickly. Divide soup into serving bowls and serve.

Rosemary Sweet Potato Medallions

Serves: 4 | Ready in about: 25 min

INGREDIENTS

1 cup water
1 tbsp fresh rosemary
1 tsp garlic powder

4 sweet potatoes
2 tbsp butter
Salt to taste

DIRECTIONS

Add water and place steamer rack over the water. Use a fork to prick potatoes all over and set onto steamer rack. Seal the lid and cook on High Pressure for 12 minutes. Release the pressure quickly.

Transfer potatoes to a cutting board and slice into ½-inch medallions and ensure they are peeled.

Melt butter in the on Sauté mode. Add in the medallions and cook each side for 2 to 3 minutes until browned. Season with salt and garlic powder. Serve topped with fresh rosemary.

Colorful Vegetable Medley

Serves: 4 | Ready in about: 15 min

INGREDIENTS

1 cup water
1 head broccoli, broken into florets
16 asparagus, trimmed
1 head cauliflower, broken into florets

5 ounces green beans
2 carrots, peeled and cut on bias
Salt to taste

DIRECTIONS

Add water and set trivet on top of water and place steamer basket on top. In an even layer, spread green beans, broccoli, cauliflower, asparagus, and carrots in steamer basket. Seal the lid and cook on Steam for 3 minutes on High. Release the pressure quickly. Remove basket from the pot and season with salt.

Spinach and Leeks with Goat Cheese

Serves: 2 | Ready in about: 10 min

INGREDIENTS

9 oz fresh spinach
2 leeks, chopped
2 red onions, chopped
2 garlic cloves, crushed

½ cup goat's cheese
3 tbsp olive oil
1 tsp kosher salt

DIRECTIONS

Grease the inner pot with oil. Stir-fry leek, garlic, and onions, for about 5 minutes, on Sauté mode. Add spinach and give it a good stir.

Season with salt and cook for 3 more minutes, stirring continually. Press Cancel, Transfer to a serving dish and sprinkle with goat's cheese. Serve right away.

Red Beans and Rice

Serves: 4 | Ready in about: 1hr

INGREDIENTS

1 cup red beans
½ cup rice,
½ tsp cayenne pepper
1 ½ cup vegetable broth
1 onion, diced

1 red bell pepper, diced
1 stalk celery, diced
1 tbsp fresh thyme leaves, or to taste
Salt and freshly ground black pepper to taste

DIRECTIONS

Add beans and water to cover about 1-inch. Seal the lid and cook for 1 minute on High Pressure. Release the pressure quickly. Drain the beans and set aside. Rinse and pat dry the inner pot.

Return inner pot to the cooker, add oil to the pot and press Sauté. Add onion to the oil and sauté for 3 minutes until soft. Add celery and pepper and cook for 1 to 2 minutes until fragrant.

Add garlic and cook for 30 seconds until soft. Add rice, transfer the beans back to the pot and top with broth. Stir black pepper, thyme, cayenne pepper, and salt into mixture. Seal the lid and cook for 15 minutes on High Pressure. Release the pressure quickly. Season with more thyme, black pepper, and salt.

Braised Greens with Farro

Serves: 6 | Ready in about: 15 min

INGREDIENTS

6 oz kale, chopped
6 oz spinach, chopped
6 oz collard greens, chopped
3 oz Swiss chard, chopped
3 oz parsley leaves, chopped

1 medium-sized leek, chopped
1 ½ cups farro
4 tbsp olive oil
5 cups vegetable broth
1 tsp sea salt

DIRECTIONS

Add in farro and 5 cups of vegetable broth. Season with salt and sea the lid. Cook on Rice mode for 9 minutes on High. Do a quick release and open the lid.

Remove farro and wipe the instant pot clean. Pour two cups of water, insert the steamer basket and place the chopped greens. Seal the lid.

Cook on Steam mode for 2 minutes on High. Do a quick release and remove the greens to a large bowl. Toss in the farro and drizzle with olive oil to serve.

Mac & Goat Cheese

Serves: 4 | Ready in about: 20 min

INGREDIENTS

1 lb elbow macaroni
2 oz goat's cheese, crumbled
½ cup skim milk
1 tsp Dijon mustard
1 tsp dried oregano, ground

1 tsp sea salt
1 tsp Italian Seasoning mix
2 tbsp extra virgin olive oil
1 tbsp vegetable oil
5 oz olives

DIRECTIONS

Add macaroni in the instant pot and pour in 4 cups of water. Add 1 tablespoon of oil. Seal the lid and cook on High Pressure for 3 minutes. Do a quick release.

Drain macaroni in a colander and set aside. Press Sauté, add olive oil, mustard, milk, oregano, salt, and Italian seasoning mix. Stir-fry for 5 minutes.

Stir in macaroni and cook for 2 more minutes. Remove from the pot and top with some fresh goat's cheese and olives. Serve immediately.

Eggplant Lasagna

Serves: 4 | Ready in about: 35 min

INGREDIENTS

1 large eggplant, chopped
4 oz mozzarella, chopped
3 oz Mascarpone cheese, at room temperature
2 tomatoes, chopped

¼ cup olive oil
1 tsp salt
½ tsp ground black pepper
1 tsp oregano, dried

DIRECTIONS

Grease a baking dish with olive oil. Slice the eggplant and make a layer in the dish. Cover with mozzarella and tomato slices. Top with mascarpone cheese. Repeat the process until you run out of ingredients. Meanwhile, in a bowl, mix olive oil, salt, pepper, and dried oregano.

Pour the mixture over the lasagna, and add ½ cup of water. In your inner pot, pour 1 ½ cups of water and insert a trivet. Lower the baking dish on the trivet, seal the lid and cook on High Pressure for 4 minutes. When ready, do a natural release, for 10 minutes.

Italian Chickpea Pot with Olives

Serves: 6 | Ready in about: 25 min

INGREDIENTS

1 cup scallions, cleaned and chopped
1 medium carrot, chopped
1 cup chickpeas, soaked
3 cups fish broth

½ cup olives, pitted
½ tsp sea salt
¼ tsp black pepper, ground
½ tsp Italian Seasoning mix

DIRECTIONS

Add all ingredients in your instant pot. Seal the lid and cook on High Pressure for 12 minutes. Release the pressure naturally, for 10 minutes. Serve warm.

Sweet Garbanzo & Mushroom Stew

Serves: 4 | Ready in about: 20 min

INGREDIENTS

1 cup chickpeas, cooked
1 onion, peeled, chopped
A handful of string beans, trimmed
1 apple, chopped
½ cup raisins
½ tbsp button mushrooms, chopped
2 carrots, chopped

2 garlic cloves, crushed
4 cherry tomatoes
A handful of fresh mint
1 tsp grated ginger
½ cup freshly squeezed orange juice
½ tsp salt

DIRECTIONS

Place all ingredients in the instant pot. Pour enough water to cover. Cook on High Pressure for 8 minutes. Do a natural release, for 10 minutes.

Buttery Chickpea Stew

Serves: 4 | Ready in about: 45 min

INGREDIENTS

6 oz chickpeas, soaked overnight
1 tomato, peeled, chopped
1 red onion, peeled, chopped
1 tbsp cumin seeds

2 cups vegetable broth
2 tbsp olive oil
2 tbsp butter
2 tbsp fresh parsley, for garnishing

DIRECTIONS

Add in the tomato, onion, cumin seeds, chickpeas, and pour in the broth. Seal the lid and set the steam handle. Cook on Soup/Broth for 30 minutes on High. Do a quick release and set aside to cool for a while. Transfer the soup to a food processor. Process until pureed and ladle to a serving dish. Stir in 2 tbsp of butter. Top freshly chopped parsley.

Quick Greek Dolmades

Serves: 4 | Ready in about: 60 min

INGREDIENTS

32 wine leaves, fresh or in jar
1 cup long grain rice, rinsed
½ cup olive oil
2 garlic cloves, crushed

¼ cup freshly squeezed lemon juice
2 tbsp fresh mint
Salt and pepper to taste

DIRECTIONS

In a bowl, mix rice with 3 tbsp of olive oil, garlic, mint, salt, and pepper. Place 1 wine leaf at a time on a working surface and add 1 tsp of filling at the bottom.

Fold the leaf over the filling towards the center. Bring the 2 sides towards the center and roll them up tightly. Grease the instant pot with 2 tbsp olive oil.

Make a layer of wine leaves and then Transfer the previously prepared rolls. Add the remaining olive oil, 2 cups of water, and lemon juice. Seal the lid and cook on High Pressure for to 30 minutes. Do a natural release, for about 10 minutes. Remove the dolmades from the pot and chill overnight.

Quinoa & Lentil Stew

Serves: 4 | Ready in about: 25 min

INGREDIENTS

1 cup quinoa, soaked overnight
1 cup tomatoes, diced
1 cup lentils, soaked overnight
¼ cup sun-dried tomatoes, chopped

1 tsp garlic, minced
4 cups beef broth
1 tsp salt
1 tsp red pepper flakes

DIRECTIONS

Add all ingredients in your instant pot. Seal the lid and adjust the steam release handle. Cook on High Pressure for 20 minutes. Release the steam naturally, for about 5 minutes.

Carrot & Bean Stew

Serves: 6 | Ready in about: 30 min

INGREDIENTS

2 cups cranberry beans, soaked overnight, rinsed
2 onions, peeled, chopped
3 carrots, peeled, chopped
3 tomatoes, peeled, diced

3 tbsp olive oil
2 tsp granulated sugar
A handful of fresh parsley
2 cups water

DIRECTIONS

Heat oil on Sauté, and stir-fry the onions, for 3-4 minutes, until translucent. Add carrots and tomatoes. Stir well and cook for 5 minutes. Stir in beans, water, sugar and seal the lid.

Cook on High Pressure for 15 minutes. Do a quick release and serve hot sprinkled with fresh parsley.

Vegetarian Paella

Serves: 4 | Ready in about: 30 min

INGREDIENTS

½ cup frozen green peas
2 carrots, finely chopped
1 cup fire-roasted tomatoes
1 cup zucchini, finely chopped
½ tbsp celery root, finely chopped
6 saffron threads

1 tbsp turmeric, ground
1 tsp salt
½ tsp freshly ground black pepper
2 cup vegetable broth
1 cup long grain rice

DIRECTIONS

Place all ingredients, except rice, in the instant pot. Stir well and seal the lid. Cook on Rice mode for 8 minutes, on High. Do a quick release, open the lid and stir in the rice. Seal the lid and cook on High pressure for 3 minutes. When ready, release the pressure naturally, for about 10 minutes.

Lemony Split Pea Stew

Serves: 4 | Ready in about: 40 min

INGREDIENTS

2 cups split yellow peas
1 cup onions, chopped
1 carrot, chopped
2 potatoes, chopped
2 tbsp butter

¼ cup lemon juice
2 garlic cloves, crushed
1 tsp chili pepper
½ tsp salt
4 cups vegetable stock

DIRECTIONS

Melt butter on Sauté, and stir-fry the onions, for 1 minute. Add the remaining vegetables and cook for 5-6 minutes, until tender. Stir in chili pepper and season with salt. Pour in the stock and seal the lid.

Cook on High on Meat/Stew for 25 minutes. Do a quick release, drizzle with lemon juice and serve.

Italian Vegetable Stew

Serves: 4 | Ready in about: 25 min

INGREDIENTS

3 zucchini, peeled, chopped
1 eggplant, peeled, chopped
3 red bell peppers, chopped
½ cup fresh tomato juice

2 tsp Italian Seasoning
½ tsp salt
2 tbsp olive oil

DIRECTIONS

Add all ingredients and give it a good stir. Pour 1 cup of water. Seal the lid and cook on High pressure for 15 minutes. Do a quick release. Set aside to cool completely. Serve as a cold salad or a side dish.

Spinach & Potato Omelet

Serves: 3 | Ready in about: 30 min

INGREDIENTS

5 eggs, beaten
1 cup spinach, torn, rinsed
1 potato, chopped
1 cup heavy cream

½ tsp salt
¼ tsp black pepper, ground
¼ tsp dried thyme
1 tbsp olive oil

DIRECTIONS

In a bowl, mix eggs, heavy cream, and potato. Sprinkle with salt and black pepper, and stir to combine. Heat oil on Sauté and cook the spinach for 3 minutes, or until wilted. Remove the spinach from the pot.

Stir in the spinach in the previously prepared mixture. Transfer all to an oven-safe dish, that fits in the instant pot. Add 1 cup of water, insert the trivet, pour 1 cup of water, and place the oven-safe dish on top.

Seal the lid and cook on High Pressure for 20 minutes. Release the steam naturally, for 5 minutes.

Chickpea Stew with Onions

Serves: 5 | Ready in about: 35 min

INGREDIENTS

1 lb chickpeas, soaked
3 purple onions, peeled and cups
2 tomatoes, roughly chopped
2 oz fresh parsley, chopped
3 cups vegetable broth

1 tbsp paprika
3 tbsp butter
2 tbsp olive oil
1 tsp salt
½ tsp ground black pepper

DIRECTIONS

Warm oil on Sauté and stir-fry the onions for 3 minutes. Add the rest of the ingredients. Seal the lid and cook on the Meat/Stew for 30 minutes on High. Do a quick release and serve warm.

Vegetable Stew

Serves: 4 | Ready in about: 55 min

INGREDIENTS

1 lb potatoes, peeled, cut into bite-sized pieces
2 carrots, peeled, chopped
3 celery stalks, chopped
2 onions, peeled, chopped
1 zucchini, sliced
A handful of fresh celery leaves

2 tbsp butter, unsalted
3 tbsp olive oil
2 cups vegetable broth
1 tbsp paprika
1 tbsp sea salt
1 tsp black pepper

DIRECTIONS

Warm oil on Sauté and stir-fry the onions for 3-4 minutes, until translucent. Add carrots, celery, zucchini, and ¼ cup of broth. Continue to cook for 10 more minutes, stirring constantly.

Stir in potatoes, cayenne pepper, salt, pepper, bay leaves, remaining broth, and celery leaves. Seal the lid and cook on Meat/Stew mode for 30 minutes on High. Do a quick release and stir in 2 tbsp of butter.

Tasty Mushroom Stew

Serves: 4 | Ready in about: 65 min

INGREDIENTS

6 oz Portobello mushrooms, chopped
1 cup green peas
1 cup onions, minced
2 carrots, chopped
½ cup celery stalks, chopped
2 garlic cloves, crushed
2 potatoes, chopped

1 tbsp apple cider vinegar
1 tsp rosemary
1 tsp salt
½ tsp pepper, freshly ground
2 tbsp butter
4 cups vegetable stock

DIRECTIONS

Melt butter on Sauté and stir-fry onions, carrots, celery stalks, and garlic, for 2-3 minutes. Season with salt, pepper, and rosemary. Add the remaining ingredients and seal the lid. Cook on High Pressure for 30 minutes. When ready, release the pressure naturally, for about 5 minutes.

Potato Balls in Marinara Sauce

Serves: 4 | Ready in about: 30 min

INGREDIENTS

2 potatoes, peeled
1 onion, peeled, chopped
1 lb fresh spinach, torn
¼ cup mozzarella cheese, shredded
2 eggs, beaten
½ tsp salt

¼ tsp ground black pepper
1 tsp dried oregano, crushed
1 cup whole milk
¼ cup flour
¼ cup corn flour

Marinara Sauce:
1 lb fresh tomatoes, peeled, roughly chopped
1 large onion, peeled, chopped
2 garlic cloves, peeled, crushed
3 tbsp olive oil
¼ cup white wine

1 tsp sugar
1 tbsp dried rosemary, crushed
½ tsp salt
1 tbsp tomato paste

DIRECTIONS

Place the potatoes in your instant pot and add enough water to cover. Seal the lid and cook on High Pressure for 13 minutes. Do a quick release. Add 1 cup of milk and mash with a potato masher.

Whisk in eggs, one at the time and mix well. Add the remaining ingredients and mix with hands. Shape into balls and set aside. Press Sauté, warm olive oil, and stir-fry onions, garlic, until translucent.

Stir in tomatoes and cook until tender, for about 10 minutes. Pour in wine, add sugar, rosemary, and salt. Stir in 1 tbsp of tomato paste and mix well. Cook for five more minutes. Place the potato balls in the cooker and seal with the lid. Cook on High Pressure for 5 minutes. Do a natural release, for 5 minutes.

Stewed Kidney Bean

Serves: 4 | Ready in about: 30 min

INGREDIENTS

6 oz red beans, cooked
2 carrots, chopped
2 celery stalks, cut into pieces
1 onion, peeled, chopped
2 tbsp tomato paste

1 bay leaf
2 cups vegetable broth
3 tbsp olive oil
1 tsp salt
A handful of fresh parsley

DIRECTIONS

Warm oil on Sauté and stir-fry the onions, for 3 minutes, until soft. Add celery and carrots. Cook for 5 more minutes, adding 1 tbsp of broth at the time. Add red beans, bay leaf, salt, parsley, and tomato paste.

Stir in 1 tbsp of flour and pour in the remaining broth. Seal the lid and cook on High pressure for 5 minutes on. Do a natural release, for about 10 minutes. Sprinkle with some fresh parsley and serve warm.

Lentil Spread with Parmesan

Serves: 6 | Ready in about: 15 min

INGREDIENTS

1 lb lentils, cooked
1 cup sweet corn
2 tomatoes, diced
3 tbsp tomato paste
½ tsp dried oregano, ground
2 tbsp Parmesan Cheese

1 tsp salt
½ tsp red pepper flakes
3 tbsp olive oil
1 cup water
¼ cup red wine

DIRECTIONS

Heat oil on Sauté and add tomatoes, tomato paste, and ½ cup of water. Sprinkle with salt and oregano and stir-fry for 5 minutes. Press Cancel and add lentils, sweet corn, and wine.

Pour in the remaining water and seal the lid. Cook on High Pressure for 2 minutes. Do a quick release. Set aside to cool completely and refrigerate for 30 minutes. Sprinkle with Parmesan Cheese.

Mushroom and Spinach Cannelloni

Serves: 4 | Ready in about: 40 min

INGREDIENTS

1 (9 oz) pack of cannelloni
12 oz spinach, torn
6 oz button mushrooms, chopped
3 oz ricotta cheese

¼ cup milk
3 oz butter
¼ tsp salt
1 tbsp sour cream

DIRECTIONS

Melt butter on Sauté and add mushrooms. Stir well and cook until soft. Add spinach and milk, and continue to cook for 6 minutes, stirring constantly. Stir in the cheese, season to taste.

Line parchment paper over a baking sheet. Fill cannelloni with spinach mixture. Gently place them on the baking sheet. Pour 2 cups of water in the instant pot and insert a trivet.

Lower the baking sheet on the trivet. Seal the lid, and cook on High Pressure for 20 minutes. Do a quick release. Remove and chill for a while. Top with sour cream and serve.

Mushroom Spinach Tagliatelle

Serves: 4 | Ready in about: 25 min

INGREDIENTS

1 lb spinach tagliatelle
6 oz frozen mixed mushrooms
3 tbsp butter, unsalted
¼ cup feta cheese

¼ cup grated Parmesan Cheese
2 garlic cloves, crushed
¼ cup heavy cream
1 tbsp Italian Seasoning mix

DIRECTIONS

Melt butter on Sauté, and stir-fry the garlic for a minute. Stir in feta and mushrooms. Add tagliatelle and 2 cups of water. Cook on High Pressure for 4 minutes. Quick release the pressure and top with parmesan.

Feta Cheese Stuffed Potatoes

Serves: 3 | Ready in about: 60 min

INGREDIENTS

6 potatoes, whole, rinsed, drained
¼ cup olive oil
3 garlic cloves, crushed
¼ cup feta cheese

1 tsp fresh rosemary, chopped
½ tsp dried thyme
2 oz button mushrooms, chopped
1 tsp salt

DIRECTIONS

Rub the potatoes with salt and place them in the instant pot. Add enough water to cover and seal the lid. Cook on High Pressure for 30 minutes. Do a quick release and remove the potatoes. Let chill for a while.

Meanwhile, in the pot, mix olive oil, garlic, rosemary, thyme, and mushrooms. Sauté until the mushrooms soften, about 5 minutes, on Sauté. Remove from the cooker and stir in feta. Cut the top of each potato and spoon out the middle. Fill with cheese mixture and serve immediately.

Leek & Garlic Cannellini Beans

Serves: 4 | Ready in about: 45 min

INGREDIENTS

1 lb cannellini beans, soaked overnight
1 onion, peeled, chopped
2 large leeks, finely chopped

3 garlic cloves, whole
1 tsp pepper
1 tsp salt

Topping:
4 tbsp vegetable oil
2 tbsp flour

1 tbsp cayenne pepper

DIRECTIONS

Add all ingredients, except for the topping ones, in the instant pot. Press Manual/Pressure Cook and cook for 20 minutes on High. Meanwhile, heat 4 tbsp of oil in a skillet. Add flour and cayenne pepper.

Stir-fry for 2 minutes and set aside. When you hear the cooker's end signal, do a quick release. Pour in the cayenne mixture and give it a good stir. Let it sit for 15 minutes before serving.

Mushroom & Rice Stuffed Bell peppers

Serves: 4 | Ready in about: 35 min

INGREDIENTS

5 bell peppers, seeds and stems removed
1 onion, peeled, chopped
6 oz button mushrooms, chopped
4 garlic cloves, peeled, crushed
4 tbsp olive oil

1 tsp salt
¼ tsp ground black pepper
¼ tbsp rice
½ tbsp of paprika
2 cups vegetable stock

DIRECTIONS

Warm 2 tbsp of olive oil on Sauté. Add onions and garlic, and stir-fry until fragrant and translucent, for about 2 minutes. Press Cancel and set aside. In a bowl, combine rice and mushrooms with the mixture from the pot. Season with salt, pepper, and paprika, and stuff each bell pepper with this mixture.

Place them in the instant pot, filled side up, and pour in broth. Seal the lid and cook on High Pressure for 15 minutes. Release the pressure naturally, for about 5 minutes.

Shiitake & Vegetable Penne Pasta

Serves: 4 | Ready in about: 25 min

INGREDIENTS

6 oz penne pasta
6 oz shiitake mushrooms, chopped
2 garlic cloves, crushed
1 small carrot, chopped into strips
6 oz zucchini sliced into strips
6 oz finely chopped leek

4 oz fresh baby spinach, finely chopped
3 tbsp oil
2 tbsp soy sauce
1 tsp ground ginger
½ tsp salt

DIRECTIONS

Heat oil on Sauté and stir-fry carrot and garlic for 3-4 minutes. Add the remaining ingredients and pour in 2 cups of water. Cook on High Pressure for 4 minutes. Quick release the pressure and serve.

Ginger & Tumeric Stew

Serves: 4 | Ready in about: 35 min

INGREDIENTS

2 cups green peas, frozen
1 large onion, chopped
4 cloves garlic, chopped
3 oz of olives, pitted
1 tbsp ginger, shredded

1 tbsp turmeric
1 tbsp salt
4 cups beef stock
3 tbsp olive oil

DIRECTIONS

Heat oil on Sauté. Stir-fry the onions and garlic for 2-3 minutes, stirring constantly. Add the remaining ingredients and seal the lid. Cook on High Pressure for 20 minutes. Do a quick release and serve.

Sweet Potato & Carrot Chowder

Serves: 5 | Ready in about: 50 min

INGREDIENTS

3 sweet potatoes, cut into bite-sized pieces
2 carrots, chopped
1 onion, peeled, chopped
6 tbsp olive oil

2 tbsp tomato sauce
1 tbsp celery, finely chopped
1 tbsp parsley, finely chopped
Salt and pepper

DIRECTIONS

Heat olive oil on Sauté mode. Add onions, carrots, celery, and potatoes. Stir-fry for 2 minutes.

Stir in 4 cups of water, tomato sauce, and the potatoes. Seal the lid and cook for 25 minutes on High Pressure. Do a quick release. Open the pot and add the other ingredients. Seal again, and cook for 5 minutes on High. Do a quick release.

Garlicy Shiitake Mushrooms

Serves: 4 | Ready in about: 45 min

INGREDIENTS

1 lb shiitake mushrooms
2 potatoes, chopped
3 garlic cloves, crushed
2 tbsp oil
1 tsp garlic powder
1 tbsp cumin seeds

½ tsp chili powder
1 large zucchini, chopped
1 cup onions
2 cups vegetable stock
1 cup tomato sauce

DIRECTIONS

Warm olive oil on Sauté. Stir-fry cumin seeds for one minute. Add onions, chili powder, garlic, and garlic powder. Cook for 3 minutes, stirring constantly.

Add mushrooms and continue to cook on Sauté mode for 3 minutes. Add the remaining ingredients and seal the lid. Cook on High Pressure for 20 minutes. When done, release the pressure naturally.

Vegan Lentils Dhal

Serves: 4 | Ready in about: 35 min

INGREDIENTS

10 oz lentils, soaked overnight
2 tbsp almond butter
1 carrot, peeled, chopped
1 potato, peeled, chopped
1 bay leaf
¼ tbsp parsley, chopped

½ tbsp chili powder
2 tbsp ground cumin
1 tbsp garam masala
3 cups vegetable stock
Salt to taste

DIRECTIONS

Melt almond butter on Sauté. Add carrots, potatoes, and parsley. Give it a good stir and cook for 10 minutes. Press Cancel and add the remaining ingredients.

Cook on High Pressure for 15 minutes. Do a quick release and serve hot.

Broccoli & Orecchiette Pasta with Tofu

Serves: 4 | Ready in about: 25 min

INGREDIENTS

1 (9 oz) pack orecchiette
16 oz broccoli, roughly chopped
2 garlic cloves
3 tbsp olive oil

1 tbsp grated tofu
1 tsp salt
¼ tsp black pepper

DIRECTIONS

Place the orecchiette and broccoli in your instant pot. Cover with water and seal the lid. Cook on High Pressure for 10 minutes. Do a quick release.

Drain the broccoli and orecchiette. Set aside. Heat the olive oil on Sauté mode. Stir-fry garlic for 2 minutes. Stir in broccoli, orecchiette, salt, and pepper.

Cook for 2 more minutes. Press Cancel and stir in grated tofu, to serve.

Easy Vegan Green Peas

Serves: 3 | Ready in about: 35 min

INGREDIENTS

1 cup green peas
1 tomato, roughly chopped
1 onion, peeled, chopped
2 carrots, peeled, chopped
2 potatoes, peeled, chopped
1 celery stalk, chopped

A handful of parsley, chopped
2 garlic cloves, crushed
4 tbsp tomato sauce, canned
2 tbsp olive oil
4 cups vegetable stock

DIRECTIONS

Add all the ingredients in the instant pot and seal the lid. Cook on High Pressure for 15 minutes. Do a natural pressure release, for about 10 minutes.

Tip: to make it thicker, cook for 10 minutes on Sauté to evaporate excess liquid.

Braised Swiss Chard with Potatoes

Serves: 4 | Ready in about: 15 min

INGREDIENTS

1 lb Swiss chard, torn, chopped, with stems
2 potatoes, peeled, chopped

¼ tsp oregano
1 tsp salt

DIRECTIONS

Add swiss chard and potatoes to the pot. Pour water to cover all and sprinkle with salt. Seal the lid and select Manual/Pressure Cook.

Cook for 3 minutes on High. Release the steam naturally, for 5 minutes. Transfer to a serving plate. Sprinkle with oregano or Italian seasoning, to serve.

Arugula Pizza

Serves: 4 | Ready in about: 20 min

INGREDIENTS

1 pizza crust
½ cup tomato paste
¼ cup water
1 tsp sugar
1 tsp dried oregano

4 oz button mushrooms, chopped
½ cup grated gouda cheese
2 tbsp extra virgin olive oil
12 Olives
1 cup arugula for serving

DIRECTIONS

Grease the bottom of a baking dish with one tablespoon of olive oil. Line some parchment paper. Flour the working surface and roll out the pizza dough to the approximate size of your instant pot. Gently fit the dough in the previously prepared baking dish.

In a bowl, combine tomato paste, water, sugar, and dry oregano. Spread the mixture over dough, make a layer with button mushrooms and grated gouda.

Add a trivet inside the pot and pour in 1 cup of water. Seal the lid, and cook for 15 minutes on High Pressure. Do a quick release. Remove the pizza from your pot using a parchment paper. Sprinkle with the remaining olive oil and top with olives and arugula. Cut and serve.

SOUPS, BROTHS AND SAUCES

Spicy Acorn Squash Soup

Serves: 4 | Ready in about: 25 min

INGREDIENTS

4 cups vegetable broth
2 tbsp butter
1 onion, diced
1 acorn squash, peeled, seeded, chopped
2 carrots, peeled and diced

½ tsp ground cinnamon
¼ tsp chili pepper
A pinch of salt
½ cup coconut milk
⅓ cup sour cream

DIRECTIONS

Melt butter on Sauté. Add onion and cook for 3 minutes until soft. Add in carrots, cinnamon, squash, salt, and chili pepper and stir-fry for 2 minutes until fragrant.

Add the stock to the vegetable mixture. Seal the lid and cook for 12 minutes on High Pressure.

Quick-release the Pressure.

Add soup to a food processor and puree to obtain a smooth consistency. Take the soup back to the cooker, stir in coconut milk until you get a consistent color. Serve hot with a dollop of sour cream.

Minestrone Soup

Serves: 6 | Ready in about: 25 min

INGREDIENTS

2 tbsp olive oil
1 onion, diced
1 cup celery, chopped
1 carrot, peeled and diced
1 green bell pepper, chopped
2 cloves garlic, minced
3 cups chicken broth
½ tsp dried parsley
½ tsp dried thyme
½ tsp dried oregano

½ tsp salt
¼ tsp ground black pepper
2 bay leaves
28 ounces canned diced tomatoes
6 ounces canned tomato paste
2 cups kale
14 ounces canned Navy beans, rinsed and drained
½ cup white rice
¼ cup Parmesan Cheese

DIRECTIONS

Warm olive oil on Sauté. Stir in carrot, celery and onion and cook for 5 to 6 minutes until soft. Add garlic and bell pepper and cook for 2 minutes as you stir until aromatic. Stir in pepper, thyme, stock, salt, parsley, oregano, tomatoes, bay leaves, and tomato paste to dissolve. Mix in rice.

Seal the lid and cook on High Pressure for 15 minutes. Do a quick release. Add kale to the liquid and stir. Use residual heat in slightly wilting the greens. Discard bay leaves. Stir in navy beans and serve topped with Parmesan Cheese.

Garden Vegetable Soup

Serves: 8 | Ready in about: 42 min

INGREDIENTS

2 tbsp olive oil
1 cup leeks, chopped
2 garlic cloves, minced
4 cups vegetable stock
1 carrot, diced
1 parsnip, diced
1 celery stalk, diced
1 cup mushrooms
1 cup broccoli florets

1 cup cauliflower florets
½ red bell pepper, diced
¼ head green cabbage, chopped
½ cup green beans
2 tbsp Nutritional yeast
½ tsp dried thyme
½ salt, or more to taste
½ tsp ground black pepper
½ cup fresh parsley, chopped

DIRECTIONS

Heat oil on Sauté. Add in garlic and onion and cook for 6 minutes until slightly browned. Add in stock, carrot, celery, broccoli, bell pepper, green beans, salt, Nutritional yeast, cabbage, cauliflower, mushrooms, potato, thyme, and pepper.

Seal the lid and cook on High Pressure for 6 minutes. Release pressure naturally, for about 5 minutes. Stir in parsley and serve.

Vietnamese Pork Soup

Serves: 4 | Ready in about: 40 min

INGREDIENTS

2 tbsp olive oil
2 yellow onions, halved
1 large piece fresh ginger, halved lengthwise
2 tsp fennel seeds
1 tsp red pepper flakes
½ tsp coriander seeds
10 black peppercorns

2-star anise
8 cups water
1 pound pork tenderloin, cut into thin strips
2 tsp salt
8 ounces rice noodles
1 Lime, cut into wedges
A handful of fresh cilantro leaves

DIRECTIONS

Warm oil on Sauté mode. Add ginger and onions and cook for 4 minutes. Add in flakes, fennel, anise, peppercorns, and coriander, and cook for 1 minute as you stir. Add water, salt, and pork into the pot.

Seal the lid and cook on High Pressure for 60 minutes. Release the pressure naturally for 10 minutes.

As the pho continues to cook, soak rice noodles in hot water for 8 minutes until softened and pliable; stop the cooking process by draining and rinsing with cold water. Separate the noodles into 4 soup plates.

Remove the pork from the cooker and ladle among bowls. Strain the broth to get rid of solids. Pour it over the pork and noodles; Season with red pepper flakes. Garnish with lime wedges and cilantro leaves.

Turkey Noodle Soup

Serves: 6 | Ready in about: 40 min

INGREDIENTS

1 tbsp olive oil
1 onion, minced
3 cloves garlic, minced
1 turnip, chopped
1 cup celery rib, chopped
1 tbsp dry basil

1 bay leaf
6 cups vegetable broth
1 pound turkey breasts, bone-in, skin on, cubed
8 ounces dry egg noodles
Salt and ground black pepper to taste

DIRECTIONS

Warm olive oil on Sauté. Stir-fry in garlic and onion, for 3 minutes until soft. Mix in celery, bay leaf, basil, and turnip.

Pour in 3 cups of broth and deglaze. Scrape any brown bits from the pan's bottom and add turkey. Seal the lid and cook on High Pressure for 10 minutes.

Naturally release the pressure for about 8 minutes. Transfer turkey breasts to another bowl. Do away with the skin and bones. Using two forks, shred the meat.

Set the cooker on Sauté. Transfer the turkey to the pot; add noodles and the remaining broth. Simmer for 10 minutes until noodles are done. Season to taste and serve.

Homemade Chicken Soup

Serves: 8 | Ready in about: 1hr 10 min

INGREDIENTS

1 ½ pounds chicken drumsticks, boneless
4 celery stalks 1 cup fennel bulb, chopped
2 onions, diced
2 carrots, diced
2 garlic cloves
3 parsley, chopped

2 bay leaves
Salt and ground black pepper to taste
½ cup matzo meal
2 eggs, beaten
2 tbsp canola oil
1 tsp baking powder

DIRECTIONS

In the pot, add drumsticks, bay leaves, onion, carrots, pepper, garlic, parsley, salt, and fennel. Add enough water such that ingredients are covered by 2 inches.

Seal the lid and cook for 30 minutes on High Pressure. Release pressure naturally, for about 10 minutes. Meanwhile, mix baking powder, eggs, oil, pepper, salt, and matzo meal, in a bowl. Use a plastic wrap to close the bowl and place in a fridge for 10 minutes.

Get rid of celery stalks. Transfer chicken to a cutting board, strip and shred it from the bones. Take back to the pot. Select Sauté and boil the soup. Roll matzo mixture into 1-inch balls and place in the boiling soup. Cook for 3 mins to heat through as you gently stir.

Cream of Pumpkin Chipotle Soup

Serves: 4 | Ready in about: 25 min

INGREDIENTS

1 tbsp olive oil
1 onion, chopped
2 chipotle peppers, seeded and finely minced
1 tsp ground black pepper
¼ tsp grated nutmeg
¼ tsp ground cloves

1 pinch ground cinnamon
1 large butternut pumpkin, cut into small pieces
4 cups vegetable broth
1 tsp salt
1 cup half-and-half

DIRECTIONS

Warm oil on Sauté and cook nutmeg, pepper, clove, cinnamon, and onion for 3 to 5 minutes, until translucent. Add pumpkin and cook for 5 minutes, stirring infrequently.

Pour in broth and add chipotle peppers and any remaining pumpkin.

Seal the lid and cook on High Pressure for 10 minutes. Release pressure quickly.

Stir in half-and-half and transfer to a blender to purée until you obtain a smooth consistency.

Cream of Mushroom and Spinach Soup

Serves: 4 | Ready in about: 25 min

INGREDIENTS

1 tbsp olive oil
8 Button Mushrooms, sliced
1 cup spinach, chopped
1 red onion, chopped
4 cups vegetable stock
2 sweet potatoes, peeled and chopped

2 tbsp white wine
1 tbsp dry Porcini mushrooms, soaked and drained
½ tsp sea salt
1 cup creme fraiche
½ tsp freshly ground black pepper

DIRECTIONS

Set on Sauté and add in olive oil and mushrooms. Sauté for 3 to 5 minutes until browning on both sides; Set aside. Add onion and spinach, and cook for 3 to 5 minutes until the onion becomes translucent.

Stir in chopped mushrooms, and cook for a further 5 minutes, stirring occasionally, until golden brown.

Pour in wine to deglaze the bottom of the pot, scrape to remove browned bits. Cook for 5 minutes until wine evaporates. Mix in the remaining mushrooms, potatoes, soaked mushrooms, wine, stock, and salt.

Seal the lid and cook on High Pressure for 5 minutes. Quick release the pressure. Add in pepper and creme fraiche to mix. Using an immersion blender, whizz the mixture until smooth. Stir in the sautéed mushrooms. Add reserved mushrooms for garnish before serving.

Cauliflower Cheese Soup

Serves: 5 | Ready in about: 20 min

INGREDIENTS

2 tbsp butter
½ tbsp olive oil
1 onion, chopped
2 stalks celery, chopped
1 large head cauliflower, cut into florets

1 potato, peeled and finely diced
3 cups vegetable broth
2 cups milk
1 bay leaf
4 ounces blue cheese

DIRECTIONS

Warm oil and butter on Sauté mode. Add celery and onion and sauté for 3-5 minutes, until fragrant. Stir in half the cauliflower and cook for 5 minutes until golden brown. Add in stock, bay leaf, and the remaining cauliflower.

Seal the lid and cook on High Pressure for 5 minutes. Release the pressure quickly.

Remove the bay leaf. Place the soup in an immersion blender, add in the milk and puree until smooth.

Spoon the soup into serving bowls and top with blue cheese before serving.

Mexican-Style Chicken Soup

Serves: 5 | Ready in about: 35 min

INGREDIENTS

5 boneless, skinless chicken thighs
5 cups chicken broth
14 ounces canned whole tomatoes, chopped
2 jalapeno peppers, stemmed, cored, and chopped
2 tbsp tomato puree
3 cloves garlic, minced
1 tbsp chili powder

1 tbsp ground cumin
½ tsp dried oregano
1 (14.5 ounces) can black beans, rinsed and drained
2 cups frozen corn kernels, thawed
Crushed tortilla chips for garnish
¼ cup Cheddar cheese, shredded for garnish
fresh cilantro, chopped for garnish

DIRECTIONS

Add chicken, oregano, garlic, tomato puree, stock, cumin, tomatoes, chili, and jalapeno peppers.

Seal the lid and cook on High Pressure for 10 minutes.

Once cooking is done, Release the pressure quickly. Transfer the chicken to a plate. On Sauté mode; cook corn and black beans. Shred the chicken with a pair of forks, and return to the pot, stirring well.

Select Keep Warm and simmer the soup for 5 minutes until heated through. Divide in serving plates; add a topping of cilantro, shredded cheese, and crushed tortilla chips.

Tomato Soup with Cheese Croutons

Serves: 6 | Ready in about: 1hr

INGREDIENTS

2 tbsp olive oil
1 onion, chopped
1 carrot, peeled and chopped
1 garlic clove, minced
Salt and ground black pepper to taste
1 cup vegetable stock
28 ounces canned tomatoes

1 cup heavy cream
4 Monterey Jack cheese, sliced
4 bread slices
2 Gouda cheese, sliced
4 tbsp butter, at room temperature
2 tbsp parsley, finely chopped

DIRECTIONS

Warm oil on Sauté. Stir-fry garlic, onion, carrot, pepper and salt for 6 minutes until soft. In the pot, add vegetable stock to deglaze. Scrape any brown bits from the pot.

Mix the stock with tomatoes. Seal the lid and cook on High Pressure for 30 minutes.

Allow for a natural release, for about 10 minutes. Transfer soup to a blender and process until smooth.

Add in heavy cream and stir; add pepper and salt for seasoning.

Place 2 slices Monterey Jack cheese onto 1 bread slice and cover with 1 Gouda cheese slice and the second slice of bread. Spread a tablespoon of butter and parsley over the top. Do the same with the rest of the cheese, bread, parsley, and butter.

Over medium heat, heat a skillet. With butter sides down, place the sandwiches on the skillet. Spread 1 tbsp butter on top of each sandwich. Cook each side for 3 to 5 minutes until browned and all cheese melt.

Transfer sandwiches to a cutting board and chop into bite-sized pieces.

Divide the soup into serving plates and apply a top with parsley cheese croutons before serving.

Ramen Spicy Soup with Collard Greens

Serves: 4 | Ready in about: 20 min

INGREDIENTS

1 tbsp olive oil
½ tsp ground ginger
2 tbsp garlic, minced
6 cups chicken broth stock
2 tbsp soy sauce
1 tbsp chili powder

1 cup mushrooms, chopped
10 ounces ramen noodles
1 (1-pound) package fresh collard greens, trimmed
A bunch of fresh cilantro, chopped to serve
1 red chilli, chopped to serve

DIRECTIONS

On Sauté, warm oil, stir in garlic and ginger and cook for 2 minutes until soft. Add stock, mix in chili powder, ramen noodles and soy sauce.

Seal the lid and cook on High Pressure for 10 minutes. Release pressure quickly. Stir in collard greens until wilted. Ladle the soup into serving bowls and add red chili and cilantro to serve.

Leek and Potato Soup with Sour Cream

Serves: 5 | Ready in about: 30 min

INGREDIENTS

2 tbsp butter
3 leeks, white part only, thinly sliced
2 cloves garlic, minced
4 cups vegetable broth
3 potatoes, peeled and cubed

½ cup sour cream
2 tbsp rosemary
2 bay leaves
Salt and ground black pepper to taste
2 tbsp fresh chives, to garnish

DIRECTIONS

Melt butter on Sauté mode. Stir in garlic and leeks and cook for 3 to 4 minutes, until soft. Stir in bay leaves, potatoes, and broth. Seal the lid and cook on High Pressure for 15 minutes. Release pressure quickly. Remove the bay leaves and cobs and discard.

Transfer soup to immersion blender and puree soup to obtain a smooth consistency. Season with salt and pepper. Top with diced chives and sour cream.

Butternut Squash Curry

Serves: 5 | Ready in about: 30 min

INGREDIENTS

1½ pounds butternut squash, roughly chopped
4 cups chicken stock
½ cup buttermilk
4 spring onions, chopped into lengths
2 tbsp curry powder
1½ tsp ground turmeric

1½ tsp ground cumin
¼ tsp cayenne pepper, or more to taste
2 bay leaves
Salt and ground black pepper, to taste
A bunch of cilantro leaves, chopped

DIRECTIONS

In the pot, stir in squash, buttermilk, curry, turmeric, spring onions, stock, cumin, and cayenne. Season with pepper and salt. Add bay leaves to the liquid and ensure they are submerged.

Seal the lid, press Soup/Broth and cook for 10 minutes on High. Naturally release the pressure for 10 minutes. Discard bay leaves. Transfer the soup to a blender and process until smooth.

Use a fine-mesh strainer to strain the soup. Divide into plates and garnish with cilantro before serving.

Hearty Winter Vegetable Soup

Serves: 5 | Ready in about: 30 min

INGREDIENTS

2 tbsp olive oil
1 onion, chopped
2 carrots, peeled and chopped
1 cup celery, chopped
2 cloves garlic, minced
5 cups chicken broth
2 turnips, peeled and chopped

28 ounces canned tomatoes
15 oz canned garbanzo beans, rinsed and drained
1 cup frozen green peas
2 bay leaves
1 sprig fresh sage
Salt and ground black pepper to taste
¼ cup Parmesan Cheese, grated

DIRECTIONS

On Sauté, warm oil, stir in celery, carrots, and onion and cook for 4 minutes until soft. Add in garlic and cook for 30 seconds until crispy.

Add vegetable broth, parsnip, garbanzo beans, bay leaves, tomatoes, pepper, salt, peas, and sage.

Seal the lid and cook on High Pressure for 12 minutes.

Allow natural pressure release, for about 5 minutes. Serve topped with Parmesan cheese.

Spicy Borscht Soup

Serves: 4 | Ready in about: 30 min

INGREDIENTS

2 tbsp olive oil
1 cup leeks, chopped
1 tsp garlic, smashed
2 beets, peeled and diced
1 tbsp cayenne pepper, finely minced
1 dried habanero pepper, crushed

4 cups beef stock
3 cups white cabbage, shredded
1 tsp salt
2 tsp red wine apple cider vinegar
¼ tsp paprika
Greek yogurt for garnish

DIRECTIONS

Warm oil on Sauté. Stir in garlic and leeks and cook for 5 minutes until soft. Mix in, stock, paprika, salt, peppers, vinegar, beets, white cabbage, cayenne pepper, and crushed red pepper.

Seal the lid and cook on High Pressure for 20 minutes. Do a quick release. Place in serving bowls and top with Greek yogurt to serve.

Two-Bean Zucchini Soup

Serves: 5 | Ready in about: 35 min

INGREDIENTS

1 tbsp olive oil
1 onion, chopped
2 cloves garlic, minced
5 cups vegetable broth
1 cup dried chickpeas
½ cup dried pinto beans, soaked overnight

½ cup dried navy beans, soaked overnight
3 carrots, chopped
1 large celery stalk, chopped
1 tsp dried thyme
16 oz zucchini noodles
Sea Salt and ground black pepper, to taste

DIRECTIONS

Warm oil on Sauté. Stir in garlic and onion and cook for 5 minutes until golden brown. Mix in pepper, broth, carrots, salt, celery, beans, and thyme.

Seal the lid and cook for 15 minutes on High Pressure. Release the pressure naturally for 10 minutes.

Mix zucchini noodles into the soup and stir until wilted. Taste and adjust the seasoning.

Creamy Quinoa & Mushroom Soup

Serves: 4 | Ready in about: 20 min

INGREDIENTS

4 cups vegetable broth
1 carrot, peeled and chopped
1 stalk celery, diced
2 cups quinoa, rinsed
1 cup mushrooms, chopped
1 onion, chopped

2 garlic cloves, smashed
1 tsp salt
½ tsp dried thyme
3 tbsp butter
½ cup heavy cream

DIRECTIONS

Melt the butter on Sauté. Add onion, garlic, celery, and carrot, and cook for 8 minutes until tender. Mix in broth, thyme, quinoa, mushrooms, and salt.

Seal the lid and cook on High Pressure for 10 minutes. Release pressure quickly. Stir in heavy cream. Cook for 2 minutes to obtain a creamy consistency. Serve warm.

Acorn Squash Soup with Coconut Milk

Serves: 6 | Ready in about: 1hr

INGREDIENTS

1 tbsp olive oil
1 onion, diced
1 stalk celery, diced
1 large carrot, diced
½ tsp salt
2 garlic cloves, minced

1 pound acorn squash, peeled diced
6 cups chicken stock
Juice from 1 lemon
1 cup coconut milk
Salt and freshly ground black pepper
2 tbsp cilantro leaves, chopped

DIRECTIONS

Heat oil on Sauté and stir-fry carrot, celery, garlic, salt, and onion, for 4 to 5 minutes until soft. Mix acorn squash with the vegetables; cook for 1 more minute until tender.

Seal the lid and cook on High Pressure for 20 minutes. Release pressure naturally, for about 10 minutes.

Add in lemon juice and coconut milk and stir. Transfer the soup to a blender and process until smooth. Divide soup into serving plates. Garnish with cilantro, black pepper, and yogurt.

Red Lentils Soup with Tortilla Topping

Serves: 6 | Ready in about: 50 min

INGREDIENTS

2 ½ cups vegetable broth
1 ½ cups tomato sauce
1 onion, chopped
1 cup dry red lentils
½ cup prepared salsa verde
2 garlic cloves, minced

1 tbsp smoked paprika
2 tsp ground cumin
1 tsp chili powder
¼ tsp cayenne pepper
Salt and ground black pepper to taste
Crushed tortilla chips for garnish

DIRECTIONS

Add in tomato sauce, broth, onion, salsa verde, cumin, cayenne pepper, chili powder, garlic, lentils, paprika, salt, and pepper. Seal the lid and cook for 20 minutes on High Pressure.

Release pressure naturally, for 10 minutes. Divide into serving bowls and add crushed tortilla topping.

Vegetarian Black Bean Soup

Serves: 6 | Ready in about: 30 min

INGREDIENTS

1 tsp olive oil
1 onion, chopped
2 celery stalks, chopped
3 carrots, chopped
2 serrano peppers, deseeded and chopped
5 cups vegetable broth

30 ounces canned diced tomatoes
1 can black beans, rinsed and drained
¼ cup chopped fresh cilantro
2 tsp ground cumin
1 tsp fine sea salt
freshly ground black pepper to taste

DIRECTIONS

Warm oil on Sauté. Add in carrots, onion, jalapeño peppers, and celery and cook for 6 to 7 minutes until soft. Mix in water, sea salt, black beans, cumin, tomatoes, cilantro, and black pepper.

Seal the lid and cook for 8 minutes on High Pressure. Release pressure naturally, or 10 minutes.

Classic Swiss Onion Soup

Serves: 8 | Ready in about: 45 min

INGREDIENTS

2 tbsp butter
8 cups onions
½ cup water
2 tbsp sugar
1 tsp salt
½ tsp ground black pepper

½ cup dry white wine
4 cups beef stock
2 sprigs fresh thyme
2 bay leaves
4 baguette slices
1 cup Swiss cheese, shredded

DIRECTIONS

Melt butter on Sauté. Add in onions and cook for 3 to 5 minutes until soft. Add water, pepper, sugar, and salt, and pepper as you stir. Seal the lid, press Poultry, and cook for 15 minutes on High.

Do a quick release. Add beef stock, bay leaves and thyme sprigs into the pot. Seal the lid cook for 4 minutes on High Pressure. Quick-release Pressure. Discard the bay leaves and thyme. Preheat the oven's broiler.

Divide into four soup bowls. Top with ¼ cup Gruyere cheese and 1 baguette slice.

Transfer the bowls to a baking sheet and cook for 2-4 minutes under the broiler until golden brown.

Chicken & Farro Soup

Serves: 6 | Ready in about: 1hr

INGREDIENTS

1 tbsp olive oil
4 boneless, skinless chicken thighs
¼ cup white wine
1 cup farro
1 large onion, chopped
2 celery stalks, cut into squares

3 large carrots, chopped
1 tsp garlic powder
1 tsp ground cumin
1 bay leaf
6 cups chicken broth
2 tsp fresh parsley leaves to garnish

DIRECTIONS

Warm oil on Sauté. Brown the chicken on all sides, for 6 minutes. Transfer the beef to a bowl. Into the pot, add wine to deglaze, scraping any brown bits present at the bottom of the cooker.

Mix the wine with farro, cumin, stock, onion, carrots, celery, garlic powder, and bay leaf. Seal the lid, press Meat/Stew and cook on High for 20 minutes.

Release pressure naturally for about 10 minutes. Divide into serving plates and add parsley for garnish.

Fire-Roasted Tomato and Chorizo Soup

Serves: 6 | Ready in about: 30 min

INGREDIENTS

1 tbsp olive oil
2 shallots, chopped
3 cloves garlic, minced
1 tsp salt
4 cups beef broth
28 ounces fire-roasted diced tomatoes

½ cup fresh ripe tomatoes
½ cup raw cashews
1 tbsp red wine vinegar
3 chorizo sausage, chopped
½ tsp ground black pepper
½ cup chopped fresh basil

DIRECTIONS

Warn oil on Sauté and cook chorizo until crispy. Remove to a to a plate lined with paper towel.

Add in garlic and onion and cook for 5 minutes until soft. Season with salt. Stir in red wine vinegar, broth, diced tomatoes, cashews, sun-dried tomatoes, and black pepper into the cooker.

Seal the lid and cook on High Pressure for 8 minutes. Release the ´pressure quickly. Pour the soup into a blender and process until smooth. Divide into bowls, top with chorizo and decorate with basil.

Chicken Broth

Serves: 16 | Ready in about: 50 min

INGREDIENTS

2 pounds chicken carcasses
4 carrots, cut into chunks
1 cup leeks, chopped
1 onion, quartered
1 cup celery, chopped

2 large garlic cloves
1 bunch fresh parsley
Salt to taste
10 peppercorns
2 bay leaves

DIRECTIONS

Add chicken, onion, pepper, celery, carrots, garlic, parsley, and bay leaves. Cover with water. Seal the lid and cook for 30 minutes on High Pressure. Release the pressure quickly.

Use a colander to drain the broth and do away with solids. Allow the broth to cool for about an hour,.

Beef Neck Bone Stock

Serves: 8 | Ready in about: 2hr 10 min

INGREDIENTS

1 carrot, chopped
2 onions, chopped
2 cups celery, chopped
2 pounds Beef Neck Bones
12 cups water, or more

1 tsp cider vinegar
2 bay leaves
10 peppercorns
Salt to taste

DIRECTIONS

Add carrot, ginger, vinegar, onion, and beef bones. Add enough water to cover ingredients. Seal the lid and cook on High Pressure for 120 minutes. Release pressure naturally for about 20 minutes.

Remove the bones and bay leaves, and discard. Use a fine-mesh strainer to strain the liquid. Allow the broth to cool. From the surface, skim fat and throw away. Refrigerate for a maximum of 7 days.

Flavorful Vegetable Stock

Serves: 10 | Ready in about: 55 min

INGREDIENTS

2 onions, chopped
2 cups celery, chopped
2 carrots, chopped
4 garlic cloves
1 cup kale
1 cup bell pepper, chopped

A handful of rosemary
A handful of parsley
10 peppercorns
2 bay leaves
Salt to taste
8 cups cold water, filtered

DIRECTIONS

Add onions, carrots, parsley, bay leaves, garlic, kale, celery, rosemary, and peppercorns. Cover with cold water. Seal the lid and cook on High Pressure for 15 minutes.

Do a natural release for 15 minutes. Use a wide and shallow bowl to hold the stock you strain through a fine-mesh strainer. Let cool to room temperature. Seal into jars and refrigerate for an up to 14 days.

Perfect Chicken Wings Broth

Serves: 8 | Ready in about: 1hr 30 min

INGREDIENTS

2 pounds chicken wings
4 spring onions, diced
2 large carrots, diced
4 cloves garlic

1 small handful fresh parsley
1 small handful fresh thyme
1 bay leaf
6 cups water

DIRECTIONS

Add chicken, carrots, parsley, thyme, onions, garlic, and bay leaf. Pour in water. Seal the lid and cook on High Pressure for 45 minutes.

Release pressure naturally, for about 10 minutes. Use a fine-mesh strainer to strain the broth and allow to cool to room temperature. Transfer the broth to containers and seal. Refrigerate for up to a week.

Spicy Beef Broth

Serves: 8 | Ready in about: 1hr 10 min

INGREDIENTS

2 pounds beef stew meat
2 leeks, chopped
1 onion, chopped
2 cups celery, chopped
2 red chilies, deseeded and chopped
2 carrots, chopped

1 tsp fresh ginger, grated
4 garlic cloves
8 cups water
1 tsp cider vinegar
Salt to taste

DIRECTIONS

In the pot, mix meat, celery, garlic carrots, leeks, onion, red chilies, and ginger. Top with vinegar and water. Seal the lid and cook on High Pressure for 45 minutes. Release pressure naturally for 10 minutes.

Use a fine-mesh strainer to strain the broth into a bowl; add season with salt. Store in sealable containers.

Basic Applesauce with Cinnamon

Serves: 4 | Ready in about: 45 min

INGREDIENTS

4 apples, cored, sliced
½ cup water

1 tsp ground cinnamon
1 tsp honey

DIRECTIONS

Add apples, cinnamon, water, and honey. Seal the lid and cook on High Pressure for 4 minutes. Release pressure naturally, for 10 minutes.

If you desire a chunky blend, stir vigorously. For smooth applesauce, puree the mixture in a blender.

Allow to cool before transferring in containers for storage.

Traditional Bolognese Sauce

Serves: 8 | Ready in about: 45 min

INGREDIENTS

4 slices bacon, chopped
1 tbsp olive oil
1 onion, minced
2 celery stalks, minced
1 carrot, chopped
1½ pounds ground beef

3 tbsp red wine
28 ounces italian canned tomatoes, crushed
2 bay leaves
Salt and pepper to taste
½ cup yogurt
¼ cup chopped fresh basil

DIRECTIONS

Set on Sauté, and cook bacon until crispy, for 4 to 5 minutes. Mix in celery, butter, carrots, and onion, and continue cooking for about 5 minutes until vegetables are softened.

Mix in ¼ teaspoon pepper, ½ teaspoon salt, and beef, and cook for 4 minutes until golden brown. Stir in the wine and allow to soak, approximately 4 more minutes.

Add in bay leaves, tomatoes, and remaining pepper and salt. Seal the lid and cook for 15 minutes on High Pressure. Release pressure naturally, for 10 minutes. Add yogurt and stir. Serve alongside noodles and use basil to garnish.

Favorite Chicken Soup

Serves: 4 | Ready in about: 40 min

INGREDIENTS

1 lb chicken breast, boneless, skinless, chopped
1 onion, chopped
1 carrot, chopped
2 small potatoes, peeled, chopped
1 tsp cayenne pepper

2 egg yolks
1 tsp salt
3 tbsp lemon juice
3 tbsp olive oil
4 cups water

DIRECTIONS

Add all ingredients to the pot, and seal the lid. Set the steam release handle and cook on Soup/Broth mode for 20 minutes on High. Release the pressure naturally, for 10 minutes.

Spicy Pork Soup

Serves: 4 | Ready in about: 65 min

INGREDIENTS

1.5 lb pork ribs
1 large leek, chopped into bite-sized pieces
1 onion, chopped
1 cup celery root, diced
½ cup parsley, chopped
4 cups beef broth

1 tsp salt
¼ tsp chili flakes
2 bay leaves
A handful of fresh basil, torn
3 tbsp oil

DIRECTIONS

Heat oil on Sauté. Add the ribs in batches and brown on all sides, for 5-6 minutes. Add the remaining ingredients. Seal the lid and cook on Meat/Stew mode on High for 30 minutes. Do a quick release.

Garlic Pork Chop Soup

Serves: 4 | Ready in about: 60 min

INGREDIENTS

2 (8-ounces) pork chops, with bones
1 tbsp cayenne pepper
1 tsp chili powder
½ tsp garlic powder
2 bay leaves
4 cups beef broth
2 tbsp oil

2 large carrots, chopped
2 celery stalks, diced
2 onions, diced
2 tbsp flour
2 tbsp soy sauce
3 tbsp butter

DIRECTIONS

Grease the stainless steel pot with oil and stir-fry the onions, until translucent on Sauté mode. Add celery stalks, carrots, cayenne, and chili pepper. Give it a good stir and continue to cook for 6-7 minutes.

Press Cancel and add pork chops, garlic, bay leaves, and soy sauce. Pour in the broth and seal the lid. Cook on Manual/Pressure Cook mode for 35 minutes on High. Do a quick release. Let chill for 5 minutes.

Broccoli and Carrot Chowder

Serves: 4 | Ready in about: 35 min

INGREDIENTS

1 head broccoli, finely chopped
1 carrot, chopped
2 tbsp sesame oil
1 onion, peeled, chopped
2 garlic cloves

1 cup soy milk
2 cups vegetable broth
¼ cup crumbled, Seasoned tofu
A pinch salt

DIRECTIONS

Heat oil on Sauté. Add onion, garlic, and stir-fry for 2 minutes, or until translucent. Pour in broth, 1 cup of water, broccoli, and carrot. Seal the lid and cook on Manual/Pressure Cook mode for 5 minutes on High.

Do a quick release. Let chill for a while, and transfer to a food processor. Pulse until creamy.

Tomato & Rice Soup

Serves: 4 | Ready in about: 25 min

INGREDIENTS

1 cup tomato puree
¼ cup rice
¼ tsp salt

2 tbsp olive oil
4 cups vegetable broth

DIRECTIONS

Add all ingredients to the pot and seal the lid. Set the steam release handle and cook on Soup/Broth mode for 30 minutes on High Pressure. Release the pressure naturally, for about 10 minutes.

Broccoli and Potato Soup

Serves: 4 | Ready in about: 45 min

INGREDIENTS

1 lb broccoli, cut into florets
2 potatoes, peeled, chopped
4 cups vegetable broth

½ tsp dried rosemary
½ tsp salt
½ cup sour cream

DIRECTIONS

Place broccoli and potatoes in the pot. Pour the broth and seal the lid. Cook on Soup/Broth for 20 minutes on High. Do a quick release and remove to a blender. Pulse to combine. Stir in sour cream and add salt.

Quick Chicken Rice Soup

Serves: 4 | Ready in about: 20 min

INGREDIENTS

1 lb chicken breast, skinless, cut into pieces
1 large carrot, chopped
1 onion, chopped
¼ cup rice
1 potato, finely chopped

½ tsp salt
1 tsp cayenne pepper
A handful of parsley, finely chopped
3 tbsp olive oil
4 cups chicken broth

DIRECTIONS

Add all ingredients, except parsley, to the pot, and seal the lid. Cook on Soup/Broth for 15 minutes on High. Do a quick pressure release. Stir in fresh parsley and serve.

Turkey Soup with Carrots & Cilantro

Serves: 4 | Ready in about: 55 min

INGREDIENTS

6 oz turkey breast, cut into bite-sized pieces
4 cups chicken broth
1 onion, chopped
3 large carrots, chopped

1 tsp salt
¼ tsp freshly ground white pepper
1 tbsp cilantro, finely chopped

DIRECTIONS

Add all ingredients in the pot. Seal the lid and set the steam release handle. Press Manual/Pressure Cook and cook for 35 minutes on HIgh. Release the pressure naturally for 10 minutes and serve immediately.

Potato & Cauliflower Soup

Serves: 4 | Ready in about: 50 min

INGREDIENTS

1 lb cauliflower, chopped into florets
1 potato, chopped
4 cups chicken broth
A handful of fresh parsley, finely chopped
½ tsp salt

¼ tsp pepper
¼ cup cooking cream
¼ cup sour cream
1 cup milk

DIRECTIONS

Add the veggies to the pot and pour broth. Seal the lid and set the steam release handle. Cook on High pressure for 20 minutes. Do a quick release. Let chill and transfer to a blender. Pulse until well- combined.

Carrot Soup with Rosemary

Serves: 3 | Ready in about: 22 min

INGREDIENTS

4 carrots, chopped
3 cups vegetable broth
1 tbsp butter

½ tsp dried rosemary
½ tsp salt

DIRECTIONS

Add all ingredients to the pot. Seal the lid and cook on Manual/Pressure Cook for 12 minutes on High. Do a natural release, for 10 minutes. Transfer to a food processor and pulse until creamy. Serve warm.

Fall Soup

Serves: 4 | Ready in about: 34 min

INGREDIENTS

3 sweet potatoes, chopped
1 tsp sea salt
2 fennel bulb, chopped
16 oz pureed pumpkin

1 large onion, chopped
1 tbsp coconut oil
4 cups water
1 tbsp sour cream

DIRECTIONS

Heat the oil on Sauté, and add onion and fennel bulb. Cook for 3-5 minutes, until tender and translucent. Add the remaining ingredients and seal the lid. Cook on High pressure for 25 minutes. Do a quick release, transfer the soup to a blender and blend for 20 seconds until creamy. Top with sour cream and serve.

Avocado & Sweet Corn Soup

Serves: 3 | Ready in about: 25 min

INGREDIENTS

1 large, ripe avocado
2 tbsp lemon juice
1 tbsp vegetable oil
4 oz canned sweet corn, drained
2 tomatoes, skinned and deseeded
1 garlic clove, crushed

1 leek, chopped
1 red chili, chopped
14 oz vegetable stock
4 oz soy milk
Shredded leek, to garnish

DIRECTIONS

Peel the avocado and mash the flesh with a fork. Stir in the lemon juice and reserve until required. Heat the oil on Sauté and add corn, tomatoes, garlic, leek, and chili. Stir-fry for 4-5 minutes, until softened.

Put half of the vegetable mixture in a food processor, add the mashed avocado and process until smooth. Transfer the contents to the instant pot. Pour in stock, soy milk, and reserved vegetables, and seal the lid.

Cook on Manual/Pressure Cook mode for 4 minutes on High. Once ready, press Cancel and release the steam naturally, for about 5 minutes. Garnish with shredded leek and serve immediately.

Spicy Parsnip Soup

Serves: 4 | Ready in about: 15 min

INGREDIENTS

2 tbsp vegetable oil
1 red onion, finely chopped
3 parsnips, chopped
2 garlic cloves, crushed
2 tsp garam masala
½ tsp chili powder

1 tbsp plain flour
4 cups vegetable stock
1 whole lemon, juiced
1 tsp salt
½ tsp black pepper, ground
Strips of lemon rind, to garnish

DIRECTIONS

Heat oil on Sauté, and stir-fry onion, parsnips and garlic for 5 minutes, or until soft but not changed color. Stir in garam masala and chili powder and cook for 30 seconds. Stir in flour, for another 30 seconds.

Pour in stock, lemon rind and lemon juice, and seal the lid. Cook on Manual/Pressure Cook for 5 minutes on High. Do a quick release, remove a third of the vegetable pieces with a slotted spoon and reserve.

Process the remaining soup and vegetables in a food processor for about 1 minute, to a smooth puree. Return to the pot, and stir in the reserved vegetables. Press Keep Warm and heat the soup for 2 minutes until piping hot. Season with salt and pepper, then ladle into bowls. Garnish with strips of lemon, to serve.

Creamy Bean Soup

Serves: 3 | Ready in about: 20 min

INGREDIENTS

1 tbsp canned beans, pre-cooked
3 cups beef broth
1 potato, chopped
½ cup heavy cream

¼ tsp sea salt
1 tsp black pepper, ground
1 tsp garlic powder

DIRECTIONS

Add all ingredients to the pot, seal the lid and cook on Manual/Pressure mode for 10 minutes on High. Release the steam naturally, for 10 minutes. Transfer to a blender. Pulse until smooth.

Return the soup to the clean stainless steel insert. Press Sauté and add a half cup of water. Cook for 5 more minutes, or until desired thickness. Let it chill uncovered for a while before serving.

Quick Beef Soup

Serves: 4 | Ready in about: 40 min

INGREDIENTS

1.5 lb lean beef, cut into bite-sized pieces
1 onion, peeled and cups
2 carrots, chopped
1 tsp cayenne pepper

¼ tsp black pepper, crushed
1 garlic clove, crushed
1 tbsp butter
4 cups water

DIRECTIONS

Melt butter on Sauté. Add onions and garlic, and stir-fry for 3 minutes, or until translucent. Add carrots and spices. Cook for 2 more minutes. Add the meat and pour in water.

Seal the lid and cook on Manual/Pressure Cook for 35 minutes on High. Release the pressure quickly.

Vichyssoise with Tofu

Serves: 4 | Ready in about: 25 min

INGREDIENTS

3 large leeks
3 tbsp butter
1 onion, chopped
1 lb potatoes, chopped
5 cups vegetable stock
2 tsp lemon juice

¼ tsp nutmeg
¼ tsp ground coriander
1 bay leaf
5 fl oz silken tofu
Salt and white pepper
Freshly snipped chives, to garnish

DIRECTIONS

Remove most of the green parts of the leeks. Slice the white parts finely. Melt butter on Sauté, and stir-fry leeks and onion for 5 minutes. Add potatoes, stock, juice, nutmeg, coriander and bay leaf. Season to taste with salt and pepper, and seal the lid. Press Manual/Pressure Cook for 10 on High.

Do a quick release and discard the bay leaf. Process the soup in a food processor until smooth. Season to taste, add silken tofu. Serve the soup sprinkled with freshly snipped chives.

Vegan Chili Beans

Serves: 4 | Ready in about: 45 min

INGREDIENTS

14.5 oz canned red kidney beans, rinsed

14.5 oz canned tomatoes
2 tbsp oil
4 cups water
2 cloves garlic, crushed

2 small fresh red chilies, finely chopped
1 green bell pepper, diced
½ cup (4 oz) tomato sauce

DIRECTIONS

Heat oil on Sauté, and stir-fry garlic, chili, and onion for 3 minutes, or until translucent. Add the remaining ingredients and seal the lid. Cook on Manual/Pressure Cook mode for 25 minutes on High Pressure.

Press Cancel and release the steam naturally, for 10 minutes and serve immediately.

Spring Lamb & Spinach Soup

Serves: 5 | Ready in about: 50 min

INGREDIENTS

1 lb of lamb shoulder, cut into bite-sized pieces
10 oz fresh spinach leaves, chopped
3 eggs, beaten

5 cups vegetable broth
3 tbsp olive oil
1 tsp salt

DIRECTIONS

Place in your instant pot along with the remaining ingredients. Seal the lid, press Soup/Broth and cook for 30 minutes on High Pressure. Do a natural pressure release, for about 10 minutes.

Pumpkin Soup

Serves: 4 | Ready in about: 35 min

INGREDIENTS

1.5 lb pumpkin, pureed
1 onion, peeled and chopped
4 cups vegetable broth
1 tbsp ground turmeric

½ tbsp double cream
½ tsp salt
A handful of fresh parsley
3 tbsp olive oil

DIRECTIONS

Add onion, pumpkin, turmeric, salt, and oil to your instant pot. Pour in broth and stir well. Seal the lid and adjust the steam release handle. Press Soup/Broth and cook for 30 minutes on High. Do a quick release.

With an immersion blender, blend until smooth. Stir in cream and top with freshly chopped parsley.

Power Green Soup

Serves: 3 | Ready in about: 35 min

INGREDIENTS

1 lb fresh brussels sprouts, rinsed, halved, chopped
6 oz fresh baby spinach, rinsed, torn, chopped
1 tsp sea salt
1 tbsp whole milk

3 tbsp sour cream
1 tbsp fresh celery, chopped
3 cups water
1 tbsp butter

DIRECTIONS

Add all ingredients to the instant pot. Seal the lid and set the steam release. Press Soup/Broth and cook for 30 minutes on High. Do a quick release. Transfer to a food processor. and blend well to combine.

Chicken Noodle Soup

Serves: 4 | Ready in about: 40 min

INGREDIENTS

1 lb chicken fillets, cut into bite-sized pieces
½ cup egg noodles
4 cups chicken broth

A handful of fresh parsley
1 tsp salt
¼ tsp black pepper, freshly ground

DIRECTIONS

Season the fillets with salt and place in the pot. Pour the broth and seal the lid. Cook on Soup/Broth for 20 minutes on High. Do a quick release. Add in the noodles and seal the lid again.

Press the Manual/Pressure Cook and cook for 5 minutes on High Pressure. Release the pressure quickly, and sprinkle with freshly ground black pepper and parsley. Serve warm.

Pomodoro Soup

Serves: 4 | Ready in about: 40 min

INGREDIENTS

2 lb tomatoes, diced
1 cup white beans, pre-cooked
1 small onion, diced
2 garlic cloves, crushed
1 cup heavy cream

1 cup vegetable broth
2 tbsp fresh parsley, finely chopped
¼ tsp black pepper, ground
2 tbsp extra virgin olive oil
½ tsp salt

DIRECTIONS

Warm oil on Sauté mode. Stir-fry onion and garlic on Sauté, for 2 minutes. Add tomatoes, beans, broth, 3 cups of water, parsley, salt, pepper, and a little bit of sugar to balance the bitterness.

Seal the lid and cook on Soup/Broth for 30 minutes on High Pressure. Release the pressure naturally, for 10 minutes. Top with a dollop of sour cream and chopped parsley, to serve.

Broccoli Gorgonzola Soup

Serves: 4 | Ready in about: 35 min

INGREDIENTS

8 oz Gorgonzola cheese, crumbled
1 cup broccoli, finely chopped
4 cups water
1 tbsp olive oil

½ cup full-fat milk
1 tbsp parsley, finely chopped
½ tsp salt
¼ tsp black pepper, ground

DIRECTIONS

Add all ingredients to the pot, seal the lid and cook on Soup/Broth mode for 30 minutes on High Pressure. Do a quick release. Remove the lid and sprinkle with fresh parsley. Serve warm.

Butternut Squash Leek Soup

Serves: 4 | Ready in about: 35 min

INGREDIENTS

4 leeks, washed and trimmed
2 cups butternut squash, chopped
¼ tsp black pepper, ground
1 tsp sea salt
1 tsp ginger, grated

1 garlic clove, crushed
4 cups vegetable broth
2 tbsp olive oil
1 tsp cumin
1 tsp ginger powder

DIRECTIONS

Stir-fry leeks and garlic for about 5 minutes, on Sauté. Add ginger powder and cumin. Give it a good stir and continue to cook for 1 more minute. Pour in the remaining ingredients and seal the lid. Cook on Soup/Broth mode for 10 minutes on High. Release the pressure naturally, for about 10 minutes.

Easy Lentil Soup with Tomatoes

Serves: 4 | Ready in about: 17 min

INGREDIENTS

2 cups red lentils, soaked overnight
1 carrot, cut into thin slices
3 tbsp tomato paste
3 garlic cloves, crushed
4 cups vegetable broth
2 tomatoes, wedged

2 tbsp parsley, roughly chopped
1 onion, diced
½ tsp dried thyme, ground
½ tsp cumin, ground
1 tsp salt
¼ tsp black pepper, ground

DIRECTIONS

Add all ingredients to the pot. Seal the lid and cook on High pressure for 7 minutes. Do a quick release.

Spring Vegetable Soup with Wax Beans

Serves: 4 | Ready in about: 18 min

INGREDIENTS

1 cup green peas
1 carrot, peeled, chopped
2 red bell pepper, seeds removed, chopped
1 cup wax beans, cut into bite-sized pieces
1 tomato, roughly chopped
2 cups vegetable broth

2 cups water
2 tbsp olive oil
1 tsp salt
½ tsp freshly ground black pepper
¼ tsp dried oregano, ground

DIRECTIONS

Stir in all ingredients in the pot. Seal the lid. Cook on High pressure for 8 minutes. Do a quick release.

Vegetable Soup

Serves: 4 | Ready in about: 22 min

INGREDIENTS

1 carrot, finely chopped
2 spring onions, finely chopped
1 red bell pepper, chopped, seeds removed
2 celery stalks, finely chopped
½ cup celery leaves, chopped
½ tsp dried thyme

2 tbsp butter
1 tsp vegetable oil
4 cups vegetable broth
1 cup milk
1 tsp salt
¼ tsp black pepper, freshly ground

DIRECTIONS

Melt butter on Sauté. Add carrot, onions, bell pepper, and celery. Cook for 5 minutes, stirring constantly. Pour in vegetable broth, seal the lid and cook on Manual/Pressure Cook mode for 5 minutes on High.

Do a quick release. Stir in all remaining ingredients and cook for 2-3 minutes, on Sauté. Serve warm.

Sweet Potato and Chili Soup

Serves: 2 | Ready in about: 20 min

INGREDIENTS

2 sweet potatoes, peeled and chopped
1 carrot, chopped
1 onion, chopped
2 cups chicken broth
2 garlic cloves, chopped

1 tsp salt
1 tbsp chilli flakes
½ tsp black pepper, freshly ground
1 tbsp olive oil

DIRECTIONS

Warm oil on Sauté, and stir-fry potatoes, onion, and garlic for 3-4 minutes. Stir in the remaining ingredients, seal the lid and cook on High pressure for 7 minutes. Do a natural release, for 10 minutes.

Bell Pepper & Lentil Soup

Serves: 4 | Ready in about: 35 min

INGREDIENTS

1 cup red lentils, soaked overnight, drained
1 red bell pepper, seeded and chopped
1 onion, peeled, chopped
½ cup carrot puree
½ tsp freshly ground black pepper

½ tsp cumin, ground
½ tsp salt
2 tbsp olive oil
A handful of parsley, to garnish

DIRECTIONS

Heat the oil on Sauté, add stir-fry the onions for 4 minutes. Add the remaining ingredients and pour in 4 cups of water. Seal the lid and cook on Soup/Broth mode for 30 minutes on High Pressure. Do a quick pressure release. Sprinkle with fresh parsley and serve warm.

Chickpea & Carrot Soup

Serves: 6 | Ready in about: 15 min

INGREDIENTS

14 oz chickpeas, soaked, rinsed, drained
2 carrots, chopped
2 onions, peeled, chopped
2 tomatoes, peeled, chopped
3 tbsp tomato paste

A handful of fresh chopped parsley
2 cups vegetable broth
2 tbsp olive oil
1 tsp salt

DIRECTIONS

Add in chickpeas, oil, onions, carrot, and tomatoes. Pour in the broth and sprinkle salt. Stir in the paste and seal the lid.

Cook on High Pressure for 6 minutes. Do a quick release and remove to a serving place. Sprinkle with freshly chopped parsley, to serve.

Cream of Broccoli and Potato Soup

Serves: 4 | Ready in about: 35 min

INGREDIENTS

⅓ cup butter
1 head broccoli, cut into florets
2 cloves garlic, minced
1 onion, chopped
2 ½ pounds potatoes, peeled and chopped

4 cups vegetable broth
½ cup heavy cream
Salt and freshly ground black pepper to taste
Cheddar cheese, grated for garnish
½ cup fresh chopped scallions, for garnish

DIRECTIONS

Melt butter on Sauté. Add onion and garlic and sauté for 5 minutes. Add in broth, potatoes, and broccoli, and mix well. Press Cancel.

Seal the lid and cook for 5 minutes on High Pressure. Release pressure naturally for 10 minutes. Transfer the potato mixture to a blender and blend until smooth.

Add in heavy cream and season with pepper and salt. Divide between bowls and top with cheese and scallions.

Quick Chicken Parsley Carrot Celery Soup

Serves: 4 | Ready in about: 10 min

INGREDIENTS

3 oz carrots, finely chopped
3 oz celery root, finely chopped
A handful of green peas, soaked
2 tbsp butter
2 tbsp fresh parsley, finely chopped
1 egg yolk

2 tbsp cream cheese
¼ cup freshly squeezed lemon juice
1 tsp salt
½ tsp pepper
4 cups beef broth plus one tbsp water

DIRECTIONS

Add all ingredients to the instant pot and seal the lid. Cook on High Pressure for 5 minutes. When done, release the steam naturally, for 10 minutes. Serve warm.

Creamy Asparagus Soup

Serves: 4 | Ready in about: 40 min

INGREDIENTS

2 lb fresh asparagus, trimmed, 1-inch thick
2 onions, peeled and finely chopped
1 cup heavy cream
4 cups vegetable broth
2 tbsp butter

1 tbsp vegetable oil
½ tsp salt
½ tsp dried oregano
½ tsp paprika

DIRECTIONS

Melt butter on Sauté, and add 1 tbsp of oil. Stir-fry the onions for 2 minutes, until translucent. Add asparagus, oregano, salt, and paprika. Stir well and cook until asparagus softens, for a few minutes.

Pour the broth and mix well to combine. Seal the lid and cook on Soup/Broth for 20 minutes on High. Do a quick release and whisk in 1 cup of heavy cream. Serve chilled or warm.

Quinoa Soup

Serves: 6 | Ready in about: 15 min

INGREDIENTS

1 tbsp canola oil
6 spring onions, chopped
2 garlic cloves, finely diced
1 carrot, chopped
2 celery stalks, chopped finely

2 chicken breasts, boneless, skinless, cut into bite-size chunks
6 cups chicken broth
1 cup quinoa
Salt and ground black pepper, to taste
2 tbsp chopped fresh parsley leaves

DIRECTIONS

Heat oil on Sauté. Add in celery, spring onion, garlic, and carrots. Cook for 5 minutes until tender. Add in chicken, quinoa, 1 tsp salt, broth, and black pepper.

Seal the lid, select Soup/Broth and cook for 15 minutes on High. Do a quick release, and add in parsley.

Homemade Vegetables Soup

Serves: 5 | Ready in about: 40 min

INGREDIENTS

2 tbsp olive oil
1 leek, chopped
2 cloves garlic, minced
2 carrots, diced
1 celery stalk, chopped
4 potatoes, quartered

1 red bell pepper, diced
¼ tsp red pepper flakes
Salt and pepper to taste
1 ½ cups vegetable stock
2 tbsp parsley

DIRECTIONS

Heat olive oil on Sauté. Add garlic and leek and sauté for 5 minutes. Add in red bell pepper, carrots, salt, potatoes, red pepper flakes, and pepper. Mix in vegetable stock.

Seal the lid and cook for 15 minutes on High Pressure. Release pressure naturally for 10 minutes. Add cilantro and coconut milk to the soup. Use an immersion blender to blitz the soup until smooth.

Sun-Dried Tomato Sauce

Serves: 4 | Ready in about: 15 min

INGREDIENTS

2 cups tomatoes, diced
½ cup tomato sauce
½ cup sun-dried tomatoes
1 medium onion, chopped
3 tbsp balsamic vinegar
3 garlic cloves, chopped

1 tsp dried oregano
½ tsp dried rosemary
1 tbsp olive oil
1 tsp sea salt
½ tsp ground black pepper

DIRECTIONS

Combine all ingredients in a mixing bowl and give it a good stir. Transfer to the instant pot and seal the lid. Cook on High Pressure for 6 minutes.

When done, remove to serving bowls and serve with pasta or rice.

Spinach Dip

Serves: 6 | Ready in about: 10 min

INGREDIENTS

2 cups cream cheese
1 cup baby spinach, rinsed, torn into pieces
1 cup mozzarella cheese
1 tsp Italian Seasoning mix

1 tsp black pepper, ground
½ cup scallions
1 cup vegetable broth

DIRECTIONS

Place all ingredients in a mixing bowl. Stir well and transfer to your instant pot. Seal the lid and cook on High Pressure for 5 minutes.

Release the steam naturally, for 10 minutes. Serve with celery sticks or chips.

Mexican Chili Dipping Sauce

Serves: 6 | Ready in about: 15 min

INGREDIENTS

1 cup sour cream
2 cups tomato sauce
½ tsp dried oregano, ground
1 cup cream cheese

1 tsp cayenne pepper, ground
½ tsp chili pepper, ground
½ tsp ground black pepper

DIRECTIONS

In a mixing bowl, add all ingredients and stir well to combine. Pour the mixture in the pot. Cook on High Pressure for 8 minutes.

When ready, do a natural pressure release, for 10 minutes. Transfer the dip into the serving bowl. Serve with carrots, celery, or tortilla chips.

Broccoli & Cheese Sauce

Serves: 4 | Ready in about: 15 min

INGREDIENTS

1 cup broccoli, chopped
1 cup cream cheese
1 cup cheddar cheese, shredded
3 cups chicken broth

1 tsp salt
½ tsp black pepper, ground
1 tsp garlic powder
2 tsp dried rosemary

DIRECTIONS

Mix all ingredients in a large bowl. Pour the mixture in the instant pot, seal the lid and cook on High Pressure for 8 minutes. Do a quick release. Store for up to 5 days.

Gorgonzola & Gruyere Carrot Sauce

Serves: 4 | Ready in about: 15 min

INGREDIENTS

1 carrot, shredded
1 cup cream cheese
½ cup gorgonzola cheese
3 cups vegetable broth

1 cup Gruyere cheese, crumbled
½ tsp black pepper, ground
1 tsp garlic powder
1 tbsp fresh parsley, finely chopped

DIRECTIONS

Combine all ingredients in a large bowl. Pour in the instant pot, seal the lid and cook on High Pressure for 8 minutes. Do a natural release, for 10 minutes. Store for up to 5 days.

Onion Gravy

Serves: 4 | Ready in about: 10 min

INGREDIENTS

1 onion, chopped
1 tsp onion powder
3 cups vegetable broth

2 cups cream cheese
2 tsp dried parsley, chopped
1 tbsp olive oil

DIRECTIONS

Heat oil on Sauté, and stir-fry the onions for 5 minutes, or until translucent.

Stir in the remaining ingredients. Seal the lid and cook on High Pressure for 5 minutes. Do a quick pressure release and serve immediately.

Bell Pepper Salsa

Serves: 3 | Ready in about: 15 min

INGREDIENTS

3 red bell peppers, seeds removed, chopped
1 cup cherry tomatoes, diced
1 onion, chopped
1 tsp garlic powder
½ cup sour cream

2 cups vegetable broth
1 tbsp balsamic vinegar
1 tbsp cayenne pepper
1 tsp salt

DIRECTIONS

Combine all ingredients in a mixing bowl. Add the mixture to the instant pot, seal the lid and cook on High Pressure for 6 minutes. Do a quick release.

Transfer to your food processor and purée until the mixture is smooth.

Parmesan Basil Sauce

Serves: 4 | Ready in about: 10 min

INGREDIENTS

1 cup fresh basil, torn
1 cup cream cheese
2 tbsp Parmesan Cheese, shredded
1 tbsp olive oil

½ tsp black pepper, ground
1 tsp salt
2 cups vegetable broth

DIRECTIONS

In a bowl, stir in all ingredients. Transfer the mixture to the instant pot. Seal the lid and cook on High Pressure for 5 minutes. Do a quick pressure release.

Goat Cheese & Tomato Sauce

Serves: 4 | Ready in about: 15 min

INGREDIENTS

1 cup goat cheese, crumbled
1 cup tomatoes, diced
3 tbsp tomato paste
1 onion, finely chopped

3 tbsp apple cider vinegar
3 garlic cloves, chopped
¼ cup mozzarella cheese
2 cups vegetable broth

DIRECTIONS

Add all ingredients to your instant pot, seal the lid and cook on High Pressure for 6 minutes. When done, press Cancel and do a quick pressure release.

Creamy Zucchini Sauce

Serves: 3 | Ready in about: 10 min

INGREDIENTS

1 zucchini, chopped
1 cup Greek yogurt
1 cup sour cream
1 tsp garlic powder

¼ cup shallots, minced
1 tbsp ground dried parsley
1 tsp salt
1 tsp ground black pepper

DIRECTIONS

In a bowl, mix zucchini, sour cream, garlic, shallots, parsley, salt, and pepper. Stir until well combined. Transfer the mixture to the pot, and seal the lid.

Cook on High Pressure for 3 minutes. Do a quick release. Remove the sauce to a bowl and stir in the yogurt. Serve chilled.

Orange Granberry Sauce

Serves: 4 | Ready in about: 15 min

INGREDIENTS

2 cups cranberries
1 tsp orange zest, freshly grated
½ cup orange juice, freshly juiced

¼ cup brown sugar
1 cup water
2 tbsp maple syrup

DIRECTIONS

Combine maple syrup, water, cranberries, and orange juice in the instant pot. Sprinkle with orange zest. Seal the lid, and cook on High Pressure for 5 minutes.

When done, release the pressure naturally, for about 10 minutes.

Press Sauté, add brown sugar and stir until thick sauce mixture is formed. Turn off the heat and transfer the sauce to the serving dish. Serve cold.

Napoli Sauce

Serves: 4 | Ready in about: 45 min

INGREDIENTS

1 lb mushrooms
2 cups canned tomatoes, diced
1 carrot, chopped
1 onion, chopped
1 celery stick, chopped
1 tbsp olive oil

2 garlic cloves
1 tsp salt
½ tsp paprika
1 tsp fish sauce
1 cup water

DIRECTIONS

Heat olive oil on Sauté. Stir-fry carrot, onion, celery, and paprika for 5 minutes. Add all remaining ingredients, except for the tomatoes, and cook for 5 minutes, until the meat is browned. Seal the lid.

Cook on High Pressure for 20 minutes. When done, release the steam naturally, for about 10 minutes. Hit Sauté, and cook for 7-8 minutes, to thicken the sauce.

Jalapeno Green Hot Sauce

Serves: 4 | Ready in about: 8 min

INGREDIENTS

4 oz green jalapeno peppers, chopped
1 green bell pepper, chopped
2 garlic cloves, crushed
½ cup white vinegar

1 tbsp apple cider vinegar
1 tsp sea salt
4 tbsp water

DIRECTIONS

Add all ingredients to the instant pot. Seal the lid and cook on High Pressure for 2 minutes. When done, release the steam naturally, for about 5 minutes.

Transfer to a blender, pulse until combined and store in jars.

Tip: Strain the mixture if you prefer more liquid sauce.

Beet Squash Sauce

Serves: 3 | Ready in about: 40 min

INGREDIENTS

3 beets, trimmed, peeled, cubed
3 carrots, peeled, cubed
2 cups butternut squash, peeled, cubed
1 cup red wine
1 tsp dried basil, ground

1 tbsp dried parsley, ground
1 tsp dried oregano, ground
½ tsp garlic powder
1 tsp black pepper, ground
1 tsp salt

DIRECTIONS

Add all vegetables in the instant pot. Pour in 2 cups of water and seal the lid. Press Steam and set the timer to 10 minutes. Cook on High Pressure. Do a quick pressure release.

Transfer to a food processor and pulse until smooth and creamy. Add the remaining ingredients and blend for a minute. Return to the pot, press Sauté and cook for 20 minutes, stirring occasionally.

BREAKFAST AND BEVERAGES

Homemade Yogurt with Walnuts

Serves: 10 | Ready in about: 18hr

INGREDIENTS

2 tbsp Greek yogurt
8 cups milk
¼ cup sugar honey

1 tsp vanilla extract
1 cup walnuts, chopped

DIRECTIONS

Add the milk, seal the lid and press Yogurt until display shows Boil. When the cooking cycle is over, the display will show Yogurt. Open the lid and check that milk temperature is at least 175° F.

Get rid of the skin lying on the milk's surface. Let cool in an ice bath until it becomes warm to touch.

In a bowl, mix one cup of milk and yogurt to make a smooth consistency.

Mix the milk with yogurt mixture. Transfer to the pot and place on your Pressure cooker.

Seal the lid, press Yogurt mode and adjust the timer to 9 hrs.

Once cooking is complete, strain the yogurt into a bowl using a strainer with cheesecloth.

Chill for 4 hrs. Add in vanilla and honey and Gently stir well. Spoon the yogurt into glass jars. Serve sprinkled with walnuts and enjoy.

Barbecue Chicken Sandwiches

Serves: 4 | Ready in about: 45 min

INGREDIENTS

4 chicken thighs, boneless and skinless
Salt to taste
2 cups barbecue sauce
1 onion, minced
2 garlic cloves, minced

2 tbsp minced fresh parsley
1 tbsp lemon juice
1 tbsp mayonnaise
1½ cups iceberg lettuce, shredded
4 burger buns

DIRECTIONS

Season the chicken with salt, and transfer into the pot. Add in garlic, onion and barbeque sauce. Coat the chicken by turning in the sauce. Seal the lid and cook on High Pressure for 15 minutes.

Do a natural release for 10 minutes. Use two forks to shred the chicken and mix into the sauce. Press Keep Warm and let the mixture to simmer for 15 minutes to thicken the sauce, until desired consistency.

Meanwhile, in a bowl, mix lemon juice, mayonnaise, salt, and parsley; toss lettuce into the mixture to coat. Separate the chicken in equal parts to match the sandwich buns; apply lettuce for topping and complete the sandwiches.

Cinnamon Pumpkin Steel Cut Oatmeal

Serves: 4 | Ready in about: 25 min

INGREDIENTS

1 tbsp butter
2 cups steel cut oats
¼ tsp cinnamon
3 cups water

1 cup pumpkin puree
½ tsp salt
3 tbsp maple syrup
½cup pumpkin seeds, toasted

DIRECTIONS

Melt butter on Sauté. Add in cinnamon, oats, salt, pumpkin puree, and water.

Seal the lid, select Porridge and cook for 10 minutes on High Pressure to get few bite oats or for 14 minutes to form oats that are soft. Do a quick release. Open the lid and stir in maple syrup. Top with toasted pumpkin seeds to serve.

Butternut Squash Cake Oatmeal

Serves: 4 | Ready in about: 35 min

INGREDIENTS

3 ½ cups coconut milk
1 cup steel-cut oats
1 cup shredded Butternut Squash
½ cup sultanas
⅓ cup honey
1 tsp ground cinnamon

¾ tsp ground ginger
½ tsp salt
½ tsp orange zest
¼ tsp ground nutmeg
¼ cup toasted walnuts, chopped
½ tsp vanilla extract

DIRECTIONS

In the cooker, mix sultanas, orange zest, ginger, milk, honey, squash, salt, oats, and nutmeg. Seal the lid and cook on High Pressure for 12 minutes. Do a natural release for 10 minutes.

Into the oatmeal, stir in the vanilla extract and sugar. Top with walnuts and serve.

Herbed Homemade Ghee

Serves: 10 | Ready in about: 17min

INGREDIENTS

8 ounces butter, softened
2 tbsp parsley, minced

1tbsp fresh chives, chopped
Sea salt to taste

DIRECTIONS

Warm butter on Sauté. Cook for 7 to 9 minutes as you stir in cycles of 3 minutes until browning.

Press Cancel and allow the butter to slightly cool. Use cheesecloth to strain the butter into a sealable container. Add the parsley, chives, and salt, and combine thoroughly.

Let cool before closing the lid. Keep in the fridge until ready to use.

Chai Latte Steel-Cut Oatmeal

Serves: 4 | Ready in about: 20 min

INGREDIENTS

3 ½ cups milk
½ cup raw peanuts
1 cup steel-cut oats
¼ cup agave syrup
1 tsp coffee
1 ½ tsp ground ginger

1 ¼ tsp ground cinnamon
½ tsp salt
¼ tsp ground allspice
¼ tsp ground cardamom
1 tsp vanilla extract

DIRECTIONS

With a blender, puree peanuts and milk to obtain a smooth consistency. Transfer into the cooker. To the peanuts mixture, add in agave syrup, oats, ginger, allspice, cinnamon, salt, cardamom, tea leaves, and cloves, and mix well.

Seal the lid and cook on High Pressure for 12 minutes.

Let pressure to release naturally on completing the cooking cycle.

Add vanilla extract to the oatmeal and stir well before serving.

Greek-Style Raspberry Yogurt

Serves: 12 | Ready in about: 23hr 20 min

INGREDIENTS

1 pound hulled and halved raspberries
1 cup sugar
3 tbsp gelatin

1 tbsp fresh orange juice
8 cups milk
¼ cup Greek yogurt containing active cultures

DIRECTIONS

In a bowl, mash raspberries with a potato masher. Add sugar and stir well to dissolve; let soak for 30 minutes at room temperature. Add in lemon juice and gelatin and mix well until dissolved.

Remove the mixture and place in a sealable container, close, and allow to sit for 12 hrs to 24 hrs at room temperature before placing in a refrigerator. Refrigerate for a maximum of 2 weeks.

Into the cooker, add milk and close the lid. The steam vent should be set to Venting then to Sealing.

Select Yogurt until "Boil" is displayed on the readings. When complete there will be a display of "Yogurt" on the screen. Open the lid and using a food thermometer ensure the milk temperature is at least 185° F.

Transfer the steel pot to a wire rack and allow cooling for 30 minutes until milk has reached 110° F.

In a bowl, mix ½ cup warm milk and yogurt. Transfer the mixture into the remaining warm milk and stir without having to scrape the steel pot's bottom.

Take the pot back to the base of the pot and seal the lid. Select Yogurt mode and cook for 8 hrs.

Allow the yogurt to chill in a refrigerator for 1-2 hrs.

Transfer the chilled yogurt to a large bowl and stir in fresh raspberry jam.

French Dip Sandwiches

Serves: 8 | Ready in about: 1hr 35 min

INGREDIENTS

2 ½ pounds beef roast
2 tbsp olive oil
1 onion, chopped
4 garlic cloves, minced
½ cup dry red wine

2 cups beef broth stock
1 tsp dried oregano
16 slices Fontina cheese
8 split hoagie rolls

DIRECTIONS

Season the beef with salt and pepper. Warm oil on Sauté and brown the beef for 3 minutes per side. Set aside. Add onions and cook for 3 minutes, until translucent. Stir in garlic and cook for one a minute until soft. Set aside. Add red wine to deglaze. Scrape the cooking surface to remove any brown sections of the food using a wooden spoon's flat edge.

Mix in beef broth and take back the juices and beef to your cooker. Over the meat, scatter some oregano. Seal the lid and cook on High Pressure for 50 minutes. Release the pressure naturally for 10 minutes. Preheat a broiler. Transfer the beef to a cutting board and slice.

Roll the beef and top with onions. Each sandwich should be topped with 2 slices fontina cheese. Place the sandwiches under the broiler for 2-3 minutes until the cheese melts.

Almond Milk

Serves: 4 | Ready in about: 20 min

INGREDIENTS

1 cup raw almonds, soaked overnight, peeled
1 cup cold water
2 dried apricots, chopped

2 tbsp honey
4 cups water
1 vanilla bean

DIRECTIONS

In the pot, mix a cup of cold water with almonds and apricots. Seal the lid and cook for 1 minute on High.

Release the pressure quickly. The almonds should be soft and plump, and the water should be brown and murky. Use a strainer to drain almonds; rinse with cold water for 1 minute.

To a high-speed blender, add the rinsed almonds, vanilla bean, honey, and 4 cups water. Blend for 2 minutes until well combined and frothy. Line a cheesecloth to the strainer.

Place the strainer over a bowl and strain the milk. Use a wooden spoon to press milk through the cheesecloth and get rid of solids. Place almond milk in an airtight container and refrigerate.

Cinnamon Mulled Red Wine

Serves: 6 | Ready in about: 30 min

INGREDIENTS

3 cups red wine
2 tangerines
¼ cup honey
6 whole cloves
6 whole black peppercorns

2 cardamom pods
8 cinnamon sticks
1 tsp fresh ginger, grated
1 tsp ground cinnamon
6 tangerine wedges

DIRECTIONS

Add wine, honey, cardamom, 2 cinnamon sticks, cloves, tangerines slices, ginger, and peppercorns. Seal the lid and cook for 5 minutes on High Pressure.

Release pressure naturally for 20 minutes. Using a fine mesh strainer, strain the wine. Discard spices. Divide the warm wine into glasses and add tangerine wedges and a cinnamon stick for garnishing before serving.

Coconut Steel-Cut Oatmeal

Serves: 2 | Ready in about: 20 min

INGREDIENTS

1 tsp coconut oil
1 cup steel-cut oats

1½ cups water
¾ cup coconut milk

DIRECTIONS

Warm oil on Sauté, until foaming. Add oats and cook as you stir until soft and toasted. Press Cancel. Add milk, salt, and water and stir.

Seal the lid and Press Porridge. Cook for 12 minutes on High Pressure. Set steam vent to Venting to Release the pressure quickly. Open the lid. Add oats as you stir to mix any extra liquid.

Homemade Apple Cider

Serves: 6 | Ready in about: 45 min

INGREDIENTS

6 green apples, cored and chopped
3 cups water

¼ cup orange juice
2 cinnamon sticks

DIRECTIONS

In a blender, add orange juice, apples, and water and blend until smooth; use a fine-mesh strainer to strain and press using a spoon. Get rid of the pulp.

In the pot, mix the strained apple puree, and cinnamon sticks. Seal the lid and cook for 10 minutes on High Pressure. Release the pressure naturally for 15 minutes.

Strain again and do away with the solids.

Valencian Horchata

Serves: 6 | Ready in about: 20 min

INGREDIENTS

2 cups water
1 cup chufa seed, overnight soak
¼ stick cinnamon

Zest from 1 lemon
2 tbsp sugar
4 cups cold water

DIRECTIONS

In the pot, combine cinnamon, chufa seed, and 4 cups water. Seal the lid cook on High Pressure for 1 minute. Release pressure naturally for 10 minutes, then release the remaining pressure quickly.

In a blender, add chufa seed mixture, lemon zest, and sugar. Blend well to form a paste. Add 2 cups cold water into a large container. Strain the blended chufa mixture into the water. Mix well and place in the refrigerator until ready for serving. Add cinnamon stick for garnishing.

Moon Milk

Serves: 2 | Ready in about: 10 min

INGREDIENTS

1 cup milk
1 tsp coconut oil
½ tsp ground cinnamon, plus more for garnish
½ tsp ground turmeric
¼ cup hemp hearts
½ tsp maca powder

1/8 tsp ground cardamom
1 pinch ground nutmeg
1 pinch ground ginger
1 pinch freshly ground black pepper
1 tsp honey

DIRECTIONS

Add milk, press Sauté and heat the milk for 3-4 minutes until the point of starting to bubble. Stir in coconut oil, turmeric, nutmeg, pepper, ginger, hemp hearts, maca powder, cinnamon, and cardamom.

Press Cancel and allow mixture to cool for about a minute. Whisk in honey.

Transfer the mixture into a mug. Add more cinnamon for garnishing!

DESSERTS

Cinnamon Apple Crisp

Serves: 5 | Ready in about: 30 min

INGREDIENTS

Topping:
½ cup oat flour
½ cup old-fashioned rolled oats

½ cup granulated sugar
¼ cup olive oil

Filling:
5 apples, peeled, cored, and halved
2 tbsp arrowroot powder
½ cup water

1 tsp ground cinnamon
¼ tsp ground nutmeg
½ tsp vanilla paste

DIRECTIONS

In a bowl, combine sugar, oat flour, rolled oats, and olive oil to form coarse crumbs. Ladle the apples into the instant pot. Mix water with arrowroot powder in a bowl. Stir in salt, nutmeg, cinnamon, and vanilla.

Toss in the apples to coat. Apply oat topping to the apples. Seal the lid and cook on High Pressure for 10 minutes. Release the pressure naturally for 5 minutes, then release the remaining pressure quickly.

Holiday Cranberry Cheesecake

Serves: 8 | Ready in about: 1hr

INGREDIENTS

1 cup coarsely crumbled cookies
2 tbsp butter, melted
1 cup mascarpone cheese, room temperature
½ cup sugar
2 tbsp sour cream

½ tsp vanilla extract
2 eggs, room temperature
⅓ cup dried cranberries
1 cup water

DIRECTIONS

Fold a 20-inch piece of aluminum foil in half lengthwise twice and set on the instant pot. In a bowl, combine melted butter and crushed cookies. Press firmly to the bottom and about ⅓ of the way up the sides of a 7-inch springform pan. Freeze the crust while the filling is being prepared.

In a separate bowl, beat together mascarpone cheese and sugar to obtain a smooth consistency. Stir in vanilla extract and sour cream. Beat one egg and add into the cheese mixture to combine well.

Do the same with the second egg. Stir cranberries into the filling. Transfer the filling into the crust. Into the pot, add water and set the steam rack at the bottom. Center the springform pan onto the prepared foil sling. Use the sling to lower the pan onto the rack.

Fold foil strips out of the way of the lid. Seal the lid, press Cake and cook on High Pressure for 40 minutes. Release the pressure quickly. Transfer the cheesecake to a refrigerator for 3 hours. Use a paring knife to run along the edges between the pan and cheesecake to remove the cheesecake and set to the plate.

New York Cheesecake

Serves: 12 | Ready in about: 1hr

INGREDIENTS

For the Crust:
1 cup graham crackers crumbs
2 tbsp butter, melted

1 tsp sugar
1/8 tsp salt

For the Filling:
2 cups cream cheese, at room temperature
½ cup sugar
1 tsp vanilla extract

Zest from 1 orange
1 pinch salt
2 eggs,

DIRECTIONS

Fold a 20-inch piece of aluminum foil in half lengthwise twice and set on the instant pot.

Spray a parchment paper with cooking spray and line to the base of a 7-inch springform pan. In a bowl, combine melted butter, salt, sugar and graham cracker. Press into the bottom and about ⅓ up the sides of the pan.

Transfer the pan to the freezer as you prepare the filling. In a separate bowl, beat sugar, cream cheese, salt, orange zest, and vanilla until smooth. Beat eggs into the filling, one at a time. Stir until combined.

Add the filling over the chilled crust in the pan. To the pan, add 1 cup water and set steam rack into the pot. Carefully center the springform pan on the prepared foil sling. Lower pan into the inner pot using sling and place on steam rack. Seal the lid, press Cake and cook for 40 minutes on High Pressure.

Release the pressure quickly. Transfer the cheesecake to a refrigerator for 3 hours. Use a paring knife to run along the edges between the pan and cheesecake to remove the cheesecake and set to the plate.

Dark Chocolate Brownies

Serves: 6 | Ready in about: 40 min

INGREDIENTS

1 ½ cups water
2 eggs
⅓ cup granulated sugar
¼ cup olive oil
⅓ cup flour
⅓ cup cocoa powder

⅓ cup dark chocolate chips
⅓ cup chopped Walnuts
1 tbsp milk
½ tsp baking powder
1 tbsp vanilla extract
A pinch salt

DIRECTIONS

Add water and set steamer rack into the cooker. Line a parchment paper on the steamer basket. In a bowl, beat eggs and sugar to mix until smooth. Stir in oil, cocoa, milk, salt baking powder, chocolate chips, flour, walnuts, vanilla, and sea salt. Transfer the batter to the prepared steamer basket.

Arrange into an even layer. Seal the lid, press Cake and cook for 20 minutes on High Pressure. Release the pressure quickly. Let brownie cool before cutting. Use powdered sugar to dust and serve.

Pumpkin Cake

Serves: 8 | Ready in about: 1hr 30 min

INGREDIENTS

3 eggs
½ cup sugar
1 cup flour
½ cup half-and-half
¼ cup olive oil
1 tsp baking powder

1 tsp vanilla extract
1 tsp ground cinnamon
½ tsp ground nutmeg
1 cup packed shredded pumpkin
½ cup chopped walnuts
2 cups water

Frosting:
4 ounces cream cheese, room temperature
8 tbsp butter
½ cup confectioners sugar

½ tsp vanilla extract
½ tsp salt

DIRECTIONS

In a bowl, beat eggs and sugar to get a smooth mixture; mix in oil, flour, vanilla extract, cinnamon, half-and-half, baking powder, and nutmeg. Stir well to obtain a fluffy batter; fold walnuts and pumpkin through the batter. Add batter into a 6-inch cake pan and cover with aluminum foil.

Into the pot, add water and set steamer rack over the water. Lay cake pan gently onto the trivet.

Seal the lid, select Cake and cook on High Pressure for 40 minutes. Release pressure naturally for 10 minutes, then release the remaining pressure quickly. As the cake cooks, beat cream cheese, confectioners' sugar, salt, vanilla extract, and butter in a mixing bowl until smooth; place in the refrigerator until needed.

Remove cake from the pan and transfer to the cooling rack to cool. Over the cake, spread frosting and apply a topping of shredded carrots.

Traditional French Squash Pie

Serves: 8 | Ready in about: 30 min

INGREDIENTS

15 oz mashed squash
6 fl oz milk
½ tsp cinnamon, ground
½ tsp nutmeg

½ tsp salt
3 large eggs
½ cup granulated sugar
1 pack pate brisee

DIRECTIONS

Place squash puree in a large bowl. Add milk, cinnamon, eggs, nutmeg, salt, and sugar. Whisk together until well incorporated. Grease a baking dish with oil.

Gently place pate brisee creating the edges with hands. Pour the squash mixture over and flatten the surface with a spatula. Pour 1 cup of water in the pot and insert the trivet. Lower the baking dish on the trivet.

Seal the lid, and cook for 25 minutes on High Pressure. Do a quick release. Transfer the pie to a serving platter. Refrigerate overnight before serving.

Lemon Cheesecake with Strawberries

Serves: 8 | Ready in about: 3hr

INGREDIENTS

Crust:

4 ounces graham crackers
1 tsp ground cinnamon

3 tbsp butter, melted

Filling:

1 pound mascarpone cheese, at room temperature
¾ cup sugar
¼ cup sour cream, at room temperature
2 eggs
1 tsp vanilla extract

1 tsp lemon zest
1 tbsp lemon juice
1 pinch salt
2 cups water
1 cup strawberries, halved

DIRECTIONS

In a food processor, beat cinnamon and graham crackers to attain a texture almost same as sand; mix in melted butter. Press the crumbs into the bottom of a 7-inch springform pan in an even layer.

In a stand mixer, beat sugar, mascarpone cheese, and sour cream for 3 minutes to combine well and have a fluffy and smooth mixture. Scrape the bowl's sides and add eggs, lemon zest, salt, lemon juice, and vanilla extract. Carry on to beat the mixture until you obtain a consistent color, and all ingredients are completely combined. Pour filling over crust.

Into the inner pot, add water and set in the trivet. Insert the springform pan on the trivet. Seal the lid, press Cake and cook for 40 minutes on High Pressure. Release the pressure quickly. Remove the cheesecake and let cool for 2 hours. Transfer to a serving plate and garnish with strawberry halves on top. Use a paring knife to run along the edges between the pan and cheesecake to remove the cheesecake and set to the plate.

Vanilla Apple Pie

Serves: 6 | Ready in about: 30 min

INGREDIENTS

2 lb apples, cubed
¼ cup sugar
¼ cup breadcrumbs
2 tsp cinnamon, ground
3 tbsp freshly squeezed lemon juice

1 tsp vanilla sugar
¼ tbsp oil
1 egg, beaten
¼ cup all-purpose flour
Pie dough

DIRECTIONS

Combine breadcrumbs, vanilla sugar, granulated sugar, apples, and cinnamon, in a bowl. On a lightly floured surface, roll out the pie dough making 2 circle-shaped crusts.

Grease a baking sheet with cooking spray, and place one pie crust in it.

Spoon the apple mixture on top, and cover with the remaining crust. Seal by crimping edges and brush with beaten egg. Pour 1 cup of water in the instant pot and lay the trivet. Lower the baking sheet on the trivet. Seal the lid, and cook on High Pressure for 20 minutes. Do a quick release and serve chilled.

Cheesecake with Cranberry Topping

Serves: 8 | Ready in about: 25 min

INGREDIENTS

2 lb Greek yogurt
2 cups sugar
4 eggs
2 tsp lemon zest
1 tsp lemon extract
½ tsp salt
1 cheesecake crust

For topping:
7 oz dried cranberries
2 tbsp cranberry jam
2 tsp lemon zest
1 tsp vanilla sugar
1 tsp cranberry extract
¾ cup lukewarm water

DIRECTIONS

In a bowl, combine yogurt, sugar, eggs, lemon zest, lemon extract, and salt. With a mixer, beat well on low until well-combined.

Grease a springform pan with oil. Place in the crust and pour in the filling. Flatten the surface with a spatula. Leave in the fridge for 30 minutes.

Meanwhile, prepare the topping by combining cranberries, jam, zest, vanilla sugar, extract, and water in the inner pot. Simmer for 15 minutes on Sauté mode. Remove to a bowl and wipe the pot clean.

Fill in 1 cup of water in the pot, and insert a trivet. Set the pan on top and pour cranberries' topping. Seal the lid, and cook for 20 minutes on High Pressure.

Do a quick release. Run a sharp knife around the edge of the cheesecake. Refrigerate overnight.

Yogurt Cake with Chocolate Glaze

Serves: 12 | Ready in about: 35 min

INGREDIENTS

3 cups yogurt
3 cups flour
2 cups granulated sugar
1 cup oil

2 tsp baking soda
3 tbsp cocoa, unsweetened
1 cup water

For the glaze:
7 oz dark chocolate
10 tbsp sugar

10 tbsp milk
5 oz butter, unsalted

DIRECTIONS

In a bowl, combine yogurt, flour, sugar, oil, baking soda, and cocoa. Beat well with an electric mixer. Transfer a mixture to a large springform pan.

Wrap the pan in foil. Insert a trivet in the instant pot. Pour in water, and place the pan on top. Seal the lid and cook for 30 minutes on High Pressure.

Do a quick release, remove the springform pan and unwrap. Chill well.

Meanwhile, melt the chocolate in a microwave. Transfer to a bowl, and whisk in butter, milk, and sugar. Beat well with a mixer and pour the mixture over the cake. Refrigerate for at least two hours before serving.

Warm Winter Apple Compote

Serves: 8 | Ready in about: 35 min

INGREDIENTS

1 lb fresh figs
7 oz Turkish figs
7 oz fresh cherries
7 oz plums
3.5 oz raisins
3 large apples, chopped

3 tbsp cornstarch
1 tsp cinnamon, ground
1 tbsp cloves
1 cup sugar
1 lemon, juiced
3 cups water

DIRECTIONS

Combine all ingredients in the instant pot. Seal the lid and cook for 30 minutes on High ´pressure. Release the pressure naturally, for 10 minutes. Store in big jars.

Honey Crème Brûlée

Serves: 4 | Ready in about: 15 min

INGREDIENTS

5 cups heavy cream
8 egg yolks
1 cup honey
4 tbsp sugar

1 vanilla extract
¼ tsp salt
1 cup water

DIRECTIONS

In a bowl, combine heavy cream, egg yolks, vanilla, and honey. Beat well with an electric mixer. Pour the mixture into 4 ramekins. Set aside.

Pour water in the pot and insert the trivet. Lower the ramekins on top. Seal the lid, and cook for 10 minutes on High Pressure. Do a quick pressure release.

Remove the ramekins from the pot and add a tablespoon of sugar in each ramekin. Burn evenly with a culinary torch until brown. Chill well and serve.

Stewed Plums with Almond Flakes

Serves: 10 | Ready in about: 20 min

INGREDIENTS

6 lb sweet ripe plums, pits removed and halved
2 cups white sugar

1 cup almonds, flaked

DIRECTIONS

Drizzle the plums with sugar. Toss to coat. Let it stand for about 1 hour to allow plums to soak up the sugar.

Transfer the plum mixture to the instant pot and pour 1 cup of water. Seal the lid and cook on High Pressure for 30 minutes. Allow the Pressure to release naturally, for 10 minutes. Serve topped with almond flakes.

Flan with Whipping Cream

Serves: 4 | Ready in about: 30 min

INGREDIENTS

½ cup granulated sugar
4 tbsp caramel syrup
1 cup water
3 eggs

½ tsp vanilla extract
½ tbsp milk
5 oz whipping cream

DIRECTIONS

Combine milk, whipping cream and vanilla extract in your instant pot. Press Sauté, and cook for 5 minutes, or until small bubbles form. Set aside.

Using an electric mixer, whisk the eggs and sugar. Gradually add the cream mixture and whisk until well combined. Divide the caramel syrup between 4 ramekins. Fill with egg mixture and place them on top of the trivet. Pour in water.

Seal the lid, and cook for 15 minutes on High Pressure. Do a quick release. remove the ramekins from the pot and cool completely before serving.

Savoury Lemon Dessert

Serves: 10 | Ready in about: 25 min

INGREDIENTS

2 eggs
2 cups sugar
2 cups vegetable oil

½ cup all-purpose flour
1 tsp baking powder

Lemon Topping:
4 cups sugar
5 cups water
1 cup freshly squeezed lemon juice

1 tbsp lemon zest
1 whole lemon, sliced

DIRECTIONS

In a bowl, combine eggs, sugar, oil, and baking powder. Gradually add flour until the mixture is thick and slightly sticky. Shape balls with hands, and flatten them to half-inch thick.

Place in a baking pan that fits in the instant pot. Pour 2 cups of water, insert the trivet and lower the pan onto the trivet. Cover the pan with foil and seal the lid. Cook on High Pressure for 20 minutes.

Do a quick release and remove the pan and foil. Cool to room temperature.

Add the remaining sugar, water, lemon juice, lemon zest, and lemon slices in the instant pot. Press Sauté and cook until the sugar dissolves. Pour the hot topping over the chilled dessert. Serve chilled.

Simple Apricot Dessert

Serves: 8 | Ready in about: 40 min

INGREDIENTS

2 lb fresh apricots, rinsed, drained
1 lb sugar
2 tbsp lemon zest

1 tsp ground nutmeg
10 cups water

DIRECTIONS

Add apricots, sugar, water, nutmeg, and lemon zest. Cook, stirring occasionally, until half of the water evaporates, on Sauté. Press Cancel and transfer the apricots and the remaining liquid into glass jars. Let cool and close the lids. Refrigerate overnight before use.

Cinnamon Pumpkin Pudding

Serves: 4 | Ready in about: 20 min

INGREDIENTS

1 lb pumpkin, peeled and chopped into bite-sized pieces
1 cup granulated sugar
½ cup cornstarch

4 cups apple juice, unsweetened
1 tsp cinnamon, ground
3-4 cloves

DIRECTIONS

In a bowl, combine sugar and apple juice until sugar dissolves completely.

Pour the mixture into the pot and stir in cornstarch, cinnamon, cloves, and pumpkin. Seal the lid, and cook for 10 minutes on High Pressure. Do a quick release. Pour in the pudding into 4 serving bowls. Let cool to room temperature and refrigerate overnight.

Vanilla & Walnut Cake

Serves: 8 | Ready in about: 15 min

INGREDIENTS

3 standard cake crusts
½ cup vanilla pudding powder
¼ cup granulated sugar

4 cups milk
1 (10.5oz) box chocolate chips
¼ cup walnuts, minced

DIRECTIONS

Combine vanilla powder, sugar, and milk in the inner pot. Cook until the pudding thickens, stirring constantly, on Sauté. Remove from the steel pot.

Place one crust into a springform pan. Pour half of the pudding and sprinkle with minced walnuts and chocolate chips. Cover with another crust and repeat the process. Finish with the lasting crust and wrap in foil.

Insert the trivet, pour in 1 cup of water, and place springform pan on top. Seal the lid and cook for 10 minutes on High Pressure. Do a quick release. Refrigerate overnight.

Pumpkin & Walnut Strudel

Serves: 8 | Ready in about: 30 min

INGREDIENTS

2 cups pumpkin puree
1 tsp vanilla extract
2 cups Greek yogurt
2 eggs

2 tbsp brown sugar
2 tbsp unsalted butter, softened
2 puff pastry sheets
1 cup walnuts, chopped

DIRECTIONS

In a bowl, mix yogurt with vanilla extract until completely smooth; set aside.

Unfold the pastry and cut each sheet into 4-inch x 7-inch pieces and brush with half of the beaten eggs. Place approximately 2 tbsp of pumpkin puree, and 2 tbsp of the yogurt mixture at the middle of each pastry, sprinkle with walnuts.

Fold the sheets and brush with the remaining eggs. Cut the surface with a sharp knife and gently place each strudel into an oiled baking dish.

Pour 1 cup of water in the pot and insert the trivet. Place the pan on top. Seal the lid and cook for 25 minutes on High Pressure.

Release the pressure naturally, for about 10 minutes. Let it chill for 10 minutes. Carefully Transfer the strudels to a serving plate.

Marble Cherry Cake

Serves: 6 | Ready in about: 30 min

INGREDIENTS

1 cup flour
1 ½ tsp baking powder
1 tbsp powdered stevia
½ tsp salt
1 tsp cherry extract

3 tbsp butter, softened
3 eggs
¼ cup cocoa powder
¼ cup heavy cream

DIRECTIONS

Combine all dry ingredients, except cocoa in a bowl. Mix well to combine and add eggs, one at the time. Beat well with a dough hook attachment for one minute. Add sour cream, butter, and cherry extract.

Continue to beat for 3 more minutes. Divide the mixture in half and add cocoa powder in one-half of the mixture. Pour the light batter into a greased baking dish. Drizzle with cocoa dough to create a beautiful marble pattern.

Pour in one cup of water and insert the trivet. Lower the baking dish on top. Seal the lid and cook for 20 minutes on High Pressure.

Release the pressure naturally, for about 10 minutes. Let it cool for a while and transfer to a serving plate.

Blueberry-Lemon Peach Pie

Serves: 6 | Ready in about: 50 min

INGREDIENTS

1 cup fresh blueberries
1 peach, sliced
1 cup flour
2 large eggs
1 tsp baking powder

½ tsp salt
¼ cup butter, softened
¼ cup powdered stevia
¼ tsp vanilla extract
2 tsp freshly squeezed lemon juice

DIRECTIONS

In a bowl, combine flour, baking powder, and salt. Mix well and set aside. In a separate bowl, combine eggs and powdered stevia. Using a hand mixer with a whisking attachment, beat well on high for 2 minutes until light and fluffy.

Place the flour mixture in a large mixing bowl. Add butter, vanilla extract, and lemon juice. Gradually add the egg mixture, beating constantly.

Transfer the mixture to an oiled baking dish. Spread the batter evenly with a kitchen spatula. Arrange the fruit on top.

Pour 1 cup of water in the pot and insert the trivet. Place the pan on top. Seal the lid and cook for 30 minutes on High Pressure. Release the pressure quickly and let chill thoroughly before serving.

Fruity Pie Cups

Serves: 6 | Ready in about: 35 min

INGREDIENTS

For the crust:
2 cups flour
¾ tsp salt
¾ cup butter, softened

1 tbsp sugar
½ cup ice water

For the filling:
1 apple
½ fresh peach
½ cup apples, chopped
¼ cup cranberries

2 tbsp flour
1 tbsp sugar
½ tsp cinnamon
1 egg yolk, for brushing

DIRECTIONS

Place all crust ingredients in a food processor and pulse until dough becomes crumbly. Remove to a lightly floured work surface. Divide into 4 equal pieces and wrap in plastic foil. Refrigerate for an hour.

Meanwhile, place all the filling ingredients in a bowl. Toss to combine and set aside.

Roll each piece into 6-inch round discs. Add 2 tablespoons of the apple mixture at the center of each disc and wrap to form small bowls. Brush each bowl with egg yolk and Gently Transfer to an oiled baking dish.

Pour 1 cup of water in the pot and insert the trivet. Place the pan on top. Seal the lid, and cook for 25 minutes on High Pressure. Release the pressure naturally, for about 10 minutes.

Berry Buckwheat Pancake

Serves: 3 | Ready in about: 15 min

INGREDIENTS

1 cup buckwheat flour
2 tsp baking powder
1 ¼ cup milk
1 egg
½ tsp salt

1 tsp vanilla sugar
1 tsp strawberry extract
1 cup Greek yogurt
1 cup fresh berries

DIRECTIONS

In a bowl, whisk milk and egg until foamy. Gradually add flour and continue to beat until combined. Add baking powder, salt, and vanilla sugar.

Grease a baking pan with oil and spoon the batter in it. Pour 1 cup of water in the pot and place the trivet. Lower the pan on the trivet. Seal the lid and cook for 5 minutes on High Pressure. Do a quick release. Top pancake with yogurt and berries. Sprinkle with strawberry extract and serve.

Vanilla Crepes

Serves: 6 | Ready in about: 20 min

INGREDIENTS

2 medium-sized bananas, mashed
1 ¼ cup milk
2 eggs
1 ½ cups rolled oats
1 ½ tsp baking powder

1 tsp vanilla extract
2 tsp coconut oil
1 tbsp honey
¼ tsp salt
Non-fat cooking spray

DIRECTIONS

Combine the ingredients in a blender and pulse until a completely smooth batter. Grease the inner pot with cooking spray. Spread 1 spoon batter at the bottom.

Cook for 2 minutes, on Sauté mode, flip the crepe and cook for another minute. Repeat the process with the remaining batter. Serve immediately.